Landscape Architecture Research

Landscape Architecture Research

Inquiry, Strategy, Design

M. Elen Deming

Simon Swaffield

WILEY

John Wiley & Sons, Inc.

For general information about our other products and services, please contact our Customer Care Department within the United States at (800) 762-2974, outside the United States at (317) 572-3993 or fax (317) 572-4002.

Wiley also publishes its books in a variety of electronic formats. Some content that appears in print may not be available in electronic books. For more information about Wiley products, visit our web site at www.wiley.com.

Library of Congress Cataloging-in-Publication Data:

Deming, M. Elen, 1956–
   Landscape architecture research : inquiry, strategy, design / M. Elen Deming, Simon Swaffield.
      p.   cm.
   Includes bibliographical references and index.
      ISBN 978-0-470-56417-2 (pbk.); ISBN 978-0-470-95065-4 (ebk.); ISBN 978-0-470-95076-0 (ebk.); 978-1-118-05708-7 (ebk.); 978-1-118-05709-4 (ebk.); 978-1-118-05710-0 (ebk.)
      1. Landscape architecture—Study and teaching.   2. Research—Methodology.   I. Swaffield, Simon, 1952–   II. Title.
   SB469.4.D46   2011
   712.072—dc22

                                                                     2010016940

Printed in the United States of America

10 9 8 7 6 5

Contents

All science should be scholarly, but not all scholarship can be rigorously scientific . . . . The terrae incognitae of the periphery contain fertile ground awaiting cultivation with the tools and in the spirit of the humanities.

—JOHN KIRTLAND WRIGHT,
cited in Yi Fu Tuan, *Topophilia*

Preface

This is a transnational project, coauthored by professors living and working on opposite sides of the world. The *translational* challenges of the work, however, far exceeded what we originally anticipated. Our international partnership has forced us to reconcile different academic cultures, practices, and standards—a microcosm of the wider challenges addressed in the text itself.

It then goes without saying that this is also an ambitious project. Both authors readily acknowledge that any book about the state of research in landscape architecture will be an incomplete, evolving project—simply by definition. It is also a work in progress in the sense that the arguments are provisional and intended as a constructive contribution to an extended debate that will continue to shape our discipline. Our propositions, classifications, and examples will no doubt provoke and stimulate varying reactions, and we look forward to our colleagues' response.

It is also important to acknowledge that we are both generalists, having been privileged for many years with an unusual vantage on contemporary research in the field of landscape architecture from the perspective of editors, educators, and scholars. This is both an advantage and a potential limitation. In reviewing and interpreting the diversity of research strategies within our discipline we have had to simplify and translate. We hope that our own process of learning the very different traditions involved has not compromised their integrity or richness, and will help others facing the same interpretive challenge.

Both of us have served as editors of peer-reviewed journals, Swaffield as founding editor of *Landscape Review* (1995–2009) and Deming first as coeditor and then sole editor of *Landscape Journal* (2002–2009). We both serve on a number of editorial advisory boards. Our exposure to authors and peer reviewers alike has inspired our approach to this book, which is to use informative examples of what researchers are already doing to illustrate the main concepts. We hope that all students and practitioners who pick up this book will share a sense of empowerment in understanding how to make a difference through research and from knowing how, exactly, their work *matters*.

We believe the most important contribution of this book is not the specific selection or elucidation of examples we have chosen but, rather, the overview and the elasticity of thinking strategically about research. The vast majority of the examples we chose were compound studies—combining, for instance, classification with logical argumentation (Fredericks 1982), description with evaluation (Francis 2002), and so on. This makes it all the more challenging for beginning researchers to develop a confident sense of understanding the relationship between strategy, design, and the need to know. In defence, we suggest that there is no such thing as a "pure" strategy—all research is constructed to address particular questions in particular contexts, and the examples reflect this process of matching approach to purpose. Similarly, research design is about fitness for purpose and the art of the possible.

However, there is a logic to developing a research strategy, and to its implementation, and we believe there has been benefit in probing the disciplinary literature in a systematic way: like an x-ray that illuminates the skeleton, it renders a more diagrammatic understanding of research strategy, design, and methods in our discipline. We hope the classification we have produced and the illustrations we have offered will open new vistas of comprehension, of analogy, and of pragmatic innovation that both inspire and guide new researchers, as well as provoke and challenge those already set in particular paradigms and conventions.

Acknowledgments

MED: Having practiced and taught for many years, when I finally returned to graduate school I was treated to a seminar in research inquiry taught by Michele Addington. In 1997, in her efforts to guide graduate students toward producing a well-crafted thesis proposal in the shortest possible time, she facilitated a remarkable discussion of research methods—an epiphany for me. The universe of possibilities that emerged in those discussions served to demystify the processes of scholarly investigation that had eluded me for so long. That liberation changed my world view.

The initial impulse to write this book simmered up a few years later, at the ECLAS conference in Ås, Norway, in 2005, where Simon Swaffield presented an early version of his paper "Theory and Critique in Landscape Architecture: Making Connections" (2006). Filled with admiration for the clarity of the rubric he constructed there, knowing the importance of the project, yet still dissatisfied with specific limits of the vision, I threw down the gauntlet on the spot: "Either you write the book, Simon, or I will." This work is the result of that early meeting of the minds, a stimulating and productive collaboration that has withstood the rigors of distance, time, training, exposure, misunderstanding, negotiation, reconciliation, and multiple stints of one or the other of us serving in administrative posts.

My work on this project was supported by financial assistance from a Wadsworth Endowment Faculty Research Award in the Department of Landscape Architecture, University of Illinois at Urbana-Champaign. The benefactors of this endowment, Jean and Brent Wadsworth, have been extraordinary friends of landscape architecture at Illinois. For well over a decade they have supported student excellence and faculty research aimed at improving the evidence base for the profession of landscape architecture and for society at large.

In part, the grant supported a research assistant, Lori Tella (MLA 2009), who helped us gather web sources on various research methods and test our initial rubric against the published literature. Debbie Huber's capable assistance at a key point in the writing is also deeply appreciated.

SRS: The origins of my interest in research strategies lie at the start of my tertiary education. In the early 1970s the Department of Geography at Cambridge University was a whirlpool of competing paradigms that opened me to the challenge of mediating between alternative ways of knowing. The confidence to chart one's own path came later, from my PhD studies at Lincoln University, under the scrutiny and with support of supervisors from three diverse disciplines—Professor Kevin O'Connor, the late Dr Angus McIntyre, and Dr (now Professor) Harvey Perkins. Preparation of a reader on theory in landscape architecture stimulated my interest in the research foundations of our professional discipline, and as Elen has explained, our collaboration grew from there.

Most of the preparation of the text has been undertaken as part of my role as Professor of Landscape Architecture at Lincoln University, and I am grateful for the support and encouragement I have received from Stefanie Rixecker as the Dean of the Faculty of Environment Society and Design, and from Neil Challenger since he took over as Head of the School of Landscape Architecture. I received support from the Lincoln University Strategic Investment Fund to gain relief from teaching in 2010, and the Velux Foundation in Denmark has supported me as a visiting professor at Copenhagen University during the latter stages of production process.

Theresa Caracausa provided essential help in identifying and reviewing examples, as a summer scholar supported by the Faculty, and her pragmatic evaluations from a student's perspective helped shape the choices. Mathew Durning prepared the authors' illustrations, with additional support from Erica Gilchrist. Michelle Collings provided invaluable help in preparing the authors' manuscript for submission.

MED and SRS: Our work on this book was made possible by many forms of mutual trust and collegiate support. We are grateful for the support and encouragement of the editors and staff at John Wiley and Sons who have guided the process from its inception, particularly Margaret Cummins and David Sassian. That this book exists at all is testament to their patient efforts.

There is also the trust between colleagues. We owe a huge debt to those authors whose work we selected to feature in this edition. They not only read and suggested improvements to our synopses of their own published work, but their encouragement and advice on the larger project was very welcome.

We especially acknowledge the kind cooperation of the editorial and administrative staff at the University of Wisconsin Press Journals Division, publishers of *Landscape Journal*. We drew many examples of research strategies from the studies published in that journal since 1982.

We offer thanks to all those members of the Council of Educators in Landscape Architecture (CELA) and the European Council of Landscape Architecture Schools (ECLAS) who provided review comments on the conference papers that helped shape the text. We also thank the key informants we approached and whose knowledge particularly informed the discussion of gatekeepers and research quality criteria.

A number of colleagues reviewed early versions of the manuscript proposal and offered helpful feedback. It goes without saying that the inevitable errors, misunderstandings and omissions remain the authors' own. James Anderson, Laura Lawson, and John Stallmeyer (College of Fine & Applied Arts, University of Illinois), Lindsay Sowman (Lincoln University), Robert Brown (University of Guelph), Cheryl Doble and Dayton Reuter (State University of New York, College of Environmental Science and Forestry), all read portions of early drafts and offered constructive criticism. Jeffrey Blankenship (Hobart & William Smith College) provided the signpost to the epigram. The most powerful and useful criticism came from former coeditor of *Landscape Journal*, James F. Palmer, who read the whole manuscript and challenged us to make it better. We are profoundly grateful for such colleagues, who are generous enough to constructively and honestly disagree with us. We hope that we have addressed the challenges they posed.

Of course, the importance of trust between coauthors cannot be overstated. As we noted in the Preface, the intellectual project represented in the text, and its writing and production, have been undertaken as a collaboration across a continent and an ocean, with a small number of working meetings, and many emails. We each acknowledge the intellect, experience, groundedness, humor, and personal generosity of our coauthor.

Simon also offers profound thanks and acknowledgement to Jenny, Matthew and Martin at home in Governors Bay in New Zealand. An author's family is the silent partner in any scholarly production, providing encouragement, love, and support when progress is slow and when things go wrong, and tolerating the intrusions into family life of the time and energy spent on the project.

Finally, we must gratefully acknowledge the mutual trust between students and their faculty. Many students have worked with us over the years and shown us the need for what we have written here. The sincerity and efforts of gifted and enthusiastic students—their capacity to generate new knowledge not from knowing exactly what to do, but from knowing how to ask the right questions—is what motivates this book.

CHAPTER 1

Introduction

1.1 Knowledge in Landscape Architecture

The "new normal" in landscape architecture is the production and consumption of knowledge. The past two decades have seen an unprecedented increase in the standards and complexity of disciplinary expertise, and with that comes increasing pressure to formalize the ways in which we seek, create, and validate knowledge. As the discipline expands and engages with other disciplines to address the profound challenges of the twenty-first century, there is pressure to include a broader base of thinking in the field and to deepen the way we think. These dynamics intersect in research.

This book offers researchers in landscape architecture a place to begin shaping their research program. It comprises a critical review of research strategies that have built and continue to build the knowledge base in landscape architecture. Its primary audience is students in higher education who are working on capstone or terminal studio projects, advanced independent studies, theses, or dissertations, as well as faculty who are supervising graduate students. As the number and size of Master of Landscape Architecture (MLA) thesis and PhD programs expand (Tai 2003), candidates and examiners require guidance and clarity of expectations about acceptable research methodology—that is, the principles, practices, and procedures of inquiry that characterize the discipline.

The career development and eventual success of academic staff also hinges increasingly upon their research agenda: its productivity, value, and impact. Universities and funding agencies demand metrics of performance and productivity that indicate the quantity and quality of research activity and dissemination, and programs are frequently ranked on this basis. In some countries, public funding for universities is tied directly to research output (Forsyth 2008), and there may be financial incentives that favor postgraduate education that involves substantial research outcomes. All of these activities involve creation of new knowledge, for which a clear strategy, or systematic process of inquiry, is needed.

An important secondary audience for the book is landscape practitioners in private-sector design, multidisciplinary or corporate consulting firms, public-sector agencies, and academia. In the design and development industry, as well as in government sectors and at not-for-profit agencies, research is becoming integral to shaping policy and practice. Indeed, success in business often depends on developing strategies for innovation in order to maintain competitiveness. "Evidence-based design" (Davies et al. 2000) is an area of fast-growing interest, as clients, public officials, and practitioners seek credible sources of knowledge of landscape and social processes upon which to base their evaluation of design proposals and policy recommendations. Forms of peer review are increasingly used in all of these situations, but they still beg the questions of which research strategies are effective and appropriate for the discipline and by what criteria should new knowledge be evaluated.

1.2 The Need for a Guide

There is at present little disciplinary guidance on research strategies. Nor is there any clear standard within landscape architecture for courses in research design and methods that are required in graduate design programs and, increasingly, taught to undergraduates. Rather than teaching from a broader "meta," or strategic, perspective, faculty members often teach research design in a way that reflects their own familiarity with a single research method or a category of methods (e.g., survey or thematic maps). Their task is made even more difficult because no single text adequately serves the landscape architecture student in finding his or her own focus of inquiry or allows the student to position his or her work in the context of a larger investigative framework. The problem is confirmed regularly in informal and formal discussions at educators' conferences in North America, Europe, and Pacific Rim countries, and we have repeatedly encountered this need in our own teaching.

Equally, there are no discipline-wide protocols or frameworks in landscape architecture by which to evaluate the validity of research proposals that seek commercial or public funding, or to assess the claims made by practitioners in the explanations of their projects, in competition entries, and in their written work. Clients in the public sector have no basis upon which to judge the validity of assumptions and presumptions made as a basis for policy advice.

This book aims to empower and inform new researchers, evaluators, and clients of research and theoretically justified work by providing a framework through which to address the following questions:

1. What research strategies are possible in landscape architecture?

2. What strategies do landscape architectural researchers tend to use?

3. How might an effective research strategy be shaped, and how might it be evaluated?

It follows that we focus primarily upon strategies rather than methods—on the configuration of an overall system of inquiry relative to the current range of epistemological and theoretical perspectives in our field, rather than upon detailed procedures, methods, and techniques that may be relevant to a particular investigation. This reflects our belief that, rather than method, it is the perspective driving an inquiry that is most fundamental in shaping any research project, and that it is the application of distinctive inquisitive strategies within particular theoretical contexts that shapes a discipline. Many methods and techniques are interchangeable across disciplines. It is the way they are used, combined, and linked to theoretical propositions and practical actions in a coherent overarching strategy that gives them a distinctive disciplinary character.

It is also important to dispel any potential confusion in the overlapping concepts of *research design* and *research strategy*. In this book, *research design* refers to the logical order or structural composition of an investigation; essentially it is a formal, or a formulaic protocol. Trochim (2006) calls research design "the glue" that keeps a research project together. Many sources suggest that there are only a limited number of possible research designs (e.g., randomized experiment, quasi experiment, nonexperiment). Research design guides the way in which an inquiry selects from and processes all possible sources of data (i.e., sampling approach) and treatments.

Research strategy, on the other hand, is essentially conceptual and is shaped by intention—not by the "how," but by the "why" of finding out. The nature of any research strategy is defined by two key dimensions that guide the process of scholarly inquiry. The first is the purpose or the relationship of the inquiry to theory—is the purpose of the investigation to build, shape, or test theory? The second dimension is the nature of the truth claims, or epistemology, that lie behind the investigation—is reality dependent upon, independent of, or interdependent between the researcher and the world?

Hence, research strategy is clearly related to, but larger and more conceptual than, research design. Research strategy subsumes research design within a larger order or agenda of thought and action. Research design is the investigative structure or logic created in the service of particular intellectual strategies; research methods are specific procedures used to advance particular research designs; research techniques are used to access and organize data (e.g., interviews) in support of particular methods.

In essence, the "strategies" that we present in this text are methodologies (studies of multiple methods) that are organized by and instrumental to an intellectual purpose and epistemological position. This guides their placement in a classification matrix (see Section 1.4). One order below that, our examples describe specific research designs, research methods, and analytical techniques that *illustrate* how these strategies operate in support of landscape architectural topics. The strategy itself is actually quite limited in its form and effect in our detailed discussions of examples, but it provides the essential context and logic for the investigation and its choice of design, methods, and techniques. Our hierarchy of terms is as follows:

1. Strategy: An agenda of thought and action for knowledge formation *(Nine strategies are classified in Table 1.1)*

2. Research design: The structure of how to choose, structure, or limit the evidence vis-à-vis the query (e.g., sampling frame or generative design)

4. Methods: Procedures of investigation, some serving more than one strategic category (e.g., historiography or survey)

5. Analytical techniques: The tools of investigation, almost all serving multiple strategies and designs (e.g., depth interview, statistical analysis, or coding)

Questions of research strategy in landscape architecture are neither new nor trivial. There have been intense debates within the discipline in recent decades as to the legitimacy of different research paradigms. Each paradigm carries its own presuppositions, and typically each commentator advocates for his or her own position. Cross-disciplinary investigation is increasingly common, yet boundaries between fields of knowledge and the validity of "borrowing" different ways of creating knowledge are increasingly contentious, particularly in relation to the closely related discipline of architecture.

As well as points of tension, there are also significant gaps in knowledge and research activity. This raises further questions: How does the discourse of "how we know what we know" shape the discipline? Which, or whose, knowledge survives this scrutiny, becoming legitimated and eventually reproduced? What questions, evidence, and ideas are excluded? And what are the implications for practice?

1.3 The Gatekeeping Dilemma in Context

Our approach to these questions of scope and legitimacy is inclusive rather than exclusive. Overall we advocate a greater focus on the conceptual logic of inquiry, explanation, and evaluation of research approach and outcomes. There have been classifications of research

Responses from Key "Gatekeeper" Informants

1. What criteria are used by your journal to evaluate the quality and validity of research and scholarship submitted for publication?

    - Scholarship—quality and insight

    - Method—coherence, integrity, and rigor

    - Outcomes—significance, relevance, and originality

    - Presentation—clarity and style

2. Does the choice and/or weighting of criteria change depending upon the topic of research, or is it standard across all submissions?

    - In principle, largely standard

    - In practice, nuanced according to the type of paper

3. Do you have an expectation or preference for certain acceptable research strategies in landscape architecture? If so, what are they?

    - A broad range is acceptable (even desirable)

    - Needs to be appropriate to the subject

4. Have you rejected any work in recent years because the research paradigm adopted is not acceptable to your journal? If so, what type of research was involved?

    - Never specifically

    - Typically, rejection occurs if the quality of work is "not good enough," or subject is not sufficiently relevant to the target journal methodology offered recently in related disciplines (Creswell 2009, Groat and Wang 2002, Laurel 2003), and within landscape architecture a conceptual framework has been proposed to reconcile the seemingly incompatible traditions of "objectivist" science and subjectivist arts (Swaffield 2006). However, the practical resolution of questions of legitimacy relies most heavily upon the judgment of "gatekeepers." These judges of research quality include, among others, academic advisors and graduate examiners, administrators and appointment committees, acquiring editors and advisory boards, editors and peer reviewers, foundation managers and granting agencies, and jurors and critics.

In the current structure of knowledge production, "gatekeepers" may wield extraordinary power. Not only do these men and women decide on career choices and success (for instance, in deciding tenure and promotion), but they also have the privilege of deciding what new knowledge is approved—and not approved—for degree completion, funding, and dissemination. Even in the context of new media and the Internet, which enables new "blog" and "wiki" formats (essentially consensual, collective efforts at knowledge production), gatekeepers are ever present.

In a recent study (Swaffield and Deming 2007), we found that in most design and planning professions, and in landscape architecture in particular, the range of acceptable

---

5. How does the research paradigm of submitted work influence selection of referees?
   - Suggests what type of expertise is relevant
   - May predispose intellectual affinity or sympathy for the approach
   - Demands a need for impartiality

6. Do you believe the situation is different in landscape architecture, as compared to more traditional disciplines? If so, how?
   - Yes—greater breadth and generality of interests
   - Yes—more contextual and cross-disciplinary emphasis
   - More frequent use of case studies
   - Lack of deeply embedded tradition or expertise in research
   - Lack of commitment to quantitative methods and mainstream science; this means limits to knowledge are, in part, self-imposed

7. Are there any other insights you could offer about the way that research and scholarship is evaluated for peer-reviewed publication in landscape architecture?
   - Need to remain cross-disciplinary requires a pluralistic approach, and also provides useful benchmarking
   - Stronger connections to practice could be fruitful, but research by design still lacks a strong research infrastructure
   - Research in the field is still inhibited by professional anti-intellectualism
   - Despite best efforts, much published scholarship is neither interesting nor stimulating
   - Need to think deeply about the nature of the audience for our scholarship—what do we want to accomplish?

modes of research are challenging even to the gatekeepers who are charged with evaluating and facilitating the dissemination of research. We asked a group of key informants among these gatekeepers—academic journal editors and advisors—to share their reflections on the role they play. Three consistent themes emerged:

- *Fitness for purpose*: methodological integrity is more important than adherence to any particular set of protocols or methodology
- *Relevance*: researchers in landscape architecture need to retain their breadth of approach, but must improve the professional and social relevance of scholarship
- *Transparency*: there is need to strengthen the quality of research reporting on the application of "mainstream" science paradigms to landscape architecture and in design-based research, each of which require transparency as well as clarity in communication

In these exchanges with key informants there were never any particular strategies or methods identified that were or were not considered worthy of publication. On the contrary, almost any research strategy or method was acceptable to the editors as long as certain other parameters of quality were upheld. This is certainly understandable: as the discipline of landscape architecture becomes increasingly diverse and ambitious in its scope and impact, its scholarship draws upon many different research traditions from related or analogous fields.

Perhaps as a consequence, however, many long-standing and unresolved contests that exist over the selection of protocols for knowledge formation and knowledge validation in other disciplines have been imported to landscape architecture. These include differences between the humanities and sciences in criteria for peer review, as well as tensions between objective and subjective claims to knowledge and disagreement over the acceptability of hybrid strategies—the so-called "emergent" methods (Hesse-Biber and Leavy 2008). The openness of the discipline to diversity in research and scholarship is commendable, but it has created a problem of validation that will not solve itself and will only increase in complexity and intensity as research efforts increase.

Most commentators upon research in landscape architecture have adopted a position of advocacy for or against a particular paradigm of knowledge or research, asserting greater legitimacy for one or another form of validation. Our position in this book is to argue, instead, that knowledge in a diverse practice-oriented discipline such as landscape architecture must be consensually produced within an intellectual and professional community. The questions that are asked and the significance reported depend on the needs of the field itself, not upon some externally referenced school of thought or normative paradigm of knowledge. In this regard, therefore, the scope and nature of research in the design fields is never "pure," abstract, or objective—rather, as with theory, it is historical, situated, pragmatic, evolving, and cumulative (Meyer 1997).

This contextuality of knowledge in the discipline highlights the critical role that gatekeepers play in the validation process. It also points to the need for greater transparency from authors in explaining the presuppositions that underpin their claims to new knowledge, and an explicit commitment to "bridging" or "translating" the traditions within the discipline. This requires authors to explain the significance of their findings in a shared (plain) language that is accessible to students as well as practitioners. Grinnell (2009, 16) notes that "in the everyday practice of science, calling things as they are is reserved for the community rather than the individual." Knowledge validation is a collective enterprise, and this is a position we advocate for landscape architecture.

1.4 Mapping the Terrain

Our primary goal in this text is to present a framework for classifying, using, and evaluating a range of research strategies in landscape architecture. Through this process, we aim to cultivate a greater understanding of what we already do and know and open researchers to the potentials of a greater number and variety of strategies for investigation than might otherwise be academically and professionally practiced. We also hope that it will help more landscape architects find research topics of interest to inform and enrich their work.

The book is therefore organized around a heuristic model of research strategies based on what actually happens in our field. We have analyzed articles published within the past decade in the main English-language peer-reviewed journals of landscape architecture and located them within a conceptual framework that is structured according to different modes of explanation and epistemology. Our purpose is to recognize, situate, and legitimize the widest range of strategies of inquiry that typically take place in, around, and through landscape architectural practice.

There is much common ground between categories of research used in the applied-design disciplines (such as landscape architecture) and those commonly used in more traditional research fields. The development of a flexible and inclusive classification for landscape architectural research does not require the reinvention of new research strategies. Instead our rubric aims to situate, expand, and augment existing practices and procedures in a way that integrates diverse traditions and attitudes from many fields of investigation into a framework of research strategies for landscape architecture. We reinforce and build on received definitions, while also allowing for greater tolerance and latitude in choices that individuals, corporations, and institutions of landscape architecture may pursue.

We have classified the strategies used in the discipline along two primary dimensions (fig. 1.1). On the one hand, we recognize the distinction between inductive and deductive research strategies. Inductive research, in broad terms, is the generation of descriptions and explanations of relationships in the world through strategies of inquiry grounded in the world of experience and empirical evidence. Deduction is the development of explanations from theory and the systematic testing of these explanations through formal processes of experimentation, evaluation, and argumentation.

The other dimension we have recognized is epistemological—between, on the one hand, an objectivist approach that presumes and seeks to understand a reality or realities in the world existing independently of the investigator and, on the other hand, subjectivist and intersubjectivist approaches that presume knowledge of reality is entirely the product

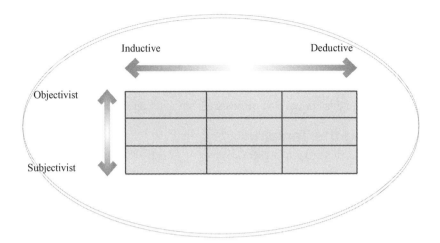

Figure 1.1 The logic of our classification of research strategies

of individuals and society. The "objectivist" position is typically associated with the natural sciences and human sciences and leads to a methodological emphasis upon how to maximize internal and external validity, for example by minimizing the influence of the researcher and by randomized sampling, respectively. The "subjectivist" position is associated with the fine arts and humanities and with a number of emerging social disciplines in which the immersion of the researcher in the systems of creating new knowledge and new realities is recognized and celebrated, and "sampling" is more concerned with the selection of particular examples and cases than with the representation of general populations.

We have expanded the classification matrix beyond the four basic possibilities created by these two dimensions, to recognize a range of transitional strategies, which in practice account for much research in landscape architecture and in other applied disciplines (fig. 1.2). Between the conventional dichotomies of induction and deduction, we recognize a "reflexive approach." In this approach, researchers move back and forth between deductive and inductive perspectives, modifying their theoretical propositions in the light of the evidence, revising their understanding of the evidence (its categories, and its meaning and significance) in light of theoretical concepts and exploring new possibilities of understanding and new ways of knowing. The pragmatic philosopher Charles Peirce used the term "abduction" to describe a way of creating knowledge that is neither inductive nor deductive: "Deduction proves that something must be; induction shows that something actually is operative; abduction merely suggests that something may be" (Peirce 1955, cited in Schobel 2006). This is described elsewhere as a "moment in the design of the world" (Bude 2000, in Schobel 2006).

We also recognize an epistemological position that lies between the objectivist and subjectivist poles that we have termed constructionist (Crotty 1998). This presumes that knowledge is generated though the interaction between the investigators (and their society) and a reality (or realities) that exists but that can never be known independently of

Figure 1.2 Reflexivity in inquiry

the presumptions of the investigators. Landscape knowledge is thus actively constructed rather than found or discovered, and it must always be interpreted in its context (Greider and Gardovich 1994). It is nonetheless anchored in some way and to some degree in a world that exists beyond the subjectivity of an individual or group of individuals (Swaffield 2006).

By expanding the two dimensions in this way we have generated a matrix of possible research strategies that contains nine broad categories (see Table 1.1). Each of these categories has been illustrated and refined in examples of published research studies that are analyzed in later chapters of this book. Having some similarity to classifications in other related disciplines, the framework also "makes sense" of the diverse research strategies we have encountered in our survey of recent research in landscape architecture. The classification is intended to help researchers locate their own interests, needs, and inclinations within a wider field and to recognize relationships with other research.

The framework is, therefore, grounded in the wider conceptual dimensions that shape research strategies across all disciplines, and in examples of research practices and outcomes that have already been executed and published in our field. However, it is not the specific selection that matters. We are more interested in the systems of knowledge formation that this sample, or any other sample, might reveal. In that sense, this book is itself a form of classification research. Another group of researchers might select a different set of examples, possibly adding specific subcategories to our major groups. However, our proposition—the basic shape of the framework—should be refined and strengthened by additional examples. This is the way we hope the framework will be used by students and

Table 1.1 Strategies of Inquiry

	Inductive (theory building)	Reflexive (theory/practice interactions)	Deductive (theory testing)
Objectivist strategies	Description	Modeling and correlation	Experimentation
Constructionist strategies	Classification	Interpretation	Evaluation and diagnosis
Subjectivist strategies	Engaged action	Projective design	Logical systems

practitioners alike—as an additive, cumulative, and, hopefully, consensual project. This, in turn, should lead to the development of improved protocols for validating research that will better integrate knowledge formation in the discipline itself.

The framework categories are described according to the distinctive principles and procedures used for knowledge production. Because most of these categories and the methods that support them are standard to many other disciplines, they have already been studied and described in dozens of methods manuals. In this book, therefore, we do not attempt to reinvent the wheel, so to speak, but simply to illustrate, highlight, and "translate" how these strategies have proved instrumental in generating new forms of knowledge and practical expertise for the design disciplines.

In laying out such a framework, this book also offers a selective survey of current intellectual conditions in the field of landscape architecture through the examples used in each chapter. The examples are taken from the past decade or so of a small sample of refereed publications associated with the discipline. The sources are limited to peer-reviewed English-language journals of landscape architecture and landscape planning. This inevitably excludes research published in a wide range of other journals, in books and nonrefereed journals, and in other languages, as well as excluding other expressions of new knowledge, such as competition entries.

The Content of the Strategy Chapters

Chapter 5: Descriptive Strategies

Direct observation, for example, field records of vegetation

Secondary description, based upon existing sources such as archival documents

Descriptive social surveys, such as polls, surveys, and questionnaires

Case studies, based on comprehensive data collection for a site or situation

Chapter 6: Modeling and Correlational Strategies

Descriptive and synthetic models

Analytical models, such as correlation

Predictive models

Dynamic simulations, including alternative futures

Chapter 7: Experimental Strategies

Classic experimentation, such as laboratory tests or field experiments

Quasi experiments, such as preference studies

Chapter 8: Classification Schemes

Collection, inventory, and catalogues

Typology and Taxonomy

The decision to narrow the sources in this way is partly pragmatic, but it also expresses our interest in the collective character of knowledge formation within the discipline and in the importance of disciplinary protocols for validation of published work. As a consequence, the selection does not include all research undertaken by landscape architecture researchers, whose publication outlets, as revealed by Gobster et al. (2010), extend well beyond the "landscape architecture" journals and include a wide range of related disciplines. Rather, it is intended to illustrate the different strategies evident within the visible "core" of the discipline in a way that enables readers to locate their own interests. It also places within the framework additional examples of research strategies that have been derived from other sources. The content of core chapters is summarized in the following list.

Each of the chapters begins with a definition and review of the characteristic strategies that led us to recognize the category. Selected approaches are exemplified by brief summaries of published research studies, with sufficient detail included for initial discussion and comparison. The examples follow a broad template that draws out their key features and enables them to be compared. These examples are intended to show how established and emerging research practices have been applied to problems of landscape architecture. Our hope and expectation is that students will access the original articles for more detailed analysis, having located and clarified their interests and questions from this overview.

Bibliography and literature reviews

Landscape assessment

Chapter 9: Interpretive Strategies

Ethnography, such as participant observation and depth interviews

Discourse analysis, such as content analysis of primary documents

Formal and iconographic analysis

Historical narrative, using primary documents and historical evidence

Chapter 10: Evaluation and Diagnosis

Parameters and Norms

Design evaluations, such as postoccupancy evaluation

Diagnostics, such as environmental impact

Chapter 11: Engaged Action Research

Pedagogy, such as service learning

Participatory action research (PAR)

Transdisciplinary action research

Chapter 12: Projective Design

Design as research, such as design experiments

Design operations

Design as interpretation

Chapter 13: Logical Systems

Logical frameworks, synthetic logic and expanded field analysis

Spatial syntax, pattern language and indexing

Template Guide for Examples

1. Title: authors, date, and short title
2. What seems to be the condition/problem/opportunity and what is known about it.
3. What question was asked and why this is relevant for the discipline.
4. What needs to be learned (e.g., what condition or event needs to be identified, measured, compared, etc.)
5. How the question was framed or positioned by conceptual, theoretical, or ideological assumptions.
6. What research strategy was adopted and why.
7. What techniques were used and what evidence was recorded; how evidence was analyzed.
8. What were the main findings or conclusions and what are their implications or applications.
9. Why this is a good example and what we can learn from it in terms of research design.

Rather than ideal examples or nearly perfect research models, we chose these examples from the published literature because they were typical and most representative of the widest possible array of research practices in our field. Indeed, several examples illustrate common design problems or errors, duly noted in their summaries. And although the selection of these studies is not intended to provide instruction in specific research methods, it does illustrate the range of methods and techniques that have helped define contemporary research practices and theory in landscape architecture.

There have been a number of interesting challenges in placing particular examples of research within the classification framework. The first is that few practical research programs sit simply and squarely within a single class or type of strategy (Abbott 2008). The majority are hybrid strategies that combine different modes of inquiry in different ways and to different degrees. In cases where the research is sequentially staged and shifts in emphasis as the investigation narrows down to a particular question, we will discuss only a portion of the study. In others, the topic requires a multifaceted approach. Sometimes (indeed, more frequently than is desirable), the strategy lacks structure or clarity due to poor design, or it is reported in a fragmented way. Our approach has been to select examples in which the strategy is clearly stated or expressed and to place the example in the classification "space" that corresponds most closely with the fundamental character of the investigation.

A second challenge has been how to deal with the fact that some types of investigation techniques are used in different ways in different strategies. Modeling and case studies are good examples of particular types of approach that can be used in a range of ways across the inductive-deductive and objectivist-subjectivist dimensions. We have noted this flexibility where relevant.

A third issue has been terminology. Many of the concepts used in research methodology have both technical and popular meanings, and in a number of cases they are used in contrasting strategies (laboratory experimentation versus design experimentation, for example). In other situations, terms are used differently in different disciplines. Simulation is an example of this plurality. We have tried to clarify our usage in the relevant places.

1.5 Building a Research-Based Discipline

As we highlighted earlier, the underlying proposition of this text is that a wide range of research practices has an important role to play in building the discipline; multiple forms of knowing are valuable and necessary in contributing to new knowledge in the field. There is far too much to learn in landscape architecture to be too fastidious about capital "R" or small "r" research or to sustain any outdated chauvinism regarding quantitative and qualitative, "hard" or "soft," inductive or deductive, or traditional or critical research. Nor is this any time to argue whether landscape architecture has its own body of research methods. Although any discipline may pioneer new applications and forms of inquiry, no discipline "owns" its research methods. However, this is not an argument for a methodological free-for-all (Feyerabend 1993). Rather, we endorse Law's position (2005, 4) in seeking "greater methodological variety" within a shared understanding of the possible research strategies and their characteristics.

New knowledge is urgently needed on all fronts, and at all levels, and each of us can and should contribute in the ways we are most capable. In the "new normal," landscape architects simply need to be smarter about producing and consuming research—all forms of research. In a *Landscape Journal* editorial, we argued that:

> current catchphrases are all about being "smart"—smart growth, smart energy, smart cars, smart cities. If we accept any part of the truism that "knowledge is power," then landscape architects might need to get smarter, too.
>
> Pursued as a trade for centuries, then regulated as a field of professional practice, landscape architecture has slowly matured into a comprehensive scholarly discipline. The term refers to an abstract body of knowledge—an evolving, semiautonomous system of learning, knowing, and praxis that is methodically and consensually produced, legitimized, and consumed. Bodies of knowledge undergo constant renewal through the processes of interrogation and investigation. Similar to a system of civil laws, academic disciplines have rules of evidence, precedent cases, and stylized, structured forms of argument. Similar to our system of litigation, we maintain and advance disciplinary knowledge in a collective, participatory process of open challenge and debate. Instead of trial by jury, however, we call it peer review.
>
> It should be emphasized that knowledge production and consumption are reciprocal processes. The production of new knowledge is never a one-way street, and expertise does not naturally flow from the academy to the profession.

After all, practical application (design and planning) is what makes science (theory and method) meaningful. But the practice of better questioning helps produce better answers—and therefore new competencies.(Deming 2009, vi)

This book is aimed at facilitating these "new competencies": not only for students but also for design and planning practitioners. In addition to providing service to clients, and solutions to problems, practitioners also must reframe practical problems as intellectual opportunities—to test theories, apply best practices, generate new realities and alternative futures, and simulate new social and environmental dynamics. This is typical in other professional fields, such as medicine, law, engineering, and business. For the discipline of landscape architecture to flourish, its professionals similarly need to disseminate and reinvest in the results of practical and theoretical research.

The process of understanding landscape architecture as a discipline begins with students. Along with other sets of skills, knowledge, and understanding, students are expected to understand the basics of research processes, including problem recognition and researchable question formation, mastery of relevant literature and the current state of knowledge, design of research strategies in response to specific knowledge needs, and a mature understanding of the impact and limitations of specific research activities. The curricular ramifications of this should be apparent, as we have argued:

> The fundamentals of research demand a skill set that ought to be taught at the undergraduate level, emphasized and honed in graduate programs, and reinforced in professional practice. Finally, the production, legitimization, and consumption of disciplinary knowledge should not grind to a halt when students enter practice. (Deming 2009)

Over the long term, students/practitioners who adopt this type of thinking about research and evidence-based design will have an impact on the intellectual culture of landscape architecture. If practitioners more fully recognize the processes of research in their own work, they ought to be able to conduct better original investigations, share what they have learned, and expand the collective body of knowledge. In the process, they will elevate their own practices, along with the practices of all others.

The suggestion that we could collectively broaden the scope of research practice by enrolling practitioners more fully is not an argument for the discipline to attempt to comprehensively investigate all dimensions of practice or to claim that all practice comprises research. Rather, it seeks an opportunity for new knowledge creation in a range of settings. Paradoxically, as the potential scope widens, there is a case to argue that specific research actions embedded in practice could benefit from a tighter focus—in the words of Wolcott, "doing less, more thoroughly" (1990, cited in Silverman 2005, 85). That means identifying an achievable research goal that may itself be modest but which, *when combined with others,* can build the discipline. All practitioners have this opportunity.

By allowing emerging techniques and voices to be recognized and given a place in the academic/professional system of knowledge production, the field will be substantially enriched. These new techniques and voices might include research strategies that have previously been misunderstood in some academic "silos," for example, site-based or phenomenological research methods associated with the arts and humanities, critical feminist investigations, narrative or exploratory methods associated with underrepresented perspectives, participatory action research, and design as research, to mention just a few. Yet these can and should be reconciled and positioned within a comparative framework of knowledge.

The book is organized in two parts. The first part establishes our approach and maps out the knowledge terrain for the discipline. Chapter 2 ("Knowing Landscape Architecture") summarizes recent surveys of the knowledge domain of landscape architecture, and its research priorities. Chapter 3 ("Theory/Research/Scholarship/Critique") then offers a similar summary of recent debates about the nature of theory in landscape architecture and its relationship with research, scholarship, and critique. These two survey chapters provide the context for developing a research strategy. Chapter 4 ("Integrating Design and Research"), the final chapter in part one, considers the practical and theoretical considerations involved in selecting and shaping a research strategy.

The second part of the book constitutes the substantive review of strategies, with nine chapters that feature specific examples of how different strategies have been applied in landscape architecture, as well as a concluding discussion of the linkage of research and practice. Chapter topics relate directly to the classification matrix set out earlier and are organized in sequence from left to right, starting at the top row of the classification (Description) and moving to the bottom (Logical Argumentation).

Finally, it is important to reiterate that this text is focused upon research strategies rather than on specific methods and techniques. Nonetheless, questions of method and technique are frequently at the forefront of students' and new researchers' concerns. We have therefore included a series of notes on method throughout the strategy chapters and have provided references to a range of relevant methods texts. For classroom use, we encourage faculty and students to supplement this book with specific methods manuals that are relevant to their project interests or curricular goals.

References

Abbott, M. 2008. *Designing wilderness as a phenomenological landscape: Design directed research within the context of New Zealand's conservation estate*. PhD diss., Lincoln University, Christchurch, New Zealand.

Bude, H. 2000. Die Kunst der Interpretation. In *Qualitative forschung*, ed. U. Flick et al., 569–77. Reinbek at Hamburg: Rowohlts Enzyklopädie.

Creswell, J. W. 2009. *Research design: Qualitative, quantitative, and mixed methods approaches*. 3rd ed. Thousand Oaks, CA: Sage.

Crotty, M. 1998. *The foundations of social research: Meaning and perspectove in the research process*. St. Leonards, Australia: Allen and Unwin.

Davies, H. T. O., S. M. Nutley, and P. C. Smith. 2000. *What works? Evidence-based policy and practice in public services*. Bristol, U.K.: Policy Press.

Deming, M. E. 2009. Editor's introduction. *Landscape Journal* 28 (2): iv–viii.

Feyerabend, P. 1993. *Against method*. London: Verso.

Forsyth, A. 2008. Great programs in architecture: Rankings, performance assessments, and diverse paths to prominence. *International Journal of Architectural Research* 2 (2): 11–22.

Gobster P. H., J. I. Nassauer, and D. J. Nadenicek. 2010. *Landscape Journal* and scholarship in landscape architecture: The next 25 years. *Landscape Journal* 29 (1): 52–70.

Greider, T., and L. Gardovich. 1994. Landscapes: The social construction of nature and the environment. *Rural Sociology* 59 (1): 1–24.

Grinnell, F. 2009. *Everyday practice of science: Where intuition and passion meet objectivity and logic*. Oxford, U.K.: Oxford University Press.

Groat, L., and D. Wang. 2002. *Architectural research methods*. New York: John Wiley and Sons.

Hesse-Biber, S. N., and P. Leavy. 2008. *Handbook of emergent methods*. New York: Guilford Press.

Laurel, B. ed. 2003. *Design research: Methods and perspectives*. Cambridge, MA: MIT Press.

Law, J. 2004. *After methods: Mess in social science research*. Abingdon, U.K.: Routledge.

Meyer, E. 1997. The expanded field of landscape architecture. In *Ecological design and planning,* ed. G. F. Thompson and F. R. Steiner. New York: John Wiley and Sons.

Pierce, C. S. 1935. *Pragmatism and Pragmaticism*. Vols. 5 and 6 of *Collected papers of Charles Sanders Peirce,* ed. C. Hartshorne and P. Weiss. Cambridge, MA: Harvard University Press.

Schöbel, S. 2006. Qualitative research as a perspective for urban open space planning. *Journal of Landscape Architecture* 1(1): 38–47.

Silverman, D. 1985. *Qualitative methodology and sociology.* London: Gower.

Swaffield, S. R. 2006. Theory and critique in landscape architecture. *Journal of Landscape Architecture* 1(1): 22–29.

Swaffield, S. R., and M. E. Deming. 2007. Embodied knowledge: Research strategies in landscape architecture. In *Negotiating landscapes: Abstracts of the 2007 annual meeting of the Council of Educators in Landscape Architecture, Pennsylvania State University, August 14–19, 2007,* ed. B. Szczgiel and M. Bose, 223–24. State College, PA: Pennsylvania State University Department of Landscape Architecture.

Tai, L. 2003. Doctoring the profession. *Landscape Architecture Magazine,* November, 64–73.

Trochim, W. 2006. *Research methods knowledge base*. Web Center for Social Research Methods.

Wolcott, H. F. 1990. *Writing up qualitative research*. Los Angeles: Sage.

CHAPTER 2

Knowing Landscape Architecture

2.1 Introduction

Integration of design and research practices in professional disciplines is a complex and vitally important challenge. While much has been written about the intellectual frameworks that support an autonomous discipline, it is generally accepted that its disciplinary status depends on whether or not it has the capacity to sustain and disseminate research and develop a specialized body of knowledge. In this chapter we first review the nature of professional disciplines. We then survey the scope of landscape architectural knowledge, based upon a synthesis of several recent surveys. Finally, we identify some research needs that have been articulated within the North American part of the discipline. These reviews are intended to provide a context for developing research questions and a research strategy (see chapter 4).

2.2 The Nature of Professional Disciplines

In summary terms, a discipline is "a branch of knowledge or teaching" that displays "a systematic and ordered study based upon clearly defined models and rules of procedure" (Snodgrass 1987, citing Clarke 1968). Like science, the word discipline thus implies a standard or characteristic method for learning and knowing. A discipline may be practically recognized as a community of thought and practice that possesses some variant of all of the following basic characteristics:

- reference or parent disciplines
- a distinctive mandate, paradigm, or worldview
- a specialized body of knowledge that produces and maintains its own literature
- a set of disciplinary principles and practices
- subthemes and study concentrations
- an active research or theory development agenda (for professional disciplines this is often based on empirical or practical problems related to the mandate)
- specialized educational programs, gatekeeper, and regulatory/advocacy groups

Typically built upon or derived from parent disciplines or combinations of other disciplines, autonomous disciplines emerge over time as unique, defined, recognizable, and distinct. They may also become catalysts for new subdisciplines. For instance, landscape architecture can trace origins in fine art, architecture, surveying, engineering, agriculture, and horticulture. It has, in turn, influenced the emergence of subdisciplines such as landscape planning.

Autonomous disciplines are typically distinguished by a distinctive point of view or mandate. Because it has been historically responsive to contextual social and environmental issues, the mandate of landscape architecture is always evolving and thus debatable. However, its basic position has consistently related to stewardship—the protection and enhancement of the conceptual, material, and phenomenal relationships between human culture and nonhuman nature. This mandate is partly what distinguishes landscape architecture from, say, architecture, but also relates it to other, synthetic or hybrid disciplines such as urban forestry.

The most important function of an autonomous discipline is the construction and maintenance of a specialized *body of knowledge*. This provides a normative, principled foundation for best practice and a platform for the acquisition of new knowledge. A discipline relies on its *research community* (Mulkay 1977) to produce and monitor its own literature for dissemination of new knowledge and critique of existing knowledge. Both self-replicating and evolutionary, we might therefore think of the body of knowledge in landscape architecture as its DNA. Disciplinary knowledge is constantly revised through both consensual and critical processes of testing, review, and recombination and re-presentation, as well as through teaching and other engaged practices.

Because of their special reciprocal relationship to practice, applied disciplines like landscape architecture draw many, if not most, academic research questions from problems and opportunities encountered by professionals in the field of practice. It should also be said that the transmission and consolidation of received knowledge are not the sole purview of institutions: this type of learning happens just as often in professional offices, ateliers, and workshops.

Maturing over time, an autonomous discipline will develop consolidated themes of activity that evolve along with the interests and concerns of its community of practitioners and researchers. A hierarchy of focal issues thus forms beneath the apparent unity suggested by professional paradigms or mandates. These issues may comprise theoretical concerns such as values and typologies, as well as practical issues of design, management, and implementation. They have their own life cycles and can sometimes be recognized as historical artefacts of the maturation of the field.

Professional disciplines are maintained and advanced by specialized professional curricula, professional societies, conferences, and peer-reviewed disciplinary journals, among other things. Both the production and reproduction of knowledge have their own processes and serve different purposes, and both are crucially important sustaining functions of an autonomous discipline. In professional courses of study, individual knowledge is guided by disciplinary taxonomies or rubrics. Such courses (United Kingdom) or programs (United States/Canada) are typically legitimized and monitored by accrediting

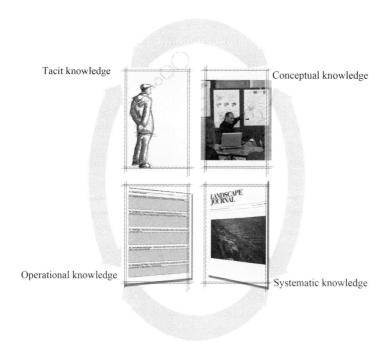

Tacit knowledge

Conceptual knowledge

Operational knowledge

Systematic knowledge

Figure 2.1 Types of knowledge
(Incorporating concepts from Nanaka and Takeuchi 1995)

bodies—gatekeeper groups that represent the interests of national or international professional organizations with a mandate of stewarding professional standards and knowledge (discussed in chapter 1).

The knowledge base of a professional discipline is, thus, in a continual process of transformation as the tacit knowledge of professional practice is encoded in scholarly work and as research investigations and theoretical speculations are tested against practice. Nanaka and Takeuchi (1995) identified four realms of knowledge in applied research situations: *tacit knowledge*, the implicit taken-for-granted knowledge of practice; *conceptual knowledge*, which makes tacit knowledge explicit and codifies it as principles and protocols; *systematic knowledge*, which is also explicit and formally expressed, validated, and integrated at the core of the discipline; and *operational knowledge,* through which systematic knowledge and conceptual knowledge are translated into different realms of practice (see fig. 2.1).

The reflexive shaping of tacit and explicit forms of knowledge shapes the emergence of the profession and underpins the development of professional institutions and teaching programs. Tacit knowledge is expressed in the everyday work of practitioners and is represented in the works described in professional journals. Explicit knowledge defines the discipline through academic publication, scholarly expression, education and accreditation, and formal professional discourse. Conceptual principles and canonical models are codified in the classic texts of the profession—such as those by Downing, Hubbard and Kimball, Eckbo, Colvin, Simonds, McHarg, Jellicoe, and others. Systematic knowledge is expressed in the peer-reviewed journals, edited texts, competitions, and research reports and theses. Operational knowledge is defined in professional competencies required for accreditation and through best-practice guidance.

Tracing this evolving and interrelated body of knowledge is the task of academic historians and is beyond the scope of this text. However, any consideration of contemporary research strategies must, of necessity, take account of the nature and scope of the field of knowledge of the discipline. In the next section, we review several recent surveys of knowledge domains in landscape architecture. The review of knowledge is partial—in particular, it is limited to a selection of English-language sources. As with the text as a whole, it must, therefore, be read alongside other accounts that focus upon knowledge formation in countries and regions whose scholarly work is published in other languages. Nonetheless, it provides a platform from which English-speaking students can build their understanding of the field and its research possibilities.

2.3 Domains of Knowledge in Landscape Architecture

The International Federation of Landscape Architects (IFLA) offers the most widely applicable statement of the scope of landscape architecture as a professional activity. This provides a global point of reference for the operational knowledge of the profession. While IFLA does not define the realm of knowledge in landscape architecture, the activities that are listed as characteristic of professional practice provide an indication of knowledge domains. They are summarized in the following list at a similar level of generality to the more explicit surveys of knowledge described later in the chapter. The terms used here are our own, based upon our interpretation of the IFLA text.

Operational knowledge domains implied by the IFLA definition of professional activity

Landscape planning, design, and management

Protected-areas management

Cultural and historic landscapes, parks, and gardens

Built environments

Infrastructure

Landscape assessment

Site analysis and planning

Landscape design and implementation

Contract administration

Research and teaching

Project management

The IFLA definition was prepared for submission to the International Labor Organization in 2003. Two comprehensive English-language surveys of professionally relevant knowledge in landscape architecture were also under way at that time. The Landscape Architecture Body of Knowledge (LABOK) project (American Society of Landscape Architects 2004) was a collaborative effort involving professional organizations, educators, and accrediting boards in North America and was aimed at defining the competencies required for landscape architectural practice. In Europe, the Le Notre project—funded by the European Commission—has been aimed at "tuning" landscape architecture education across Europe (Bruns et al. 2009).

LABOK focused upon identifying the core knowledge and competencies that characterized landscape architecture and defining the point in the development of a professional landscape architect at which these types of knowledge and competencies should be mastered. The survey report draws a distinction between core and contextual knowledge acquired and expected in first professional degrees, in postprofessional degrees, and in practice. It therefore included conceptual, systematic, and operational realms of knowledge. The study was structured around nine knowledge domains in the discipline, set out as follows.

LABOK knowledge domains

Landscape architecture history and criticism

Natural and cultural systems

Design and planning theories and methods

Public policy and regulation

Design, planning, and management

Site design and engineering

Construction documentation and administration

Communication

Values and ethics in practice

Not all of the LABOK domains were assessed as equally important at each stage in the formation of a professional landscape architect. Predominantly operational knowledge on construction, documentation, and administration, for example, was judged to require less emphasis in the first professional degree. Nor were all domains assessed as equally important within the discipline: at that time public policy and regulation, for example, was seen as a relatively low priority overall. Similarly, within each of these domains there were subject areas that were more or less important at different stages in the professional formation of a landscape architect.

A second survey that provides insight into the knowledge domain of the discipline was undertaken as part of the Le Notre project (www.le-notre.org). Le Notre is a European Thematic Network in the field of landscape architecture that is organized by the

European Council of Landscape Architecture Schools (ECLAS), with support from the European Commission. It is associated with the "Bologna" process, which is aimed at establishing a common framework of tertiary education across Europe through a process described as "tuning." The Le Notre working document on tuning (Bruns et al. 2009) describes the field of landscape architecture and its areas of expertise and is intended to provide terms of reference for European educational programs in landscape architecture. The focus is, therefore, educational, rather than professional accreditation, although accreditation is recognized as a longer term potential outcome.

The Le Notre project was a continuing process of collaborations through conferences, workshops, and subject-based working groups. It also included a survey of students, academics, and practitioners. The tuning report recognized two linked areas of core competency in landscape architecture—(1) knowledge of and skills in planning, design, and management and (2) knowledge and understanding of landscape change. The report cites Steinitz's (1990) framework for classifying the types of knowledge in the discipline, with a focus upon planning, design, and management, and uses the European Landscape Convention as a point of reference for understanding landscape.

The project identified a substantial list of generic competencies and competencies related to landscape architecture. Like the LABOK study, Le Notre incorporates conceptual, systematic, and operational knowledge. The categorization (Table 2.1) specifically distinguishes knowledge and expertise about *theory and practice* of landscape architecture; the *activities* of design, planning, and management; specific *landscape types*; and *technologies and materials*. Within this framework twelve core areas of knowledge and expertise are identified.

A survey of scholarly publications in North America (Powers and Walker 2009) provides a useful link between these professionally oriented frameworks of knowledge and the process of validation for the systematic knowledge of the discipline. *Landscape Journal* is a peer-reviewed journal published on behalf of the Council of Educators in Landscape Architecture (CELA). It has been a primary vehicle for the codification of landscape architecture knowledge in North America since 1982. Powers and Walker's

Table 2.1 The Le Notre "tuning" project: key areas of knowledge and expertise

Theory and practice	Activities	Landscape types	Technologies, materials
Theory and methodology	Landscape planning	Urban open space	Materials and construction
Professional practice	Landscape design	Cultural landscapes	Vegetation and plant material
History and conservation	Landscape management	Infrastructure projects	Information technology

survey reviewed the content of published articles for its first quarter century, from 1982 to 2007. The categories they used were based on "track themes" that had evolved through the peer-review and presentation process for the CELA annual conferences.

The following list shows the categories of published work in *Landscape Journal* in descending order of frequency of publication. As with the LABOK and Le Notre frameworks, the categories are broad and inclusive, and they disguise many potential shades of interpretation. However, the survey provides a snapshot of the areas of systematic knowledge emerging from research and scholarship that is explicitly and directly associated with landscape architecture in North America.

Categories of scholarship published in *Landscape Journal* (after Powers and Walker 2009)

History and culture

Landscape planning and ecology

Human and environment relationships

Design theory

Urban design

Landscape design and implementation

Communication and visualization

Methods of inquiry

Sustainability

Landscape architecture profession

Design education and pedagogy

Gobster et al. (2010) have significantly extended this analysis with an investigation of peer-reviewed publication by landscape architecture faculty in North America. Their aim was to evaluate the performance of *Landscape Journal* (LJ) relative to its own goals and to the contributions of other scholarly journals. In addition to reviewing the content of *Landscape Journal,* the investigators evaluated its impact as indicated by the number of citations, and compared this with the extent and impact of research published by landscape architecture faculty in other landscape-related journals.

The review of content largely reinforced the findings of Powers and Walker, highlighting the dominance of historical and theoretical topics. However, further analysis by Gobster and colleagues found that much of the more applied (and arguably socially relevant) research in the discipline—in areas such as environmental management and landscape planning—was more likely to be published in the journals of related disciplines and to receive higher impact ratings. They conclude that the discipline needs to strengthen the relationship of its specialist journals with the wider world of research and scholarship.

Finally, there are also a number of classifications of the knowledge base of the discipline offered by individual commentators. Howett (1987), for example, identified three broad areas of knowledge that she argued are central to landscape architecture: systems ecology, semiotics, and environmental psychology. Our own review of theoretical writing in recent Anglo-American literature (Swaffield 2002) identified five core themes: (1) design process, (2) the interpretation of meaningful form, (3) landscape representation, (4) ecological design and aesthetics, and (5) the integration of site, place, and region. Each of these themes has been the subject of more detailed and focused syntheses by others. This review reinforced awareness of the breadth of knowledge in the discipline, while Howett's article highlighted connections with a diverse range of other disciplines.

Overall, the categories of knowledge we have drawn from these sources were not constructed with identical assumptions and are not, therefore, strictly congruent, either practically or conceptually. Taken together, however, they provide an impression of the field of knowledge that constitutes the core of the discipline, both in North America and Europe, and, through the IFLA statement, globally.

Table 2.2 provides a synthesis of the categories of knowledge domains drawn from the different institutional sources and analyses outlined above. Even at this abstract level, it reveals a relatively high degree of commonality. The LJ/CELA classification is least well aligned with the others, largely because it is more narrowly focused upon the systematic knowledge that is formalized through peer review and academic publication, whereas the professional knowledge frameworks include the conceptual and operational knowledge of practice. The LJ/CELA classification also includes several categories that do not appear at a macro scale in the LABOK and Le Notre classifications, but which would be found as subthemes in these wider frameworks, such as pedagogy (knowledge about teaching).

In some cases, minor differences between systems are a consequence of subtle variations in the logic of the groupings. For example, criticism is associated with history in the LABOK categories, but with theory and method in Le Notre. A more noticeable difference is the result of a decision within the Le Notre framework to group some areas of knowledge according to the type of setting for practice (e.g., infrastructure, urban open space, cultural landscapes), for which there is no direct equivalent in LABOK. However, these functional groupings do appear in the IFLA rubric. It is also notable that the IFLA classification of professional activity (which is broadly indicative of the operational knowledge of the discipline) aligns very well with the more comprehensive surveys of all forms of knowledge, as well as with the more narrowly focused expression of systematic knowledge published in the academy.

The LABOK and Le Notre reviews recognize the extensive realms of knowledge that are expressed within the specialist areas of practice and research, as well as the knowledge that is associated with postprofessional degrees. The boundaries of the profession and discipline are expanding, driven by a number of dynamics, including interdisciplinary forms of knowledge, agendas to better integrate science and public policy, business opportunities and imperatives, the individualization of work, and the curiosity of practitioners, scholars, and researchers. Landscape architecture educators and researchers typically

Table 2.2 Core domains of knowledge in landscape architecture

IFLA	LABOK	LE NOTRE	LJ/CELA
Cultural and historic landscapes, parks, and gardens	Landscape architecture history and criticism	History and conservation	History and culture
Protected areas management	Natural and cultural systems	Cultural landscapes	Human and environment relationships
Landscape assessment	Public policy and regulations		Sustainability; perception
Site analysis and planning	Design and planning theory and method	Landscape planning	Landscape planning and ecology
		Theory and methodology	Design theory, methods of inquiry
Research and teaching			Design education and pedagogy
Built environments infrastructure		Urban open space infrastructure projects	Urban design
Landscape planning, design, and management	Design, planning, and management	Landscape design; Landscape management	Landscape design and implementation
Landscape design and implementation	Site design, engineering	Materials and construction	
		Vegetation and plant material	
Contract administration, project management	Construction documentation and administration	Professional practice	Landscape architecture profession
	Values and ethics		
	Communication	Information technology	Communication and visualization

cite work from journals in a wide range of disciplines other than landscape architecture, which indicates the highly permeable nature of the discipline. One outcome of this expansion of perspective is the wide range of research strategies adopted by the discipline.

2.4 Research Needs

Identification of the research needs of the discipline—the domains where new knowledge is required—is much less well articulated than is the existing realm of knowledge. It is an almost taken-for-granted presumption in discussion over research in the discipline that there is a gap between the expressed research needs of practice and the perceptions of need of academic researchers. However, there are no formal processes by which such needs are identified, or responses shaped, or the two mapped against each other.

In the United States, for example, LABOK was seen as a "snapshot," not a plan for the future (ASLA 2004), although it could be a useful starting point for a knowledge strategy. Although it does not yet formally publish a research agenda for the profession, the American Society of Landscape Architects (ASLA) expresses its priorities through advocacy on key issues. These issues currently include, among other topics, economic recovery, transportation, sustainable design, livable communities, water and storm water, and historic landscapes. In addition, seventeen professional practice networks (PPN) include specialties such as campus planning and design, children's outdoor environments, healthcare and therapeutic design, housing and community design, reclamation and restoration, and women in landscape architecture.

Professional research needs may be articulated in other ways—for example, through networks and foundations that develop working research agendas. One example is the Landscape Futures Initiative, an ambitious project supported by the U.S.-based Landscape Architecture Foundation (LAF). Beginning in 2002, a series of seven symposia analyzed the processes of landscape transformation that are likely to affect the design professions in the coming decades. Seven drivers of global landscape change were identified: urbanization, culture and technology, connectivity, politics and economy, global environmental threats, population and social dynamics, and leadership trends. The concluding conference, "Leadership in Landscape Change," drew together the overall findings of the series (as our text goes to press, the final conference report has not been published).

LAF maintains a call for research for its *Land and Community Design Case Studies Series* in order to systematically build documentation for design projects using the template developed by Francis (2001) (see example 5.7). In a recent extension of this, LAF has launched the *Landscape Performance Series,* a web-based resource intended to provide a quantitative evidence base for designers and decision-makers. Stated objectives for the case studies and landscape performance series highlight the Foundation's research focus on the contributions made by scholars and designers to livable communities, sustainability, and environmental protection.

In 2009, CELA established a new executive leadership position charged with research coordination, in part aimed at forming a research agenda by and for educators in the field.

In a recent informal survey, CELA members identified a number of priorities for new research in landscape architecture. The following list reveals a set of concerns that are decidedly practical and do not differ substantially from the LAF and LABOK agendas. The categorization is our own.

Research priorities of CELA landscape educators

Sustainability and biophysical process

Natural hazards such as tropical storms, hurricanes, tsunamis, etc.

Water quality

Design to maximize energy efficiency in buildings (or minimize energy use in buildings)

Identification of, and design for, appropriate microclimatic environments for plants and nonhuman animals

Soil erosion and sediment control

Stream corridor restoration

Social and cultural process

Cross-cultural issues in design

Collaborative design

Public perceptions/visual analysis/visual design in forestry and rural/wild lands

Health and well-being

Environmental design and urban health

Active living

Design of outdoor spaces for human thermal comfort

Urban regeneration

Landscape urbanism (umbrella topic)

Brownfield redevelopment

Storm water management

Tools and technologies

Emerging digital design media, e.g., software that models natural forces such as gravity, wind, soft bodies, and water

Internet-based video presence

Visualization methods/ethics

Climate-change visioning tools/processes

Combining the case-study priorities of the Landscape Architecture Foundation with the ASLA and CELA lists of research priorities provides an initial impression of research priorities in the North American discipline (Table 2.3). As with the synthesis of knowledge

Table 2.3 Research agendas in North America

ASLA advocacy agenda	LAF case study priorities	CELA research priorities
Sustainable design	Green infrastructure	Sustainability and biophysical process
Water and storm water	Water quality and source protection	
Historic landscapes		Social and cultural process
Livable communities	Healthy communities	Health and well-being
	Open space	
Economic recovery	Urban redevelopment of brownfields	Urban regeneration
		Tools and technologies

domains earlier in the chapter, a pattern can be identified. Here, it is focused on four areas: design and planning of sustainable landscape systems; understanding social and cultural values and processes in landscape; healthy and livable communities; and urban regeneration. In addition, educators recognized the need for enhanced tools and technologies.

In the European context, the Le Notre tuning project does not explicitly address research needs, although it recognizes the need for the teaching of research competencies in educational programs. The European Landscape Convention, sponsored by the Council of Europe, is providing a major stimulus for individual and multicountry research investigations of "landscape" as defined by the convention. Work on "landscape" studies more generally and upon research needs related to multifunctional land use are being pursued under the auspices of the European Science Foundation. However, to the best of our knowledge there is as yet no overarching survey or statement of the research needed to support or expand the specific knowledge base of landscape architecture as a discipline within Europe.

One feature of the emerging collective agenda for the United States is its instrumental and pragmatic focus. There is as yet little sense of a collective theoretical agenda for the discipline as a whole. That is not to say that a theoretical agenda is altogether absent from the discipline, however. Many individual commentators and some leading practices have advocated particular directions of theoretical exploration. Some themes can be seen recurring in the literature, including theorization of the landscape planning and design process within the late modern global city, the phenomenological exploration of individual experience within an increasingly diverse and interconnected world, the deepening understanding of site, and the interface between perception and ecology.

Furthermore, some areas of major activity in related disciplines receive little explicit attention in the landscape architecture literature. Most noticeable of these is the relative lack of attention to the challenge of climate change adaptation and mitigation at multiple scales (Swaffield and Swanwick 2008). At the precise moment when the practice of landscape architecture is becoming more vital to our collective survival, its lack of a coherent research agenda and its lack of relative impact in the wider field of published knowledge make it vulnerable to becoming sidelined in the global academy. The discipline clearly needs a broader and better-organized professional research agenda to guide its initiatives, a clearer practical understanding of what it means to be a research-based, rather than a service-driven profession, and a stronger focus upon effective dissemination of the knowledge it creates (Gobster et al. 2010).

References

American Society of Landscape Architects. 2004. *Landscape architecture body of knowledge study report.* Washington, DC: American Society of Landscape Architects.

Bruns, D., V. Ortacesme, R. Stiles, J. De Vries, R. Holden, and K. Jörgensen. 2009. *Tuning landscape architecture education in Europe* (draft version 25). http://www.le-notre.org (accessed January 2010).

Clarke, D. L. 1968. *Analytical archaeology.* London: Methuen and Co.

Francis, M. 2001. A case study method for landscape architecture. *Landscape Journal* 20 (1): 15–29.

Gobster P. H., J. I. Nassauer, and D. J. Nadenicek. 2010. *Landscape Journal* and scholarship in landscape architecture: The next 25 years. *Landscape Journal* 29 (1): 52–70.

Howett, C. 1987. Systems, signs, sensibilities. *Landscape Journal* 6 (1): 1–12.

Mulkay, M. 1977. Sociology of the scientific research community. In *Science, technology and society: A cross-disciplinary perspective,* eds. I. Spiegel-Rosing and D. D. S. Price. London: Sage

Nanaka, I., and H. Takeuchi. 1995. *The knowledge creating company: How Japanese companies create the dynamics of innovation.* New York: Oxford University Press.

Powers, M., and J. Walker. 2009. Twenty-five years of *Landscape Journal*: An analysis of authorship and article content. *Landscape Journal* 28 (1): 96–110.

Snodgrass, A. M. 1987. *An archaeology of Greece: The present state and future scope of the discipline.* Los Angeles: University of California Press.

Steinitz, C. 1990. A framework for theory applicable to the education of landscape architects. *Landscape Journal* 9 (2): 136–43.

Swaffield, S. R. 2002. *Theory in landscape architecture: A reader.* Philadelphia: University of Pennsylvania Press.

Swaffield, S. R., and C. Swanwick. 2008. Climate change and landscape architecture: A practice and research agenda. In *New landscapes—new lives: New challenges in landscape planning, design, and management. ECLAS Annual Meeting, Sept. 14, 2008*, ed. I. Sarlov-Herlin. Alnarp, Sweden: Swedish Agriculture University (SLU).

CHAPTER 3
Theory/Research/ Scholarship/Critique

3.1 Introduction

In this chapter we briefly review the debates over the nature of theory that have characterized the discipline over the past twenty-five years, and explore their implications for our understanding of research and its connections to scholarship and critique. Presumptions made about the nature of theory shape the type of systematic knowledge upon which a discipline is based. This, in turn, shapes the way in which a discipline defines its research activity and scholarship—the relationship between research and practice, the character of its research endeavors, and the strategies it adopts.

Questions and debates over the theoretical base of landscape architecture have emerged regularly over its long evolution as a profession and discipline. Corner (1990) argued that theory can be both a "stabilizer" and a "disruptive mechanism." It can be a stabilizer in the sense that some types and applications of theory express the codified conceptual and operational knowledge of a discipline, described by Eckbo (1950) as "the generalization of social experience"—knowledge drawn from practice and upon which much practice is itself based. Theorizing can also provoke change in thinking and practice and can be understood as a critical act that challenges assumptions about the nature of practice and about the world in which we practice. Corner (1991) identified and advocated a third, hermeneutic, role for theory that systematically and reflexively draws out relationships and significance.

All of these roles have been expressed and articulated in recent debates. In an earlier review (Swaffield 2002), we summarized them as *instrumental* theory aimed at prediction, control, and practical action, *critical* theory that challenges the status quo and stimulates change, and *interpretive* theory that enhances understanding of meaning and context (fig. 3.1).

Alongside the debate about the role and nature of theory, there has been a parallel debate about the nature of research in the discipline and its relationship to scholarship and practice. The two debates are linked through the way that particular interpretations of the nature of theory are associated with particular paradigms of research. Just as there

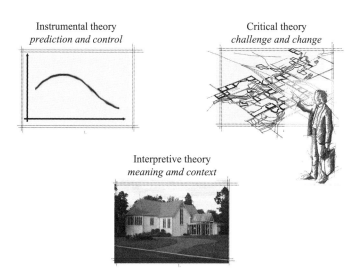

Instrumental theory
prediction and control

Critical theory
challenge and change

Interpretive theory
meaning amd context

Figure 3.1 The nature of theory in landscape architecture

are different possible interpretations of theory, so there have been different interpretations of what constitutes research. Some commentators advocate a narrow definition, aligned with the conventions of the natural sciences, while others seek to widen it to include design activity.

In the more restrictive approach to research, the role of scholarship is elevated in importance to provide legitimacy for activities that have been excluded from the research domain. The stance adopted over theory and its relationship to research and scholarship also influences the interpretation of the nature and role of critique. Marc Treib has been reported to say, "There is an idea structure behind criticism. This is the link between criticism and theory" (cited in Berrizbeitia 1997, 10). Hence, theory, research paradigms, and traditions of scholarship and critique are all inextricably linked and influence the strategies of inquiry we adopt.

3.2 Competing Ideals of Theory

Debates over the nature and content of theory in landscape architecture have characterized the discipline from its origins, but have been particularly intense during periods of socioeconomic and intellectual transformation. Theories of humankind and our relationship to nature were deeply implicated in the shifting fashions of the gardens of the elite during the political conflicts over different types of governance in Europe in the seventeenth and eighteenth centuries (Jellicoe and Jellicoe 1987). Contested theories of landscape perception and taste were part of the intellectual and practical reshaping of rural estates in Northern Europe during the modernization of agriculture in the eighteenth century (Hunt 1992). Theories and metaphors of human physiology and well-being influenced the creation of public parks and "Garden Cities" during the rapid urbanization of industrial countries in the late nineteenth and early twentieth centuries. There were calls for new theoretical understandings of the relationship between society and technology to guide the landscape design contribution to the growth and rebuilding of western economies following the Second World War (Eckbo 1950). In each case the three roles of theory—as instrumental stabilizer, critical disrupter, and interpreter of change—were all evident and in tension.

Questions of the nature of landscape design theory in a late modern world emerged in the 1980s and 1990s, stimulated both by the intellectual ferment of post-structural thinking in related disciplines and by the rapid urban transformations that were driven by globalization of societies and economies. This latest period of debate has been intensified by changes taking place within the universities themselves, as corporate management and public-choice models of funding have demanded explicit measurement of "research" activity (Forsyth 2008). This has, in turn, encouraged landscape educators to seek to widen the scope of what is defined as theory in the discipline.

Early contributions to the most recent phase of debate over theory focused upon the need to renew and broaden the theoretical basis of teaching and practice in landscape architecture. They typically argued for a reorientation from an established "modern" approach, characterized as instrumental, uncritical, and lacking in originality or insight (Krog 1981, 1983), to a more open-ended, creative, environmentally and socially responsible, "postmodern" orientation (Krog 1981; Koh 1982; Meeus and Vroom 1986). Other influential commentators (Howett 1987; Spirn 1989) focused upon the substantive content of theory, proposing different agendas for further development and typically drawing upon emerging movements in related disciplines.

In 1990 one of the key gatekeepers of the discipline in North America shifted the grounds of the debate. Taking up a new role as editor of *Landscape Journal,* Robert Riley threw down a challenge. In the transition from a profession to a discipline, he argued, the concept of theory had become misused. Frequently plagiarized from other disciplines, theory was used to justify decisions about style. "Anything concerned with what to do or why to do it, instead of how to do it, is proudly proclaimed as theory. This is not theory; it is pseudotheory," he claimed (Riley 1990, 48).

Citing a framework presented by Amos Rapoport, Riley advocated a more restricted and "precise" use of the term theory that was drawn from the hypothetico-deductive model of science. According to this view, theory is a formal statement that explains real-world phenomena and has been built and tested through systematic experimental research. In contrast, the sets of ideas typically called theory in landscape architecture, and used to justify particular strategies or actions, should be more correctly termed frameworks. Having defined the terms, Riley argued that the discipline could then proceed to build a more valid and useful theoretical foundation.

It is important to note that Riley's charge of pseudotheory did not question the potential value of concepts and understandings drawn from other disciplines per se. Nor did he argue against diversity in research and scholarship. However, he did argue for a more tightly defined understanding of the term theory and of the process of research by which it is developed. A number of other subsequent commentators on the discipline have reinforced and reiterated similar arguments (Chenoweth 1992; LaGro 1999; Milburn et al. 2003).

The argument that the definition and construction of theory in the discipline should be aligned with the conventions of modern science has itself not gone unchallenged. In particular, influential commentators such as Corner (1990, 1991) and Meyer (1997) offered tightly argued agendas for a "situated" understanding of knowledge. In his extensive two-part essay, Corner offered an historically situated interpretation of theory in which he argued that the emergence of modern science had privileged an instrumental, utilitarian approach to knowledge, and suppressed the "forgotten rule" of theory, which, he suggested, is indeed to provide the poetic motivation for action.

In his critique, Corner expressed a concern similar to Riley's (1990) about the problem of making claims for theoretical justification based upon the "creative adrenaline in risk, novelty, and polemical experiment" of the avant-garde (1991, 121). Like Riley, Corner challenged the dominance of form over content that is frequently associated with fashionable new design movements. However, he also attacked the suggestion that theory in landscape architecture should be based upon the model of positivist science, in which it is assumed that "factual data alone will automatically lead to a logical and credible synthesis" (1991, 117). Instead, Corner advocated an interpretative approach to theory, as a form of knowledge that is "always situated within particular contexts" (1991, 126). Corner framed this as a phenomenological project that would enable the discipline to reconnect technical action with the "poetics" of dwelling. In later work (1999) this stance was expanded to position landscape architecture as a "strategic agent of culture." This suggests that theory and theory making may also be a contingent, reflexive, and inclusive enterprise.

Meyer (1997) extended the case for regarding theory as knowledge that is specific rather than general. Arguing that in landscape architecture knowledge is always "situational—it is explicitly historical, contingent, pragmatic, ad hoc" (1997, 71), she sought to ground the knowledge base of the discipline in its engagement with particular sites. Landscape theory, Meyer suggested, "finds meaning, form and structure in the site as given" (1997, 71). Theory making—research—is thus a critical inquiry into "the immediate, the particular, and the circumstantial" (1997, 71). One consequence of such a grounded approach to the nature of theory in the discipline is that it opens the way to an argument that creative work—the real and imagined design projects of the discipline—can have theoretical status in and of themselves (Armstrong 1999). As an example of this, Corner (1999) identified a range of types of contemporary design projects with a theoretical orientation.

The question of whether "design" can claim status as a way to generate theoretical knowledge became the focus of intense debate at the end of the 1990s, as it struck at the heart of presumptions and presuppositions about the nature of theory and research. As De Jong and Van de Voordt (2002) pointed out, the challenge of generalizing and inducing knowledge from many particular but complex cases is not unique to design. It shares common ground with humanities disciplines such as history, whose subject matter is always particular and situated. This creates a rather different context from the definition of theory that is assumed in the natural sciences, where it is typically formalized through the deductive process.

3.3 Representing Theory

One of the frequently unspoken presumptions of the "science" model of theory is that important relationships can be expressed in numerical symbols. In contrast, knowledge in the humanities and many emerging social disciplines is expressed through the logical arrangement of words into a compelling narrative. Some advocates for an approach to theoretical knowledge that incorporates creative production have explored the representational challenges in theorizing knowledge in a design discipline (see fig. 3.2). Dee (2002), for example, argued that there is also knowledge embedded in the visual realm. The *European Journal of Landscape Architecture (JOLA)* includes a section—Thinking Eye—that promotes the sharing of knowledge through graphic expression. Curated collections, such as the Eco-Revelatory Design exhibition (Brown 1998), and peer-evaluated (juried) competition entries are other ways in which graphic expressions of ideas are given independent status as shared knowledge.

The relationship of representation to landscape experience and the creation of systematic knowledge is profoundly complex and central to the future of the theorizing in the discipline. Corner (1992) argued that drawing is "an integral part of the landscape project" and focused, in particular, upon the role of analogical and metaphorical representations, through which new ways of knowing and acting can be invented. As he later pointed out (1999), the power of landscape lies in its eidetic content—in its ability to evoke ideas upon which to base insight and action—but the discipline has little systematic theoretical understanding of either the processes or the outcomes. At present (and with a few exceptions, as noted above), the formalization of knowledge through peer-reviewed publication relies largely upon discursive interpretation of graphics, images, and numerical symbols.

Figure 3.2 Representing landscape theory

In a closely related discipline (architecture), Chi (2007) identified the gap between "design and discursive argument" as a critical consideration in design-based research (2007, 9). She argued the need for *translation*—"a double procedure upon a work of design: compression in perceptual, semantic space, and expression from unique to collective time" (2007, 9). "At its best," she suggested, "the reflective, analytical effort involved in this second creation can be more than an exercise in communication" (2007, 10). It becomes a "generative medium" in itself (2007, 10). This highlights a critical part of the tension of developing theory in a design discipline (explored further in section 3.6): To what extent are the authors of claims to new knowledge created through design activity required to articulate and explain the significance of their findings to the wider discipline, and by what language protocols should this be undertaken?

In science and in the humanities there are clear requirements upon authors of published work to provide a textual narrative using shared concepts. In the fine arts, however, this translation role is typically undertaken not by the artist, poet, or performer, but by curators and critics. In discussing architecture, Chi argued that the author/designer and the critic/editor each have a responsibility, and she sees positive potential in the process of translation.

3.4 Theoretical Conversations

The past twenty-five years therefore have seen continuing and still unresolved debates about the appropriate way to frame systematic knowledge in the discipline. On the one hand, there are advocates for a model of theory and theorizing that draws particularly upon the formal conventions of the natural sciences. There are those who advocate for a more grounded and situated approach that would draw more upon the humanities, and those who seek alignment with emergent methodologies from new social disciplines, while yet others emphasize the relevance of the creative arts. Each carries different assumptions and implications about the way in which knowledge is created, codified, and validated, and each sees different implications for the way theory is defined and constructed.

McAvin et al. (1991) suggest that the only effective strategy to develop theory and critique in the discipline will be to promote conversations and dialogue between alternative positions—a "shared reflective process." With this in mind we have previously offered a heuristic classification of knowledge claims within the discipline, as a way to help situate particular examples, and to encourage greater mutual understanding (Swaffield 2006). This provisional classification (fig. 3.3) was designed to highlight the "presuppositions" (Harrison and Livingstone 1980) that underpin different ways of thinking about the world, of knowing it, of expressing that knowledge in conceptual terms, and of investigating new understandings through distinct research strategies and methods. The hope was that making the importance of presuppositions clear would enable a more effective and constructive exchange of ideas about the nature of theory and its particular applications in design and critique.

In this text we adopt a position that is more inclusive than the formal approach to theory promoted by the champions of empirical science. However, we acknowledge the

Assumptions about Knowledge & the World	The Purpose of Knowing	Examples of Theoretical Perspective	Examples within Landscape Architecture	Typical Research Strategies	Typical Research Methods	Predominant Modes of Representation
Objectivism	**Instrumental/ Predictive** *What, where & how?*	[Post]positivist natural sciences	Landscape perception studies Landscape ecology.	Descriptive survey Modeling Experimentation & Quasi-experiments	Measurement and mapping Questionnaire surveys Statistical analysis Alternative futures	Mathematical symbols, with written interpretation
[Social] Construction	**Interpretive** *Who, when and why?*	Pragmatism Hermeneutics Symbolic Interaction Phenomenology	Design process Place studies Community studies Historical studies Project evaluations	Classification Ethnography Discourse Analysis Iconography Historiography Evaluation and Diagnosis	Close observation Interviews and focus groups Documentary analysis Life histories Post Occupancy Evaluation	Written narrative, with illustrative diagrams and photographs
Subjectivism	**Critical** *What are the consequences?* *How might things be done differently?*	Critical Inquiry Post-structuralism Feminist	'Expressivist' Theory 'Critical Visual Studies' Design scenarios	Action Research Projective Design Logical systems & argumentation	Deconstruction Reflection Creative Intervention	Diverse media -written -graphic -aural -performance

Figure 3.3 Foundations for knowledge claims
(Derived from Swaffield 2006)

continuing validity of Riley's observations about the frequently loose and opportunistic use of the term theory within landscape architecture, and we do not endorse a linguistic and epistemological "free for all." Instead, we take the view articulated by Silverman, a leading qualitative social scientist, who defines theory as "plausible relationships between concepts" (2005, 98). This rather more open definition recognizes the differences between intellectual traditions and their characteristic forms of representation of knowledge. Most importantly, however, we advocate a position of transparency, in which the onus is upon the author and editor of work to make clear and explain the presumptions they have used in making their claims to new knowledge. Drawing from Meyer and Corner, we, therefore, argue for the claims to be situated in their historical, geographical, and social contexts.

3.5 Research and Scholarship

In advocating for a more precise and narrower definition of theory, Riley also offered a critique of the claims that people make to be undertaking "research" in the discipline. As with theory, his charge was that the term research was used too broadly. He understood the reason for this—as he noted, "research is a magic word" that has credibility in the university and in the wider community (1990, 47). But through broadened use, he believed, its meaning had become debased, and "the idea of scholarship ha[d] gotten lost" (1990, 47). The point was reinforced by Chenoweth (1992), who criticized the tendency by landscape architecture educators to elevate whatever activity they are undertaking to the status of research by "inserting words such as 'action' or 'design' or 'holistic'" (1992, 121). The argument was reiterated by LaGro (1999) and again by Milburn et al. (2003), both questioning the broad use of the term research. More specifically, both challenged a claim that has gained increasing currency in a range of disciplines over the past couple of decades—in effect, that design itself can constitute research.

The case for design *as* research (see fig. 3.4) was encapsulated in a research paper from the Royal College of Art in London (Frayling 1993). It was reiterated by two leading

Into Design.   Through Design.   For Design.

Figure 3.4 Research into, through, and for design

design theorists from the 1960s, Nigel Cross and Bruce Archer, who advocated for the legitimacy of "research into, for and through design" (cited in Bowring 1999). In architecture, Groat and Wang (2002) examined the relationship between design and research. They identified ways in which design can be the *subject* of research and outlined several models of how research might be *situated within* design activity. They stopped short of arguing that design could constitute research. However, other architectural educators have been less cautious in their advocacy, and a theme issue of the *Journal of Architectural Education* (*JAE*) in 2007 included more wide-ranging claims.

The *JAE* contributors covered a spectrum of positions. They included those who argued that conventional research methodologies should be placed at the core of design practice (Kieran 2007); those who claimed that architectural field work and experimentation within "research" studios had been generating valid and valuable knowledge for many years (Furjan 2007); and those who advocated that architecture to "become a leader in changing and broadening how research is understood in academe" (Wortham 2007). A similar range of claims were made in 2003 in a collection of essays drawing mainly upon product design (Laurel 2003).

The argument for design as research builds from the observation that design necessarily involves empirical research to understand the context of a project and to develop a design program. This is an important foundation, but not sufficient in itself to justify the claim that design *is* research. However, the argument then adds another strand to the case by noting the growing importance of theorizing through design exploration and testing. Further justification is drawn from the way that theoretically informed design frequently involves the discovery and creation of new ideas, concepts, configurations, and products, as in "research and development." Finally, the reflexive and reflective nature of design thinking is identified as a key feature that indicates its "research" credentials.

From here, advocates for design as research follow diverging lines of argument. One group argues that design has all the attributes of research, broadly defined, and should, therefore, claim status and validity as research. Others argue that design is a new and different form of research, with its own legitimacy. According to Lunenfeld, "Design research is a method of investigation that sides with finding out rather than finding the already found" (2003, 10). It is "a rational practice, but . . . one in which the emotional is allowed its own power and intelligence" (2003, 12). The first pathway is well illustrated by the way in which advocates arguing that design has the attributes of research frequently adopt the language of science, talking of "design experiments" (Steenbergen 2008). In contrast, others are careful to distinguish design research from science (Lunenfeld 2003, 13), while still making claims for its legitimacy as research.

These debates have also emerged within landscape architecture. As in architecture and design, the positions vary (Selman 1998; Bensar 1998). Some commentators (e.g., Milburn et al. 2003) have argued that the fundamental nature of research excludes design-related activities. Defining research as "rigorous endeavors which attempt, through generally accepted methods of data collection and analysis, to reduce data into a compelling, authentic, and meaningful statement that extends our understanding of a given state, issue, perspective or action, and which is critically peer reviewed, universally accessible, and provides a new or substantially improved insight," they suggest that there is support for the notion of "design as a topic of research but excludes design as a research method" (Milburn et al. 2003, 122). Others have taken the position that design *is* research, by virtue of its theoretical orientation and the way it creates new knowledge, insights, and possibilities (Barnett 2000).

The consequence of adopting a narrow definition of research in landscape architecture that excludes design and creative activity raises serious questions about the long-term viability of the discipline within university systems where advancement and funding is based upon research performance. It is precisely this type of concern that has been a major dynamic behind the "design as research" agenda. To address this problem, advocates for a restrictive view of research—such as Milburn et al. (2003)—have turned to the more traditional notion of scholarship, and in particular to the arguments presented by Boyer (1990, 1996). Drawing upon the work of Schön on the "Reflective Practitioner" (1983), Boyer presented a framework aimed at recognizing the intellectual values and contributions of teaching and practice. He focused particularly upon the concept of "scholarship" and proposed expanding its definition to cover four categories—discovery, integration, application, and teaching.

Boyer's categories of scholarship

Discovery—the traditional definition of investigative research

Integration—the synthesis of knowledge and interpretation of its significance

Application—the engagement of new knowledge with practice

Teaching—the communication of research findings to a wider community

By recognizing a definition of scholarship that includes but extends beyond research, those promoting this framework in landscape architecture seek to provide a way to validate a wider range of "scholarly" activity without compromising the credibility of "true" (traditional) research. Boyer's framework has received considerable attention from educators in North America, where assessment of research and scholarship remains largely vested within individual institutions. However, it is less widely recognized elsewhere, where assessment has become more centralized within governmental bureaucracies. Ironically, it is in centralized assessment systems, such as in the United Kingdom, Australia, and New Zealand, that demands from the design disciplines to be judged as legitimate researchers on their own terms have gained most ground.

Furthermore, and notwithstanding appeals to Boyer's framework as a way to validate scholarly activity, the "design is *not* research" position remains firmly grounded within the conventions of science. It underplays the fact that there are many disciplines in the humanities, fine arts, and related disciplines whose scholarly production is recognized as research within the academy, but which, like the design disciplines, do not follow experimental or quasi-experimental research protocols. This has led to the exploration of an alternative position that design *could be* research, depending upon how it is undertaken and presented.

3.6 Studio Design as a Research Setting

Advocates for the recognition of design as a form of research typically emphasize the unique status of the design studio as a setting for research. Armstrong (1999) identified three possibilities. First, the design studio may be a site for research *into* design process and learning. Here, the studio is, in effect, a case-study setting for research on design. Second, the studio can be structured as part of a larger research program, a "forum for speculative ideas taken through to a degree of resolution" (1999, 10). In this situation it becomes a generator of theoretical insights and propositions. Third, the studio can be seen as a "master class," following the model of the performance arts, a workshop for "theorized creative work." Others have used the term design "laboratory," seeking to align the design process more closely with science (fig. 3.5), and the idea of "design laboratories" has become widespread in universities and practices, as sites of design "experiments."

The role of the studio as a setting for investigation is expressed in the concept of the refereed studio (Bowring 1997, 1999). The use of the concept in Australasia in the late 1990s provides a useful illustration of its strengths and limitations. Armstrong (1999) argued that the origins of the refereed studio drew upon the strategy adopted by the creative artists in Australia, who strengthened their scholarly culture "through theorizing creative

Figure 3.5 Design studio as "laboratory"

LANDSCAPE
REVIEW

Theme:
The issue of the refereed studio

Contributors:

Helen Armstrong, Design studios as research: an emerging paradigm for landscape architecture

Ann Forsyth, Henry Lu and Patricia McGirr, College students and youth collaborating in design: research on the design studio

Sue-Anne Ware, Research by design; honouring the Stolen Generation – a theoretical anti-memorial

Helen Armstrong and Debbie Robbins, Design Through Debate: a new studio

1999:5(2)

A JOURNAL OF LANDSCAPE ARCHITECTURE

Figure 3.6 The refereed studio as published research

works and the traditional scholarship associated with the critic" (1999, 6). Drawing upon this precedent, the Committee of the Heads of Australian Schools of Architecture began publication of an annual report in which design studios were subject to peer review; this allowed studio leaders to formalize their work as peer-reviewed research. However, peer review raises the critical question: by what criteria should these studio investigations be evaluated? Two issues of the Australasian journal *Landscape Review* explored the proposition in landscape architecture (see fig. 3.6).

In the first call for submissions of "refereed studios," Bowring (1997) set out relatively conventional criteria for assessment that are compatible with the definition of research subsequently proposed by Milburn at al. (2003). Articles seeking publication as refereed studios were required to include a statement of objectives, a critical review of the substantive focus of the work, an explanation of process, and a summary of outcomes that demonstrate originality and new insights. Examples were published in 1999 and again in 2003.

Although the published articles revealed a range of creative work and insights, the initiative was not an unqualified success. Commenting upon the submitted articles, three highly experienced peer reviewers noted that authors seemed unwilling or unable to articulate the context, rationale, or results of an investigation in a way that enabled the work to be positioned within a systematic body of knowledge (Berger et al. 2003). The nature of the research objectives, strategy, and methods—and what new knowledge was added to the discipline—were frequently left unclear, despite the efforts of editors and referees. At the time, this lent support to Thwaites' (1998) observation of the limitations that result from the lack of research training among landscape educators.

Ten years on, the relationships between research and design deserve reconsideration within the discipline. There are a number of ways in which studio- or practice-based design projects can be framed within established research methodologies—for example, as case studies. In recent years there have been an increasing number of published works that place design explorations within a wider research framework in the way envisaged by Armstrong, and there is a growing record of reflective theoretical writing based upon the outcomes of design interventions. Chapter 12, therefore, examines projective design and its proposition as a research strategy.

3.7 Theory and Critique

Arguments for the recognition of some forms of design activity as having research status or that design can be part of a valid research strategy make frequent use of the terms "critique" and "critical reflection," and they draw support from the scholarship traditionally associated with the critic (Armstrong 1999). Critique, or criticism in the academic sense, implies a self-aware and systematic scrutiny of a situation or work from a particular perspective (McAvin et al. 1991). It is aimed at the "explication of content and context" (Meyer 1991, 155), through a process of "baring, exposing and evaluation of . . . implicit presuppositions" (Tzonis 2003, 20–21). It is, therefore, deeply engaged with theory and requires an acute awareness of the "pre-suppositional hierarchy" (Harrison and Livingstone 1980) of knowledge and knowledge formation discussed in previous sections.

Bowring defined design critique as "the practice of evaluating design in an informed manner, based on an understanding of the content and context of the work, and the design languages upon which it draws" (2000, 42). Drawing upon Attoe (1978), she recognized three styles of critique in landscape architecture: descriptive, interpretive, and normative. The *descriptive* role involves providing a systematic and theoretically informed account of a work, the intentions of its creator, and its disciplinary and landscape context (Riley 1991). Descriptive critique has much in common with the research strategy we describe later as descriptive case studies and may also provide the foundation for other types of more evaluative critique.

Interpretive critique may express a more creative role (McAvin et al. 1991) in the way that the commentary can reveal new understandings and perspectives upon a work, and hence provide insight upon the wider discipline and society. Interpretive criticism contrasts and compares particular projects and may frequently use metaphor and analogy to throw new light upon a design (Eaton 1990). As such it extends the work beyond its own frame of reference and creates new knowledge and understanding by bridging and mediating in the way proposed by Meyer (1997).

The third, normative dimension of critique makes and communicates judgments upon designed works, performance, or other creative acts such as writing. It evaluates the success or otherwise of a work, both on its own terms and in relation to wider disciplinary agendas and imperatives. It may also offer comment upon the appropriateness of its objectives and strategies (Riley 1991). Commenting upon the field of landscape assessment, Carlson (1993) suggested that the critic's role may even extend beyond evaluation to formulating positions and arguments that *justify* particular ways of acting or particular actions.

The three types of critique are complementary and may be interwoven within a single narrative. They all link closely to research. Descriptive critique has much in common with descriptive research through case studies. Interpretive critique may inform transformative action, interpretive research, and design proposition. Normative critique is closely aligned with evaluative research strategies.

3.8 Conclusion

Shaping a research strategy implies taking a position on a number of related issues. These include consideration of the nature of theory in landscape architecture and the characteristics of research and how it relates to other dimensions of scholarly activity, including critique. Debates in the discipline over the past two decades or so have tended to polarize around three positions. One is a conservative, or traditional, approach that draws particularly upon the conventions of the natural sciences, in which theory and research are defined narrowly and thus exclude much intellectual activity in the discipline. Advocates of this position seek alignment of the discipline with the protocols of mainstream science and suggest validating design-related investigative activity under the title and status of scholarship.

An alternative position, typically less well-articulated but certainly evident in much of the writing of the avant-garde in the discipline, is to adopt an inclusive position that validates a wide range of designerly activity and products as theory and research. This position aligns itself with a broad range of creative disciplines and places landscape architectural research within the realm of emergent paradigms that challenge the hegemony of science (Hesse-Biber and Leavy 2008). For these commentators, the lack of congruence between research in design disciplines and more traditional definitions of research is not "our" problem (Barnett 2000).

A third position—and one which we ourselves have adopted in this text—is to seek ways to mediate between the poles of the debate. We do this partly in a spirit of "realpolitik," because we acknowledge the institutional and bureaucratic power of the conservative position on research in many institutions in which landscape architecture programs are based. However we also recognize the diversity of scholarly activity recognized as research within disciplines outside science. More fundamentally, we see widespread evidence of a deepening understanding of the different ways in which knowledge about the world can and should be created and expressed. As we indicated in chapter 1, we believe there is a range of productive ways for our discipline to engage with knowledge formation, and we see no reason to privilege one pathway over another. Instead, we seek more robust ways to combine an inclusive approach to the expression of theoretical understanding, and openness to possibilities of different research strategies, with an expectation for a high level of rigor and transparency in the explanation and justification of whatever approach is adopted.

The means of representation of new knowledge and insights created through research clearly becomes a central issue in an inclusive approach to the definition of research in landscape architecture. The hypothetico-deductive model of science privileges formal theory that is expressed in mathematical terms and explained in text. The inductive and interpretive models of the social sciences and humanities utilize textual narratives supplemented with figurative illustrations and sometimes descriptive statistics. The creative and fine arts are expressed in a wide range of media—from sound and bodily performance to figurative and abstract visual imagery, typically (but not always) interpreted through a textual narrative of a critic who is independent of the artist. Landscape architecture interfaces with and draws upon all these traditions and frequently combines different media and modes of representation. Determining an appropriate mode and medium of representation is thus a critical consideration in undertaking research in the discipline, and is a question that interweaves through all the research strategies.

References

Armstrong, H. 1999. Design studios as research: An emerging paradigm for landscape architecture. *Landscape Review* 5 (2): 5–25.

Attoe, W. 1978. *Architecture and critical imagination*. Chichester, U.K.: John Wiley and Sons.

Barnett, R. 2000. Exploration and discourses: A nonlinear approach to research by design. *Landscape Review* 6 (2): 25–40.

Berger, A., L. Corkery, and K. Moore. 2003. Editorial: Researching the studio. *Landscape Review* 8 (1): 1–2.

Berrizbeita, A., ed. 1997. Landscape architecture criticism. *LandForum* (Fall/Winter) 1997: 9–10.

Bowring, J. 1997. Research by design: The refereed studio. *Landscape Review* 3 (2): 54–55.

———. 1999. Editorial: The issue of the refereed studio. *Landscape Review* 5 (2): 1–4.

———. 2000. Increasing the critical mass: Emphasizing critique in studio teaching. *Landscape Review* 6 (2): 41–52.

Boyer, E. L. 1990. *Scholarship reconsidered: Priorities for the professoriate*. Princeton, NJ: The Carnegie Foundation for the Advancement of Teaching.

Boyer, E. L., and L. D. Mitgang. 1996. *Building community: A new future for architecture education and practice.* Princeton, NJ: The Carnegie Foundation for the Advancement of Teaching.

Brown, B., ed. 1993. Eco-revelatory design: Nature constructed/nature revealed. Special issue, *Landscape Journal* 17 (2).

Carlson, A. 1993. On the theoretical vacuum in landscape assessment. *Landscape Journal* 12 (1): 51–58.

Chenoweth, R. 1992. Research: Hype and reality. *Landscape Architecture Magazine,* March, 47–48.

Chi, L. 2007. Translation between design research and scholarship. *Journal of Architectural Education* 61 (1): 7–10.

Corner, J. 1990. A discourse on theory I: Sounding the depths—origins, theory and representation. *Landscape Journal* 9 (2): 61–78.

———. 1991. A discourse on theory II: Three tyrannies of contemporary theory and the alternative of hermeneutics. *Landscape Journal* 10 (2): 115–33.

———. 1992. Representation and landscape: Drawing and making in the landscape medium. *Word and Image* 8 (3): 243–75.

———. 1999. *Recovering landscape: Essays in contemporary landscape architecture.* New York: Princeton Architectural Press.

Dee, C. 2002. 'The imaginary texture of the real. . .': Critical visual studies in landscape architecture. *Landscape Research* 29 (1): 13–30.

De Jong, T. M., and D. J. M. van der Voordt. 2002. *Ways to study and research: Urban, architectural and technical design.* Delft, The Netherlands: Delft University Press Science.

Eaton, M. M. 1990. Responding to the call for new landscape metaphors. *Landscape Journal* 9 (1): 22–27.

Eckbo, G. 1950. *Landscape for living.* New York: F. W. Dodge.

Forsyth, A. 2008. Great programs in architecture: Rankings, performance assessments and diverse paths to prominence. *International Journal of Architectural Research* 2 (2): 11–22.

Frayling, C. 1993. Into, through, and for research: Research in art and design. *Royal College of Art Research Papers* 1(1) (cited in Lunenfeld 2003).

Furjan, H. 2007. Design/research: Notes on a manifesto. *Journal of Architectural Education* 61(1): 62–68.

Groat, L., and D. Wang. 2002. *Architectural research methods.* New York: John Wiley and Sons.

Harrison, R.T., and Livingstone, D.N. 1980. Philosophy and problems in human geography: A presuppositional approach. *AREA* 12 (4): 25–31.

Hesse-Biber, S. N., and P. Leavy. 2008. *Handbook of emergent methods.* New York: Guilford Press.

Howett, C. 1987. Systems, signs, sensibilities. *Landscape Journal* 6 (1): 4–12.

Hunt, J. D. 1992. *Gardens and the picturesque: Studies in the history of landscape architecture.* Cambridge, MA: MIT Press.

Jellicoe, G., and S. Jellicoe. 1987. *The landscape of man.* London: Thames and Hudson.

Kieran, S. 2007. Research in design: Planning doing monitoring learning. *Journal of Architectural Education* 61 (1): 27–31.

Koh, J. 1982. Ecological design: A post-modern design paradigm of holistic philosophy and evolutionary ethic. *Landscape Journal* 1 (2): 76–84.

Krog, S. 1981. Is it art? *Landscape Architecture Magazine,* May, 373–376.

———. 1983. Creative risk taking. *Landscape Architecture Magazine,* June, 70–76.

LaGro, J. A. 1999. Research capacity: A matter of semantics? *Landscape Journal* 18 (2): 179–86.

Laurel, B., ed. 2003. *Design research: Methods and perspectives.* Cambridge, MA: MIT Press.

Lunenfeld, P. 2003. The design cluster. In *Design research: Methods and perspectives,* ed. B. Laurel, 10–15. Cambridge MA: MIT Press.

McAvin, M., E. K. Meyer, J. Corner, H. Shirvani, K. Helphand, R. B. Riley, and R. Scarfo. 1991. Landscape architecture as critical inquiry. *Landscape Journal* 10 (1): 155–72.

Meeus, J. H. A., and M. J. Vroom. 1986. Critique and theory in Dutch landscape architecture. *Landscape and Urban Planning* 13: 277–302.

Meyer, E. 1991. Landscape architectural design as critical practice. *Landscape Journal* 10 (1): 156–59.

———. 1997. The expanded field of landscape architecture. In *Ecological design and planning,* ed. G. F. Thompson and F. R. Steiner. New York: John Wiley and Sons.

Milburn, L. A., R. D. Brown, S. J. Mulley, and S. G. Hilts 2003. Assessing academic contributions in landscape architecture. *Landscape and Urban Planning* 64: 119–29.

Riley, R. 1990. Editorial commentary: Some thoughts on scholarship and publication. *Landscape Journal* 9 (1): 47–50.

———. 1991. Response. *Landscape Journal* 10 (1): 167–169.

Schön, D. 1983. *The reflective practitioner: How professionals think in practice.* New York: Basic Books.

Selman, P. 1998. Landscape design as research: An emerging debate. *Landscape Research* 23 (2): 195–204.

Silverman, D. 2005. *Doing qualitative research: A practical handbook.* 2nd ed. London: Sage.

Spirn, A. 1989. The poetics of nature: Towards a new aesthetic for urban design. *Places* 6 (1): 82–93.

Steenbergen, C. 2008. *Composing landscapes: Analysis, typology, and experiments for design.* Basel: Birkhauser Verlag.

Swaffield, S. R., ed. 2002. *Theory in landscape architecture: A reader.* Philadelphia: University of Pennsylvania Press.

———. 2006. Theory and critique in landscape architecture. *Journal of Landscape Architecture* 1: 22–29.

Thwaites, K. 1998. Landscape design as research: An exploration. *Landscape Research* 23 (2): 196–98.

Tzonis, A. 2003. Introducing an architecture of the present: Critical realism and the design of identity. In *Critical regionalism: Architecture and identity in a globalized world,* ed. A. Tzonis and L. Lefaivre, 8–21. Munich: Prestel.

Wortham, B. D. 2007. The way we think about the way we think: Architecture is a paradigm for reconsidering research. *Journal of Architectural Education* 61(1): 44–52.

CHAPTER 4

Integrating Design and Research

4.1 Introduction

In environmental design disciplines such as landscape architecture, urban planning, architecture, and engineering, the interconnections between academic and professional practices create a fertile intellectual environment for research. Opportunities for the production of meaningful new knowledge occur in professional offices as well as in graduate professional and postprofessional programs. This chapter aims at the needs of new researchers, both in graduate schools and in practice, as an aid to understanding some of the possibilities, procedures, and challenges involved in the development of research proposals.

As such, the chapter also serves as a "bridge" between the more theoretical discussion of the research context and needs of the discipline (forming the first part of this book) and the accounts of situated research practices contained in the next nine chapters (the second part). It is intended as a conceptual guide, not a "how-to" manual, but it does include discussion of the essential concepts, dynamics, and standards of research. This chapter concludes with a set of questions and responses that are intended to help new researchers shape their own research projects.

4.2 Problems and Purpose

Whether it appears in the form of a need or an opportunity, *all* research and design projects share the same beginning—an awareness, articulation, and acceptance of a problem (Koberg and Bagnall 1976). Whenever there seems to be an insufficiency, an inadequacy, or an imbalance of some sort, a researcher is motivated to respond. Curiosity and a desire to learn about the world are quite powerful incentives for research. The recognition of a new research topic (i.e., an opportunity to learn) is, therefore, the first step in generating new knowledge. All projects also require the development of a precise research question in order to frame an orderly and useful investigation. What exactly do we want to find out? A research question is already narrower and more synthetic than the original topic; it is the result of a necessary intellectual choice.

Because needs and opportunities to learn announce themselves differently, there are a variety of ways to articulate the motivation to "find out" as a relevant research question. As so many research manuals and guides to proposal writing attest, this can take some practice. Among other ways, a research topic may appear through the presence or absence of landscape resources (such as public space, habitat, energy, biodiversity, food and fiber, and so on), through a desire to improve or better understand landscape performance or conditions (efficiency, resilience, comfort, proximity, permeability, etc.), through insufficient knowledge (information, skills, understanding, principles, etc.), or through conflicting or inconsistent values (such as beauty, justice, equity, inclusion, etc.).

We do not find it useful in this book to distinguish between practical or professional topics and academic topics, because most research in landscape architecture includes elements of both. Instead, we focus upon purpose and strategy: what *motivates* someone to seize a research opportunity, and what intellectual path do they decide to take in pursuing it.

At its most fundamental, research in a design discipline expresses one of three broad motives: intellectual (to know more or know differently), opportunistic (to respond or manage differently), and ethical (to value or allocate resources differently). In many academic disciplines, the classic research questions are intellectual. They arise from not understanding a phenomenon well enough. Choosing a research strategy for intellectual problems often depends on the extent of current knowledge: not knowing anything is an entirely different kind of research challenge than not knowing enough and should be met with different research strategies—scoping and exploration, as opposed to detailed analysis of a specific relationship.

Environmental design disciplines respond to constant change in the real world, and change produces opportunities for forming new understandings and interventions. Whether by natural or human process, both destruction and development can offer opportunities to improve interpretation, performance, or knowledge of landscape events and phenomena. Design is a special type of opportunistic response—a projection of a possible future landscape in response to a change in condition or need. Although it has profound investigative potential, design projection is one of the most synthetic and least understood of all research motives and strategies.

Many environmental designers are ethically motivated to help resolve life's largest and most intractable socioenvironmental problems—such as poverty, injustice, and global climate change. However, compound problems like these are impossible to understand unless and until they are broken down into discrete research components, or variables. As was noted in chapter 1, our capacity and choices concerning how to frame social or environmental problems as researchable questions are inextricably guided by our assumptions about the nature of the world and about ways of knowing and investigating.

In our experience, graduate professional students in landscape architecture are increasingly motivated by the opportunity to address ethical questions, rather than by intellectual questions. However, no matter which of these imperatives inspires us, the starting point for research is the same: what, precisely, do we need to learn and why? How do we identify a research topic clearly and narrowly enough so that an appropriate investigation may be developed and undertaken with the skills, time, and resources available and a meaningful outcome achieved? The more precisely a question can be articulated as a "need or desire to know," the more effectively a research strategy can be selected and shaped to generate the new knowledge that is sought.

In the preceding chapters we argued that in landscape architecture a broad range of research strategies are not only intellectually legitimate but may also be necessary to accelerate disciplinary knowledge formation. Indeed, all of the categories we identified in chapter 1 can be adapted for landscape architectural research, and several lend themselves particularly well to graduate research in institutional settings, as well as professional research conducted in public- and private-sector offices. In the following paragraphs we consider each in turn.

Descriptive research produces new knowledge by systematically observing, collecting, and/or recording new information (data set). The scale, magnitude, or time frame for descriptive work is also quite often discretionary; thus, descriptive research strategies are easily adaptable to the level of skill and scale of action that is feasible in graduate research. One of the most common research designs adopted for graduate theses is the descriptive case study, which has been proven many times to be able to provide a clearly defined and achievable result. It is also widely used in practice-based research. Chapter 5 includes discussion of descriptive case studies.

Modeling and correlational research identifies and measures relationships between specific variables and constructs simplified representations (models) of their structure and dynamics. Graduate researchers in the social and biophysical sciences will frequently use correlational strategies to conduct statistical analyses on data sets, and this can also be of value in a professional setting where an evidence base for design actions is sought. There are several examples in chapter 6. Modeling is typically more demanding and is usually associated with larger research teams, although simple descriptive and synthetic models can be a viable basis for a graduate research project.

Of the strategies we have identified, the various types of experimentation are perhaps the most challenging for graduate and practice researchers, because of the difficulties of creating a credible and practical experimental design for landscape problems. Nonetheless, quasi-experimental research designs can be realistically adopted and may offer very fruitful lines of inquiry for new researchers, provided that the focus is tightly defined. Several of the examples in chapter 7 describe quasi-experimental projects coauthored by graduate students and their supervisor.

Classification schemes produce knowledge by structuring or weighting data sets around a shared pattern, system, theme, or organizational structure. This is a frequently employed strategy by which formal principles are sought in a body of work, or data is organized in preparation for conducting a larger study. Examples in chapter 8 suggest that classification can be a fruitful and achievable form of graduate research, provided the scope is realistic. It is also well suited to practice-based research that seeks a greater understanding of particular types of phenomena.

Interpretive research produces knowledge by identifying, naming, and assigning new significance or meanings to dimensions, themes, or narratives within a data set. Chapter 9 presents several useful examples. Many graduate theses have been prepared as a result of interpreting primary material such as archived correspondence, by interpreting the values or experiences of key informants, or by "reading" the meaning encoded into a set of design practices or forms.

Evaluative research produces knowledge by comparing landscapes and landscape practices to accepted norms, rubrics, or new standards—"does this condition or action perform as it should?" Next to descriptive research, this group of strategies (presented in chapter 10) is perhaps the most popular among graduate students, because it allows for the exploration of professional situations by reference to relatively fixed and controllable normative values or parameters. It can be valuable in practice, for example in postoccupancy evaluation.

Engaged action research produces new researchable questions based on processes of social transformation. In schools with a strong mission of community engagement and outreach, action research is increasingly popular and accepted. Some of the examples in chapter 11 suggest that because of human contingency, participatory action strategies may follow unpredictable trajectories, in terms of resources and time expended and of results obtained, particularly for inexperienced researchers. It can, therefore, be higher risk, although the rewards to graduate researchers may be worthwhile.

Design research projects new configurations, relationships, possibilities, and, thus, new "realities." It is important to recognize the difference between design as a service or problem-solving endeavor and design framed as an investigative strategy. As demonstrated in chapter 12, projective design undertaken as research sets out to address a specific research question that is linked to, and part of, a wider disciplinary framework. To be considered research, its findings must contribute to the development of the discipline. It can be particularly challenging for researchers who are also designers to distinguish between various types of applied and conceptual design and design as research, and this can be a source of tension and risk.

Logical systems research (chapter 13) creates new knowledge by shaping, reflecting upon, and transforming the relationships between categories and concepts. In this way it enables new ways of seeing, knowing, and acting. A classic example is expanded field analysis that may offer a new perspective on the relations between design practices and other values. This type of synthetic argumentation can be a challenging strategy that requires deep understanding of a topic as well as a creative and penetrating intellect. It is not typically recommended as a strategy for graduate study during the first professional degree.

There is another approach to applied research that we have not identified as a distinct strategy, but which holds perennial interest for graduate student researchers. Exploratory (both subjective and pragmatic) research produces conjectural knowledge—potential questions— by direct encounter and reflection upon phenomena. While it is not always accepted as a strategy for research—largely because it is difficult to report in a way that satisfies the basic parameters of research quality—in some schools of thought, exploratory research is accepted as a sort of protoresearch that can bring valuable new phenomena, relationships, or opportunities to light. However, it requires maturity of thought and understanding, and there is a risk that studies of this kind by new researchers can be seen as naïve.

4.3. Framing a Research Question

In introducing the range of strategies that can be used by new researchers, we emphasize the importance of understanding "the need and desire to know." The most common question from a research advisor is typically "what is the question your research attempts to address?" Several excellent manuals are available to guide the development of research proposals (Booth et al. 1995; Barrett 2003; Creswell 2009; Rudestam and Newton 1992; Van Wagenen 1991; among others), and it is not our intention to repeat their principles here. However, it is commonplace to recommend that new researchers practice a narrative script for thinking through their initial purpose statement and their motives (rationale). The following is a modified version of such a checklist (Booth et al. 1995), reshaped to highlight the choice of research strategy as a response to motive and orientation.

Framing research questions

1. *Topic:*   I am investigating (what) _____

2. *Question:* Because I want to find out (who/why/how) _____

3. *Strategy:*   I am using (name the research strategy) _____

4. *Motive:*   In order to understand/contribute to (what kind of knowledge is needed)

This type of checklist of questions has been widely used by Carl Steinitz in his landscape planning research and teaching (1990, 1995). It is a potentially useful exercise to practice when reading published research by others because it can help tease out the means and ends of research. The most useful work that can be done at the outset of any project is understanding or rearticulating the "real" focus of investigation, rather than the "given" problem or the one that superficially presents itself. For instance, a landscape performance problem might mask an intellectual question about how landscape is conceptualized; a perceived ethical question may turn out to be an issue of resource allocation (or vice versa). Indeed, in both design and research, the clarity and insight brought to bear on problem definition will make the difference between an average project and a truly superlative one. Great designers and great scientists alike seem to have the insight to reframe practical questions as intellectual opportunities—a chance to investigate ideas that are fresh, unique, or profound.

One of the chief differences between design and research lies in the way an investigation is motivated and framed. There is a clear difference between finding a specific design solution to a situated problem and identifying a general principle that may reliably and clearly inform others in future, analogous situations that are, at present, unknown. This is the basic difference between design (as it is commonly practiced) and research (as it is commonly understood). In the first case, what is needed is an adaptation of service, resource, or commodity (a specific situation): call this design. In the second case, what is needed is a process of investigation that contributes to theory (an autonomous body of knowledge): call this research.

When design is framed as an investigation, so that some form of new knowledge is sought, produced, and disseminated, we can envisage design process as research. When design is undertaken as a way of solving a practical problem using only conventional "rules of thumb" or idiosyncratic or arbitrary responses, we cannot. In other words, in order to transcend basic instrumentality as an end in itself and become a legitimate strategy for research, design practices and processes must aim for larger investigative and theoretical ends, supported by logical and disciplined means.

Despite the distinction we have just drawn, and depending on how clearly it is framed, design activity *may* be effectively integrated with, and very often depends upon, research activity. Opportunities to extend design beyond instrumental goals always exist; the challenge is how to recognize them. As was discussed in previous chapters, the binary relations between theory and practice, and research and design, quickly recede before the very rich gradation of hybrid possibilities that stretches between the two extremes. In every case, and at the very least, design and research can and should inform each other.

In "doing" or "making" design, one typically adopts a creative problem-solving role—one seeks to change present reality into a future, more desirable one. Design projects typically involve many different processes of discovery, and there may or may not be a component of generalizable learning involved in every design. However, in "doing" or "conducting" research, one seeks principally to know what is hitherto unknown, and one must also *communicate* it to others as a generally reliable or valid new thought about some problematic aspect of the world. The process of communication is critical to the validation and subsequent application of the research, and this introduces the question of how research is presented and evaluated.

4.4 Degrees of Research

Most graduate research is framed within the context of a higher degree. In landscape architecture, at present, the professional master's degree (MLA) is still considered the terminal degree in landscape architecture, while the PhD is generally regarded as an academic, scholarly degree required only by the faculty of research-focused schools. However, there is growing speculation (Taylor 2000) that the MLA will someday become the new industry standard for professional competency (replacing the bachelor of landscape architecture degree, or BLA), and the PhD or professional doctorate will become the terminal degree for academic purposes. If and when this happens, it will have major significance for the discipline, as the level of the degree determines the nature and sophistication of the research activity of graduates and the skills they develop.

The thesis or dissertation is the primary vehicle by which graduate research is undertaken, presented, and evaluated. Most legitimate graduate colleges and universities publish generic requirements for the qualities sought in the graduate thesis. Typically, most departments will gauge their master's or doctoral degree candidates against equivalent standards of the college or faculty of which they are part, whether that is engineering, agriculture, fine arts, architecture, or natural resources. Thus, depending on institutional context, unit mission, faculty background, department culture, and curriculum, the requirements for the research thesis in landscape architecture may differ from school to school.

For instance, the policies of the College of Environmental Science and Forestry at the State University of New York, Syracuse, include language that is characteristically "scientific."

> [S]tudents must investigate a problem that initiates, expands, or clarifies knowledge in the field and prepare a thesis based on this study. Students are required to define an appropriate problem for investigation; review relevant information; develop a study plan incorporating investigative techniques appropriate to the problem; implement the plan; and relate the results to theory or a body of knowledge in the field.

Within that academic culture, every candidate for a master of science degree, in any discipline, is required to

> successfully defend the thesis. The objectives of the defense examination are (1) to probe the validity and significance of the data and information presented in the thesis or dissertation, (2) to assess the student as a critical thinker and data analyst, (3) to evaluate the student's scientific creativity, including the student's ability to relate research results to scientific theory within the chosen field, and (4) to present the results effectively in writing. (College of ESF 2010)

This policy serves equally well to guide students of environmental science or urban forestry, as well as postprofessional students in landscape architecture (MSLA). However, research expectations for first professional degree (MLA) graduate students in landscape architecture are considerably more open. "Master of Landscape Architecture students must complete an integrative experience, participate in the capstone studio during the final semester of the program, and disseminate the results of their integrative studies through capstone seminars" (College of ESF 2010). In this scientific academy, therefore, the generation of new knowledge is not necessarily a standard to which professional students in landscape architecture are strictly held.

A set of standards from the bylaws of a department of landscape architecture at a college of fine and applied arts expresses the expectation that MLA students will "make a contribution" to knowledge in a variety of ways:

> One of the major objectives of the Master of Landscape Architecture Program is to prepare students . . . to make a contribution to the store of knowledge

and/or skills of the field that furthers work or understanding in a particular subject matter.

As a culmination of master's level study and as a demonstration of achievement of the above objective, each student, under the supervision of a committee, is to pursue independently, and in depth, a work of particular relevance for landscape architecture which will accomplish one or more of the following goals:

1. demonstrate an innovative application of knowledge within the field;
2. analyze, critically examine, and/or empirically test ideas/theories; and/or
3. creatively synthesize, expand and/or develop ideas/theories.

A thesis proposal must clearly explain how the topic, issue and/or question under investigation will accomplish at least one of the above and the completed thesis must reasonably justify that it has been achieved. (Department of Landscape Architecture 1999)

A more complete survey of graduate programs would, no doubt, turn up quite as many different articulations of basic thesis standards as there are departments. Although there is typically a great deal of latitude in the definition, purpose, and form of a graduate thesis in landscape architecture, the basic components tend to be very similar. At a minimum, a graduate thesis or dissertation must articulate a research question, explain what is already known about it and why this research is needed, choose a research design, describe and apply a credible methodology, report upon new findings, and explain their significance within the wider body of knowledge in the discipline.

In some programs (quite commonly in design schools or landscape architecture programs nested in schools of architecture), the thesis may also be expected to involve professional-level demonstration of the techniques of placemaking, planning, or management, as appropriate to the course of study. Although demonstrated mastery of practical techniques, conventional knowledge, or even best practices are not usually considered adequate as achievements of *research*, to apply these same practical techniques in a new way or to evaluate received knowledge in new variations or circumstances may be perfectly acceptable to many, if not most, programs.

The distinction between demonstrating mastery of design and planning processes and applying them in a new or novel way to create new knowledge of wider significance can and does create confusion for design and planning students (and faculty) in professional degree programs with a thesis requirement. Depending on what faculty perceive as their adjacent or reference disciplines, for instance, it may be difficult to come to agreement on basic standards, as well as appropriate topics and methods for advanced study. Unfortunately, depending on the degree of clarity or shared acceptance of thesis standards, graduate students sometimes get caught up in standoffs when faculty debate the priorities of professional mastery versus research value. Given the particular paradigmatic stance of an academic community, standards may be continually updated along a spectrum designed to achieve greater rigor or adaptability or to find some balance in between.

4.5 Assessing Research Quality

Just as within the discipline itself, standards and expectations of research quality are hotly debated among faculty and students, as well as between faculty and alumni. In reviewing the familiar concepts below, our purpose is to find a middle way, a neutral ground allowing both innovation and rigor in the work of new researchers.

The *value,* or quality, of a graduate student's academic thesis or dissertation may be assessed by the same yardsticks used to measure the quality of any other research project—together with the added dimensions of increased analytical or projective skill, intellectual maturity, and personal growth for the student. Citing a scheme by Guba (1981), Groat and Wang (2002) discuss four common standards of research quality: truth value, applicability, consistency, and neutrality. Depending on the research strategy in play, it is interesting to note that each of these standards may be observed, measured, and described differently.

Truth value relates to forms of internal validity (in objectivist research) or credibility of the findings. Synonyms for valid include appropriate and meaningful. Note that the words "true" or "accurate" are not usually given as synonyms for "valid." In research design and measurement processes, the term valid promises only that the collection and interpretation of data is strategically logical, procedurally defensible, and equivalent to the phenomena they measure. For analysis to be considered credible, data sources must be identified and analyses confirmed through multiple pathways (for example, through triangulation or inter-rater reliability in the context of investigation) or through the compelling logic of the process and its outcomes.

Applicability refers to forms of external validity or generalizability, where procedures and/ or findings may be extended or are transferable to a wider context or analogous situation. This derives particularly from the choice of research design and its implementation.

Consistency refers to the concepts of reliability, stability, or dependability. "Reliable" means a stable result or finding that is not dependent upon contingent factors. It also means a measurement or observation that is precise and free from technical error. If error or instability is experienced or expected, it should be trackable or traceable to its source. It is said that "reliability is a necessary but not sufficient condition for validity"; that is, a reliable or consistent measurement may still be *invalid* for a given purpose or use (Pedhazur and Schmelkin 1991, 81).

Transparency relates to the lack of hidden bias of the researcher. In the sciences, this is expressed as objectivity or neutrality, where observations are structured in a way to be as independent of the values of the researcher as possible. In the humanities and emergent social sciences, there is an expectation of sincerity or of other manifestations of the investigator's intellectual openness and honesty.

In addition to these standards, we suggest there are at least four other criteria that should be considered in evaluating both graduate and practical research in landscape architecture as well as any other discipline—significance, efficiency, clarity, and originality.

Significance is always relative to the stated goal or purpose of the research problem and its likely contribution to new knowledge. Significance may be stated as the response to the dreaded "So what?" question—"Why does this study matter?" What are the implications or projected impact of the research on the phenomenon under study, the larger context of the problem, or on the discipline itself?

Efficiency means a kind of intellectual fitness—an appropriate economy of research means fitted to theoretical ends. Simply put, any researcher needs to pay attention to, and husband, scarce resources such as time, energy, and money in an effort to advance new knowledge. This is probably even more true for student researchers.

Clarity of organization is essential for clear communication—not an insignificant virtue. Sample formats for thesis proposals abound in the literature, as well as on the Web sites of graduate colleges around the world. At the end of this chapter we include a model that we have used. Use of the prompts associated with its component parts allows this format to be personalized or adapted for almost any type of research proposal. That being said, virtually all proposal formats will include the same basic components:

- identification of phenomenon (topic)
- literature review, summarizing the current state of understanding
- problem definition (in the context of conceptual constructs)
- research design and rationale
- description of strategy, methods, techniques, and tools
- expected findings and significance
- analysis, interpretation, and discussion
- logistical and ethical concerns

Without clarity of organisation and expression, it is impossible to assess whether other criteria of quality have been achieved.

Originality means that the ideas or knowledge that result from a research or design activity are emergent and new, as in unique or unprecedented. Among its many other qualities, research is valued as a form of "original knowing," a different kind of newness that is (assumed to be) new to all. In the world of research, new knowledge requires shared verification of its originality and subsequent legitimization of its collective value via the peer-review process. It can be difficult for beginning researchers to adjust to the inverted standards of "originality" for design and research. In design, originality is stereotypically sought introspectively or subjectively, sometimes in deliberate isolation, and it may be measured by the emergence of a unique and unprecedented solution to a problem. In research, originality is sought by paying the closest possible attention to what has already been done, thought, and known and is measured by the emergence of an original question about a phenomenon and the discovery of some new knowledge or insight into its condition. It is worth noting, however, that these stereotypes are increasingly breaking down, so that some designers are deliberately working more like researchers, and researchers are beginning to accept more intuitive approaches to research as problem solving.

The criteria described above are not absolute. There is no "correct" way to meet them, and in many situations the actions needed to maximize upon one criterion may compromise achievement of another. Assessment of research quality—in developing a strategy and design and in evaluating completed work—is a process of weighing and balancing different needs and imperatives. We return to this issue in chapter 14. One of the reasons for our focus in this text upon strategy, rather than on design or method, is that a key test for publication, as highlighted by the key informants reported in chapter 1, is the overall integrity and coherence of the research—its fitness for purpose—which is, fundamentally, a strategic rather than a technical consideration.

4.6 A Developmental Heuristic

As the criteria of research quality signal, the process of developing and shaping a research strategy is a complex, reflexive, and lengthy exercise. It has very little in common with writing a term paper. Just as with a significant design project, shaping a research study is neither a linear process nor does it correspond to any particular topology or scale of thinking. Some students begin with a convenient or interesting site or an archive that has received little previous attention, for which they must develop an original question or problem to pursue. Others begin with a body of theory, critical perspective, or design work for which they devise a way to draw out and apply principles. There are those students who identify a phenomenon, experience, or trend they wish to explain. Still others may find a ready-made thesis topic embedded in a larger research project that they have been engaged to support as part of a research team or institute.

For any graduate student, however, it is necessary to assume some analytical distance on his or her own intellectual processes. Otherwise, it can be very difficult to separate personal discovery and skill building from the rigor of research. It may help students to achieve this sense of perspective by thinking of research not as belonging just to themselves, but rather as contributing to collective learning for the greater good. Valuable new knowledge may sometimes result from a personal journey, but learning is of greater value and may become part of a wider research agenda when it can be applied to problems in other places and times or used by others facing similar or analogous problems.

Table 4.1 below comprises a set of questions and responses designed to assist in shaping a graduate-level research strategy. It is offered as a provisional aid to working through the self-discovery and logical decisions needed to narrow, clarify, and justify the research agenda for a thesis. As a process model, it focuses upon the reflexive thought patterns demanded of the beginning researcher. Our intent here is to help new researchers tease out and develop their own awareness of the relationships between pragmatic and strategic responses to a "need to know." When treated as a written exercise, the questions may also contribute to the development of a research proposal. To that end, a model proposal format follows Table 4.1 at the conclusion of the chapter. These questions and the model format can also be used as a guide to practice-based research projects.

An important motivation behind the development of this decision model is to encourage deeper consideration of the relationships between motives and strategy in research inquiry. The questions set out above can be usefully undertaken by small teams. They do

Table 4.1 **Questions and responses to aid in definition of a research project**

Intellectual need/question/motive	Strategy/response/rationale
Situation: *What seems to be happening/interesting/missing/wrong?*	Identify general subject/scale/scope/sector of study: i.e., place, paradigm, perception, process, or policy.
Mission: *What is the cause/position/identity you assume?*	Reflect upon and articulate your motivation for this investigation.
Relevance: *Where/what/who benefits from this new knowledge, or loses from the lack of it?*	Describe project significance: i.e., impact/contribution to affected parties, places, or conditions.
Discipline: *To what body of knowledge do you seek to contribute?*	Establish the field of study/practice for your inquiry (landscape architecture, resource management, environmental behavior, planning policy, etc.).
Epistemology: *How will you claim your new knowledge?*	Clarify the presuppositional framework for the study (Is the approach objectivist, constructivist subjective/pragmatist? Why?). This will be determined partly by the context of the study, partly by the significance (the risks of getting it wrong and who carries those risks), and partly your intellectual style.
Context and scope: *When or where did/ how has the problem become apparent?*	Conduct literature search (select, review, and synthesize) for background information and precedent cases.
State of current knowledge: *What do we already know about the topic, and how has our knowledge evolved?*	Conduct literature search (select, review, and synthesize) of known theoretical approaches—both general/related theory and specific applications.
Strategic framework: *What type of inquiry would make it possible for you to find out something new about your phenomenon?*	Develop a purpose statement with goals and logic for a research strategy vis-à-vis your topic, its context, your skills and motivation, and specific theoretical concepts.

Continued

Table 4.1 (Continued)

Intellectual need/question/motive	Strategy/response/rationale
Research(able) questions: *What can you learn and what do you most need to find out?*	Articulate a question that precisely identifies sites/cases/subjects/samples/evidence/data types for the phenomena you want to investigate.
Research(able) design: *What type of data do you seek, and how will you access it in a way that is most appropriate for your skills, site, scope, and time limits of the study?*	State the variables/parameters you need to investigate and develop a research design that will enable you to access relevant data.
Research methods: *How exactly do you propose to describe, measure, evaluate, or interpret the data?*	Select and test methods—detailed procedures, techniques, and units for data collection, analysis, and evaluation.
Expected findings: *What do you expect to find out?*	Anticipate the projected findings (try to imagine both positive and negative results).
Demonstration: *How will you know when you have answered the original question?*	Return to the original research question(s); articulate any additional questions that emerged in the course of the investigation; show how they are related to or supportive of the larger, general questions (or not).
Relevance: *So what will the discipline learn from your work and why does it matter?*	Describe how your research questions, methods, or findings might be extended to other sites/situations by other researchers; reflect upon how the study findings will meet publication criteria and note its limitations.
Feasibility: *Can you achieve it with the time and resources available?*	Outline precise steps, travel, products, and other pragmatic requirements that need to be accomplished within the cost limits, time frame, and scope of the study.

not have to be taken in order—some responses may become clear when other questions are still being shaped. A good technique is to move back and forth between the prompts and corresponding responses until a statement can be articulated that is meaningful, efficient, and clear. From there, discussion can move up or down the different ranges until a more comprehensive understanding of motive and strategies emerges.

Asking questions to shape an investigation also prefigures the preparation of a more formal statement of intent, known as a proposal. It is normal practice in graduate programs to require students to prepare a formal thesis or dissertation proposal, and this may often be presented at an open seminar. The proposal is, in effect, an explanation, justification, and work plan for the proposed research. It helps structure discussions between student and adviser, provides the basis for approval of a topic, and also serves to guide the preparation of the final thesis. A number of texts offer advice upon how to prepare a thesis or research proposal. Here we include a model format drawn from our own work.

Table 4.2 Model outline for a thesis/research proposal*

Covers:	Front and back (refer to appropriate templates/policies)
	Flyleaf or frontispiece (if desired)
Front Matter:	Page nos. i-xv, etc.
	Title page: Refer to appropriate templates/policies
	Abstract: Describe topic; problem/purpose of research; goals and objectives; general methods; results expected; significance/impact—all in terse and condensed language, generally between two hundred and four hundred words
	Table of contents
	Lists of figures and/or tables
	Preface: Acknowledgments, naming mentors, motivations, funding sources, etc.
A. Research Overview:	A brief statement that summarizes the mission/goals and central research topic in a few short paragraphs.
	1. The "hook": Craft a compelling opening statement that engages the reader with your topic. This will depend upon the context.
	2. Situation: Briefly explain what is, or seems to be, happening at the proposed focus of your study.
	3. Motive: Explain what is, or seems to be missing or "broken," what opportunity is being missed, and why the research is needed.
	4. Identify key concept(s): Introduce the concepts or perspective that will frame the research—perhaps summarized as a "big idea" upon which it is focused.
	5. Question(s): State precisely what you aim to find out.
	6. Strategy: Briefly explain the conceptual approach to your research.
	7. Hypothesis (if strategy is deductive) or proposition (if strategy is inductive or abductive): Suggest a potential relationship between phenomena and governing concepts that can be explored.
	8. Design: Outline the basic structure or logic of how data (evidence) will be sampled and/or generated and analyzed in order to implement your strategy and address the hypothesis or proposition.
B. Topical Background:	A literature review of the specific topic or issue that details exactly what situation, context, or place is under investigation.
	1. Historical overview of issue/problem: Explain how the topic/situation has developed over time (diachronic) and how it is related to other parallel situations (synchronic).
	2. Literature review of relevant applications (case studies or examples): Explain what is already known about the place, issue, problem, or situation and what best practices or models could be applied.

Continued

Table 4.2 (Continued)

C. Theoretical Context:	A literature review of relevant theory that expands on the purpose statement to explain exactly what ideas, strategies, or arguments are being explored, extended, tested, or challenged. 1. Existing theories, models, or claims to knowledge: Critically review what is directly relevant to the topic under investigation. 2. Inadequacy of existing models: Use citations, observations, or other evidence to indicate gaps or flaws in the available knowledge base. 3. Research context: Place your research in the context of previous work. 4. Theoretical framework: Explain how your general constructs will be applied to the specific issue.
D. Objectives and Rationale:	A summary of the question, existing knowledge claims from the literature, and your objectives to improve understanding. 1. Rationale: In the context of what is known (or knowable), justify how your proposal is reasonable, necessary, and useful. 2. Significance and/or contributions of the research: Explain why we need to know. 3. Research objectives: List succinct, specific, achievable objectives (no more than three to five) that are measurable or able to be evaluated.
E. Research Strategy:	The rationale for a research strategy that shapes the type of investigation to the specific need to know and the possible ways of knowing. 1. Explanation and justification of strategy: Explain the intellectual and practical agenda, its relationship to theory, and the presuppositions you have made and why.
F. Research Design:	Explain the way in which you will approach the task of collecting and analyzing data. Identify specific phases and tasks of the research process, and explain how the sampling methods fit the specifics of the problem. 1. Overall design: Explain how the strategy is expressed in a particular research design and choice of methods and why have you chosen to work this way. 2. Sampling approach: Identify the case(s), target sample, or population that you will investigate. 3. Data collection: Specify and justify the data collecting techniques and instruments for each research task. 4. Data recording methods: Describe and explain. 6. Ethics: Explain any ethical issues or social concerns and how you are addressing them.
G. Data Analysis:	Identify the specific phases and tasks for analysis of each data set and explain how the analysis fits the question, i.e,. what do you need to find out?
H. Feasibility:	Show how the research can be undertaken with the time, resources, and skills available. 1. Pilot testing: Explain any "dry-run" models, presurveys, test cases, sample analyses, and provide illustrations and diagrams as needed. 2. Work plan and scheduling: Time line, duration, and task order.

	3. Budget: List anticipated expenses, such as travel, communications, reprographics, equipment, wages, access, etc. Show how these will be met from different funding sources.
I. Significance:	Explain the expected contributions and implications of research.
	1. Projected outcomes: Explain what you hope to learn and why this matters. The discussion should reflect the research objectives.
	2. Potential impacts: Identify the contributions to theory and/or to practical problems.
	3. Future needs: Identify opportunities or obligations to follow up.
J. Dissemination:	Explain your plans for reporting the results.
	1. Intended audiences: Explain who will be interested in the results. This may include people you have engaged with during the process.
	2. Communication intentions: Identify possible journal(s) or forums or other mechanisms for presentation, publication, or reporting of results.
K. Supporting material:	1. Endnotes (if appropriate).
	2. References cited.
	3. Appendices and exhibits.
	4. Any applicable institutional disclaimers/ethical justifications.
	5. Personal/professional curriculum vitae.

To be adapted as necessary to meet specific graduate school or funding agency policies.

This model thesis proposal outline concludes the first part of the book. In the second part, nine chapters will review and exemplify different research strategies, grounded in the peer-reviewed literature. It should be reiterated that besides their illustrative clarity or other qualities we found interesting, the articles selected for these chapters are not intended to be definitive exemplars. There are scores of other articles that might have been equally suitable examples, including some that may be in press and published after this book has been finished. Indeed, students and beginning researchers may very profitably explore the concepts of this book by using these categories to select, sort, and analyze their own reading material. Above all, the purpose of the texts we have chosen is simply to illustrate a wide range of strategies and to stimulate a researcher's imagination with their adaptive possibilities.

References

Barrett, S. 2003. *A short guide to writing about art.* 7th ed. New York: Longman.

Booth, W., G. Colomb, and J. Williams. 1995. *The craft of research.* Chicago: University of Chicago Press.

College of ESF (College of Environmental Science and Forestry), State University of New York, Syracuse. 2010. http://www.esf.edu/graduate/graddegreq.htm (accessed July 2010).

Creswell, J. W. 2009. *Research design: Qualitative, quantitative, and mixed methods approaches.* 3rd ed. Thousand Oaks, CA: Sage.

Department of Landscape Architecture, University of Illinois at Urbana-Champaign. 1999. 7.3.8: Thesis. In Policies of the department of landscape architecture (unpublished in-house document). Last revised July 7, 1999.

Groat, L., and D. Wang. 2002. *Architectural research methods.* New York: John Wiley and Sons.

Guba, E. 1981. Criteria for assessing the trustworthiness of naturalistic inquiries. *Education Communication and Technology Journal* 29 (2): 76–91.

Koberg, D., and J. Bagnall. 1976. *The all new universal traveler: A soft systems guide to creativity, problem-solving, and the process of design.* Rev. ed. Los Altos, CA: W. Kaufmann.

Pedhazur, E. J., and L. P. Schmelkin. 1991. *Measurement, design, and analysis: An integrated approach.* Hillsdale, NJ: Lawrence Erlbaum Assoc.

Rudestam, K. E., and R. R. Newton. 1992. *Surviving your dissertation: A comprehensive guide to content and process.* Newbury Park, CA: Sage.

Steinitz, C. 1990. A framework for theory applicable to the education of landscape architects (and other environmental design professionals). *Landscape Journal* 9 (2): 136–43.

———. 1995. Design is a verb; design is a noun. *Landscape Journal* 14 (2): 188–200.

Taylor, P. 2000. Re: search: The generation of knowledge in landscape architecture. *Landscape Journal* 19 (2): 102.

Van Wagenen, K. 1991. *Writing a thesis: Substance and style.* Englewood Cliffs, NJ: Prentice Hall.

CHAPTER 5

Descriptive Strategies

5.1 Introduction

Landscape relates primarily to the human scale—it can be seen, touched, and smelled, moved through, and experienced. Landscape architectural practice is expressed in everyday actions such as drawing, mapping, constructing, and planting. This makes both landscape and landscape architecture accessible to empirical description, the most basic research strategy. Empiricism is a philosophical tradition that dates back to Aristotle and places emphasis upon knowledge gained from direct observation and experience of the physical senses (McIntyre 2005). Description refers literally to the "writing" of information. Descriptive research strategies thus produce new knowledge by systematically collecting and recording information that is readily available to the investigator and does not require complex analysis in order for it to be understood.

This chapter examines four types of descriptive research strategy widely applied within landscape architecture—observation, secondary description, descriptive social surveys, and complex description (including case studies). Descriptive strategies are well suited for practices looking to build up applied knowledge in support of their professional activities and for use by students as they develop an interest in research and undertake exploratory studies. Description is also frequently the first stage of a higher-level research program. In the social sciences, for example, observation is widely used by experienced researchers as part of more theoretically oriented investigations, and description is frequently used as a strategy to open up new areas of investigation about which little is known. Decisions about what to describe and how to record descriptive information about landscape and landscape architecture may, therefore, underpin the validity and value of a wider research program.

Descriptive research is deceptively straightforward. After all, what could be simpler than to record the features and characteristics of a site or landscape as we find it, or to ask people what they value in a landscape, or to describe how landscape architects practice? However, a strategy based upon description raises many fundamental questions of research design and method. How do we order and name what we observe? In what ways do previous knowledge and the language and graphics we use shape what we observe and record? How can we record the complexity of landscape without losing its essential character? If we are using secondary sources such as documents, how complete is the record? Can we believe it? If we ask people for their knowledge and views, can we believe what they tell us? Indeed, can we believe and trust what we ourselves observe and record? The notes in this chapter briefly introduce two important questions about methods in descriptive research and their relationship to strategy and design: how to record descriptive information and the role of pilot testing surveys. Notes in subsequent chapters deal with other, related questions.

5.2 Observation

Many historical precedents demonstrate how the foundation knowledge of the discipline has been built upon the work of careful and acute observers who prepared firsthand accounts and inventories of the rich diversity of landscape phenomena in the world. In the early eighteenth century, Alexander Pope advised landowners to "consult the genius of the place" as the basis for designed improvement, and observation and analysis of site features and characteristics have subsequently provided the foundation for the discipline (Meyer 2005). As Cooper Marcus and Francis have also noted (1998), observation can be a very efficient way to gain insight into the character, use, and performance of places already designed.

There are several types of research design based upon observational strategies that are particularly relevant to landscape architecture. First, observations and records can be ordered by reference to a particular *site,* or place. Place is a location where biophysical features, human activities, and social and cultural meanings and values combine (see fig. 5.1) to create a distinct identity (Relph 1976). These broad categories can usefully provide a basis for observation and inventory of both site and place.

Site or place inventories are an integral part of landscape architecture, but they can also provide knowledge that is more widely used in the discipline as the basis

Figure 5.1 Place—the community of Rapaki, Aotearoa, New Zealand

for classification and typology. In the first research example (Goličnik and Ward Thompson 2010) (Example 5.1), observation and mapping techniques are used to describe the locations of activity in relation to the biophysical layout of several parks (fig. 5.2). These types of descriptive technique enable the researcher to record the nature and location of human activities and analyze their relationship to park design, as a contribution toward a wider strategic investigation into the role of public open space in community well-being.

A second type of research design for observational research is to describe an imaginary or actual section, or *transect*, across a landscape. The section was widely used by Ian McHarg to describe landscape relationships in *Design with Nature* (1969), and the example of historiography by Ward Thompson (2006) featured in chapter 9 highlights

Example 5.1:
Design and Use of Urban Spaces
(Goličnik and Ward Thompson 2010)

This research was undertaken as a PhD study that was part of a larger program investigating the role and design of public parks and open space. The article is focused upon the need for practical and effective ways to observe and record the relationship between the design of parks and their patterns of use.

The objective of the research was to explore the effectiveness of GIS for spatial annotation, analysis of data, and visualization of patterns of human behavior in urban public parks. The strategy was descriptive, and it used a research design involving site observations and measurements of map data in selected case-study locations. Three case-study examples were reported in the published article, located in Edinburgh, Scotland, and Ljubljana, Slovenia.

The research developed observation and recording techniques to record the nature, location, and duration of activity in the case-study parks. The park layout was derived from various sources and on-site and was entered into a GIS using the ArcView software. Basic numerical measures of human characteristics and activity were recorded and located on the maps, as well as collated in tables. The field observations took place on a number of days in early summer at specified time periods, and both daily and composite maps were prepared to record spatial patterns of activities.

The results from the observations of activities were interpreted and discussed in relationship to the spatial character and pattern of the parks, with the investigators concluding that there are a limited number of key design cues that shape use. From these conclusions, tentative design guidelines were developed that focused upon the importance of edge effects, personal space, activity spaces, and buffer zones.

The value and interest of this project as an example of a descriptive research strategy is the way it adopted a case-study design using conventional observation and recording techniques to build an effective empirical understanding of the way that landscapes are used. It generates practical knowledge about an important aspect of practice and provides tangible evidence to support future design proposals.

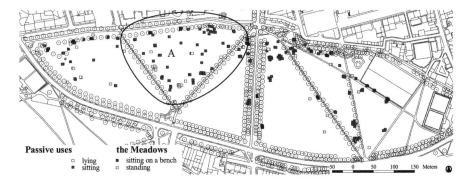

Passive uses · the Meadows
□ lying ■ sitting on a bench
■ sitting □ standing

Figure 5.2 Map of park users, Edinburgh, Scotland
(Reprinted from Goličnik and Ward Thompson (2010). Copyright 2010. Used with permission from Elsevier.)

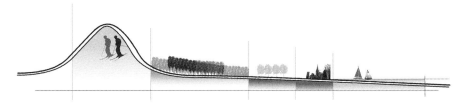

Figure 5.3 A transect
(Inspired by Patrick Geddes' concepts of the Valley Section. Illustrated in Ward Thompson 2006.)

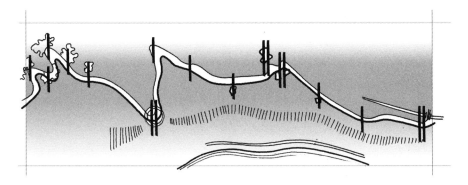

Figure 5.4 An experiential journey
(Inspired by Georges Descombe's 1991 sketch of the "Swiss Way" published in Descombes 1999).

the Valley Section used by Patrick Geddes to analyze and describe landscape characteristics (fig. 5.3).

A third research design option is to describe a *journey* through a landscape (fig. 5.4).
This is one of the oldest types of landscape description, but it is gaining renewed attention
in contemporary theory. Sequential descriptions also underpin the use of virtual landscape simulations.

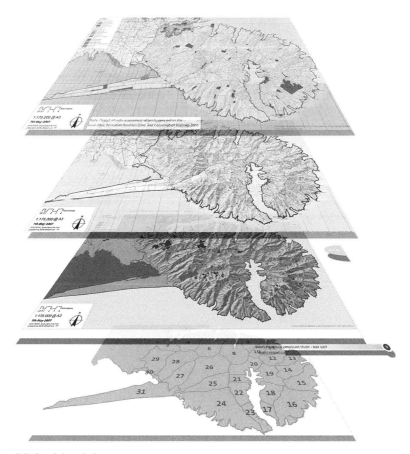

Figure 5.5 Areal description

(Incorporating transformed maps from Banks Peninsula Landscape Study, prepared by Boffa Miskell Ltd. for Christchurch City Council)

A fourth approach to research design for descriptive observation is to record how land-scape phenomena may be distributed spatially across and throughout a wider district, territory, or region (fig. 5.5). Several types of *areal* landscape description can be identified (Mabbutt 1968). The most familiar is known as the "landscape" approach, which is based upon the investigator's identification of common characteristics or features that give an area its overall distinctive appearance. In contrast, a "parametric" approach describes singular dimensions of the area—such as soil or vegetation patterns—as discrete sets of data.

Parametric data may be combined in a *layered* approach, which overlays different parametric descriptions so that their coincidence in space can be represented. Once undertaken as separate hand-drawn overlays, this now provides the basis for geographic information systems (GIS), and as more and more landscape information is digitized (see below), the parametric layered approach to landscape description has come to be more and more dominant.

A *genetic* approach is focused upon describing the processes that have created the landscape. These are frequently based upon geomorphological features—for example, describing a landscape in terms of floodplains, erosion fans, and so on—but they may also refer to vegetation types, such as old growth or secondary forest.

Increasingly, landscapes are being described in terms of *networks*, which portray the functional or symbolic relationships that bind different places together within a wider landscape (Stephenson et al. 2009).

As a descriptive strategy becomes more sophisticated, it becomes more dependent upon the combination, classification, and interpretation of different sources of data (see Notes on Method 5.1). This is a question that is discussed further in chapter 8 (Classification Schemes).

Words are good at describing qualities, but they are less good at describing quantity. Some words provide an indication of relative quantity (more or less, bigger or smaller), but research strategies that are confined to purely qualitative descriptors are limited in their ability to manage large and complex amounts of data and face all manner of challenges in dealing with consistency over time and across situations (what does "big" actually mean? Does it mean the same to different researchers?). Hence, even qualitative researchers find it useful to incorporate simple numerical techniques into their research design—that is, to use simple *measurements*. As Silverman (1985) noted, numbers are helpful when making sense of everyday phenomena.

The next example of descriptive research is focused upon an areal description of an indicator of biodiversity, bird species, within a particular landscape element,

Notes on Method 5.1: Recording and Representation

Describing is the process of putting some aspect of the world into words, based upon observation or sensation (touch, smell, etc.). But what words do we use to describe and "make sense of" the complexity of phenomena within landscape? Do we describe the leaf, twig, branch, tree, or forest? Indeed, what differentiates a tree from a forest, or the wood from the trees? Philosophers and linguists have spent their lives considering such questions. Descriptive research strategies adopt a practical stance, and most empirical description adopts "natural" categories, taken from everyday life. It treats as given the categories that occur in language, and where some additional definition is needed, this is done by reference to other everyday terms.

In the contemporary world, with multicultural societies, ease of travel, and global media, the implications of using natural categories are increasingly under scrutiny, as the language used to describe a phenomenon and the meaning it has for the subjects of the research within their culture and society inevitably frames the research from a particular cultural perspective. This requires researchers using descriptive strategies to be aware and sensitive to the assumptions they make. In chapter 9 (Interpretive Strategies) the question of "whose words and in what context" becomes a central focus for investigation.

Habitat strategy	1977	No.	1999	No.
Interior species	American Redstart Haley Woodpecker Pileated Woodpecker Veery	4	White-breasted Nuthatch	1
Interior/edge species	Blue Jay Eastern Towhee Grey Catbird Northern Cardinal Northern Flicker Yellow-throated Vireo	6	Black-capped Chickadee Blue Jay Carolina Wren Downey Woodpecker Eastern Towhee Eastern Wood Peewee Great Crested Flycatcher Great Horned Owl Grey Catbird Northern Cardinal Northern Flicker Red-eyed Vireo Wood Thrush	13

Figure 5.6 Numerical inventory: bird counts

(Reprinted from McWilliam and Brown 2001, with permission from the publisher, Taylor and Francis. Copyright 2001.)

a forest (see fig. 5.6 and Example 5.2). McWilliam and Brown (2001) demonstrate the use of basic numerical inventory and mapping of the species biodiversity in a setting affected by new housing. An interesting aspect is that the survey followed an earlier predevelopment survey and so enabled comparisons to be made over time, as a form of postoccupancy evaluation. Example 5.2 illustrates the value of repeating a survey to enable comparisons over time. Change in landscape is fundamental to landscape architecture, and the description of a series of events is a distinctive type of strategy, with its own particular challenges in research design.

In diachronic research based upon empirical observation, temporal descriptions are derived from a series of field observations by the investigator. Example 5.3 illustrates an innovative way to report upon systematic field observation of the changing seasonal color of landscape (Stobbelaar et al. 2004). It shows a phenology diagram of an organic farm in Drenthe, illustrating the color changes in the field and field verges. The rows on the diagram indicate the various plots; the height of a row represents the relative area. The vertical lines are the moments of observation (fig. 5.7).

5.3 Secondary Description

The second type of descriptive research strategy we highlight in this chapter is the use and summarization of observations or information that has been recorded by people other than the investigator. Research designs for secondary description typically use documentary sources and descriptive categories that are "found." That is, they have

Example 5.2:
Effect of Housing Development on Bird Species Diversity
(McWilliam and Brown 2001)

The context for the study was the development of new housing in formerly rural land around the town of London, Ontario, in Canada. The area included significant forest fragments, and the implications of land development for bird species diversity had been raised as a concern during predevelopment hearings. There was insufficient existing knowledge to be able to make reliable predictions of likely effects. However, a rapid baseline survey of species had been undertaken before construction commenced. This study replicated the survey postdevelopment and asked what the effects of housing development had actually been upon bird species diversity.

The research design was a rapid field description of a defined area, based upon landscape ecological concepts that linked species to distinctive types of habitat.

The field survey recorded the presence of bird species as indicated by their distinctive songs. (Although more robust techniques are now available, this was the method used in the original survey and was retained to ensure consistency in measurement.)

not been created by the researcher. However, they are not necessarily natural categories, as they may have been created by others for different purposes. Typical found sources for secondary description include archival documents and maps, diaries, media reports, and previous studies. Example 5.4 (Kim and Pauleit 2009) illustrates a design in which data from a series of aerial photographs of a locality are used to describe changes in landscape pattern over time due to urbanization.

5.4 Descriptive Social Surveys

Descriptive landscape questions cannot always be answered by direct observation of the phenomena in question or from recorded secondary sources. They may require information that can only be found by asking what other people have seen or experienced. In this situation it can be fruitful to develop a strategy based upon a descriptive social survey. We use this term for a descriptive strategy in which an investigator designs the research to systematically ask other people to provide information on the topic of interest, using a formal survey instrument such as a questionnaire or an interview that is structured around a standard set of questions (fig. 5.9). The categories are, therefore, those selected by the researcher. There are other types of social survey—such as open-ended interviews—in which the response is shaped by the subjects and their interaction with the researcher. These "interpretive" strategies are explored in chapter 9. Other types of strategy involving social surveys place primary focus upon removing the influence of the investigator. The use of experimental and quasi-experimental research strategies is examined in chapter 7.

Recordings were made at dawn and dusk and during vegetation inventory. The vegetation was mapped to identify the areas and locations of different types of habitat. The inventory was organized using categories based upon the habitat preference of species (interior, interior/edge, edge).

The postdevelopment survey results revealed an overall numerical increase in species, but there was a shift from interior to edge/interior and edge species. The decrease in interior species was anticipated, as the habitat survey had revealed a major decline in interior core habitat. However, the significant increase in interior/edge species was unexpected, because as the forest edge conditions expanded they had also become less complex.

The research provided useful evidence of the effect of changing landscape pattern upon species composition, and the authors argued for more pre- and postoccupancy studies to build practical knowledge of the effects of change. However, they also noted the methodological limitations of the original baseline survey, which may have underestimated species numbers.

The study illustrates both the advantages and disadvantages of a descriptive strategy using a design based upon rapid field descriptive techniques. It highlights the value of a postoccupancy survey but also demonstrates the challenge of ensuring consistency in measurement over time when field techniques are continually being improved.

Example 5.3:
Phenology of the Landscape:
The Role of Organic Agriculture
(Stobbelaar et al. 2004)

Phenology is the study of recurring phenomena; this research investigated the influence that organic farming has had upon the changing color of an agricultural landscape. The catalyst for the work was the growing public and commercial interest in organic farming and the claims made for it in respect to the positive effects it might have upon landscape quality. Quality was defined in this study in terms of the legibility and coherence of a landscape. The specific focus of the research was upon the seasonal coherence of color as an indicator of natural rhythms. It asked whether organic farming resulted in different and higher-quality patterns of landscape color.

The research adopted a description strategy using a research design based upon comparison of field observations made at the "high point" of each season in three different study regions. Photographs, drawings that removed evidence of weather, and ground plans of crops were made in each study region. The colors of the landscape were recorded and the data summarized in tables and diagrams. Both organic and conventional farms were surveyed.

The research then moved from description to evaluation, and farms were ranked according to the degree of seasonal development evident in their fields. (In this summary, the descriptive dimension is highlighted.) The research found that in two of the three regions, the organic farms showed much more evidence of seasonal change than did the conventional farms. However, in reviewing the research the investigators recognized that the evaluative phase of the design was based upon expert evaluation.

The interesting feature of this example as a descriptive strategy is the way it shows how a design using basic field observation techniques and systematic collation of data can be used to build a sophisticated understanding of a dynamic phenomenon.

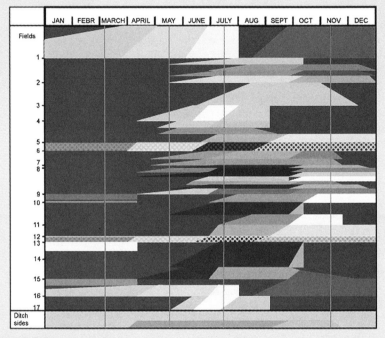

Figure 5.7 Phenology diagram

(Reprinted from Stobbelaar et al. 2004, with permission from the publisher, Taylor and Francis. Copyright 2004.)

The key research design decisions in a descriptive social survey strategy relate to the framing of the questions, the selection of the people who will be asked to respond, and how to gain access to them. Questions need to be clear, direct, and unambiguous. If the questionnaire is "closed," then the range of possible answers must be considered. For example, using a Likert scale, a set of words or numerical values are provided for the respondent to choose from. Options might range along a five-point scale from "strongly prefer" to "strongly dislike" (fig. 5.10). Alternatively, respondents may be asked to indicate their strength of feeling or opinion on a numerical scale ranging from one to ten.

If the questionnaire is "open" it gives respondents the chance to choose their own words in reply to the question. Open questionnaires present more challenges in analysis,

Example 5.4:
Woodland Changes and Landscape Structure
(Kim and Pauleit 2009)

The context for this project was the effect of urbanization and agricultural intensification upon woodlands in South Korea. The research investigated recent changes in landscape structure in the rapidly growing Kwangju City region.

The aim of the research was to assess the extent of change in spatial characteristics of woodlands in the city region. The strategy adopted was secondary description based upon a research design that measured changes in landscape structure over time. The regional landscape was described using a methodology adopted from the Landscape Character Assessment approach developed in the United Kingdom. Four study landscapes were selected, representing contrasting landscape types (urban, urban fringe, agricultural, and mountain). Changing land cover in each area was determined based upon existing aerial photographs taken on four dates over a twenty-six-year period.

The spatial characteristics of woodland cover were described using three landscape ecological metrics: a patch shape index, a patch distribution index, and a patch density index. Changes in seminatural land cover around woodlands were also measured as an indicator of habitat change.

Absolute changes and annual rates of change in the areas and indices were identified over the study period and presented in tabular and map form. The results reveal that woodland areas are highly dynamic features, with an overall loss in area as well as fragmentation. The landscape ecological metrics revealed that while there were variable changes in each of the landscape types, the relationship with changes in woodland area were complex and sometimes counterintuitive. The authors then speculated on possible dynamics and identified needs for further research and possible conservation strategies.

As a descriptive research strategy, the example demonstrates how change in a landscape can be traced using data from a secondary source. The design shows how landscape ecological concepts are used to generate descriptive indices that can be derived from delineation of areas in the aerial photographs and used to track change over time. The process is a simple description of a series of time slices and differs from a modeling strategy as it does not analyze dynamic relationships among variables.

Figure 5.8 Woodland change in Korea

(Reprinted from Kim and Pauleit 2009, with permission from the publisher, Taylor and Francis. Copyright 2009.)

Lincoln University **September 2002**

Christchurch Visitor Itinerary Planning and Perception Survey (VIPPS)

3D: How long will be your stay in Christchurch this time? (Just record hours for day visitors only)

Hours? ________________ Days? ________________

3E: Could you please tell us about the main places on your holiday itinerary before Christchurch?

Region	Route/Transport mode	Duration

3F: Could you please tell us about the main places on your holiday itinerary after Christchurch?

Region	Route/Transport mode	Duration

3G: What were the main reasons for including Christchurch as a stop on your itinerary?

1. ________________________________
2. ________________________________
3. ________________________________
4. ________________________________
5. ________________________________

3H: Are there any things in the Canterbury region you would like to do but have not had the time?

1. ________________________________
2. ________________________________
3. ________________________________
4. ________________________________
5. ________________________________

GO TO PART C

Figure 5.9 A typical social survey instrument

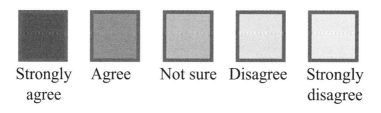

"I Like My Neighbourhood"

Figure 5.10 A Likert scale

as it becomes necessary to "code" the replies into a form that can be summarized and analyzed. In simple descriptive surveys (see Example 5.5), the results are typically presented as basic lists or tables, with a numerical summary of the replies in each category. As noted in chapter 6, it is important to understand the measurement scale used in a survey instrument, because that will determine the types of statistical analyses that can be used legitimately. It is also always vital to pilot test descriptive survey instruments to ensure that they work in the field and deliver useful information (Notes on Method 5.2).

The selection of whom to ask in a descriptive social survey depends upon the information sought and how it will be used. Example 5.5 illustrates a straightforward and effective research design for a descriptive social survey in which the overall aim of the research was to find out about use of plant species in the profession (Hooper et al. 2008). The investigators, therefore, approached landscape architects and nurseries. The choice of whom to ask determines the possibilities and practicalities of how to administer the survey—by mail, email/Web, telephone, person to person (e.g., by calling at houses), or through "intercepts" (which are person to person, but carried out on an opportunistic basis—for example, stopping and talking to whomever happens to be coming along a street). All have their own advantages, disadvantages, and idiosyncrasies. Sampling is considered further in a Note in chapter 8.

5.5 Complex Description

There are many possible sources of empirical data about landscape and landscape architecture. A complex descriptive strategy using a research design that combines different sources (fig. 5.11) can build up a rich understanding by providing complementary accounts of different aspects of a landscape topic. There are many reasons for using a strategy based upon multiple sources. The combination of different observation techniques builds up a richer and more complete account. For example, a wider landscape description can provide a context to place-based description, by overlaying a description of critical relationships, supplying a narrative account of a crucial route, and providing historical perspectives. Different descriptive sources can also reveal different types of information.

Example 5.5:
Theory and Practice Related to Native Plants: A Case Study of Utah Landscape Professionals

(Hooper, Endter-Wada, and Johnson 2008)

This research investigated how landscape professionals selected and used native plants in their professional practice. The authors noted that the use of native plants is now an integral part of ecological design, as well as green building practices and ecological restoration, but there has been controversy surrounding the definition of native plants and how they should be used.

The focus of the research was, therefore, to better understand the relationship between theory and practice in the use of native plants by landscape professionals. The strategy was a descriptive social survey, and the design involved two stages. The first consisted of a questionnaire survey of all current members of the Utah Chapter of the American Society of Landscape Architects. The second part involved interviews with customers of a nursery who were selected for their involvement in and knowledge of the native plant industry. The questions sought information on the participants, their experiences using native plants, their views on the use of native plants, the limitations to using native plants, and information needs.

Survey results were coded and analyzed using the Statistical Package for the Social Sciences (SPSS for Windows 2006) and results compiled into charts and tables. Themes in the tables included the professional background of respondents and their experiences and views regarding native plants.

The findings indicated that survey participants expressed a general commitment to using native plants. However, they encountered challenges and constraints related to native plant availability, lack of customer receptivity, limitations in their own knowledge, issues over the ability of native plants to meet diverse and complex project objectives, and market forces within the landscape design and nursery industries.

The investigators concluded that the findings raised questions about how regional design aesthetics evolve, the relationship between landscape design and nursery market trends, and how best to educate landscape architects to deal with the issues.

The research is interesting because it illustrates how descriptive social surveys can be used to improve understanding of an emerging area of practice.

Notes on Method 5.2: Pilot Testing

Undertaking a "'proof of concept" trial is a critical part of any applied research. It can range from checking the practical availability and compatibility of information to running through a desk exercise to test the feasibility of the process and timetable to undertaking trial interviews or questionnaires on a smaller number of people. The scale and organization of the pilot test depends upon the nature of the main survey. Structured interviews with a modest number of landscape architects might be effectively pilot tested with colleagues or adjunct teachers, while a large questionnaire survey may require a larger and more systematic pilot test. There is extensive published experience and both theoretical and practical guidance available within the social sciences upon preparation of questionnaires (e.g., Rea and Parker 2005), all of which is transferable to landscape architecture.

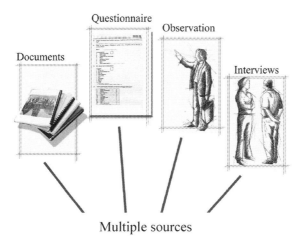

Multiple sources

Figure 5.11 Multiple sources of information

Multiple sources may also provide greater certainty and precision about particular phenomena through triangulation (fig. 5.12). The term triangulation comes from geometry and is used in surveying in a way that will be familiar to all researchers in landscape architecture. In the context of research, triangulation in a research design means that we look for evidence from different data sources that are mutually reinforcing—for example, evidence of similar values being expressed about a landscape that occur in closed questionnaires as well as in-depth interviews. It is important to realize, however, that not all research data can be triangulated, as it may have been collected using different assumptions. Silverman (2005), therefore, cautions investigators to ensure that any multiple-methods approach adopts clear ground rules, so that any combination of data from different sources can be justified theoretically as well as practically. This means that if we add a description of apples to a description of oranges, then we must be certain to describe the result in terms of fruit and not presume that apples are the same as oranges in every respect.

The following example of a complex descriptive strategy uses complementary multiple sources—primarily descriptive, but also including quantitative measures—to build up an account of the values of urban woodlands in Scotland. In Example 5.6, Ward Thompson et al. (2005) combine a number of user surveys to provide an overview of the social values associated with an important type of landscape. The research design incorporates some correlational and content analyses (see the following chapters), which enable the findings to contribute to a wider and more robust theoretical understanding. However, the study is included here because it builds upon a foundation that starts with a descriptive strategy.

5.6 Descriptive Case Studies

Many research strategies used in the natural sciences and the naturalistic social sciences achieve explanatory value by narrowing the focus of investigation. For example, experimental strategies (see chapter 7) adopt designs that aim to isolate key factors that can be

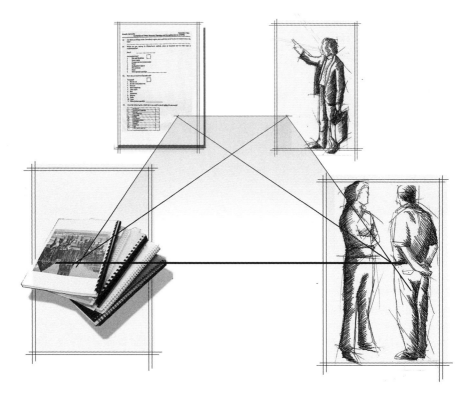

Figure 5.12 Triangulation

controlled and their relationships manipulated, in order to derive formal measures that can be analyzed using statistical methods. These, in turn, can be used to test formal models and theories. However, landscape is a complex phenomenon that is very hard to break up into pieces in order to investigate using experimental techniques—particularly as it involves people and social relationships as well as biophysical relationships. In situations where the subject of research is complex and involves the interaction of both human and biophysical relationships, many applied disciplines adopt a case-study strategy (Yin 2005, Gerring 2007).

Case studies are complex multifaceted investigations into a particular place, project, organization, or landscape. Yin (2005) defines them as "empirical" inquiries into "contemporary phenomena within a real life context" and notes that they are particularly useful when there are no clear boundaries between the focus of research and the context. He identifies three types of case study: descriptive studies, exploratory studies, and explanatory studies. According to Yin, the key factors in selecting a case-study strategy are the type of question, the degree of control over the situation, and the type of phenomenon, particularly over time.

In this chapter the descriptive role of case studies is emphasized. However, it is important to note that case studies can also be used in a strategy to explore new topics, and

Example 5.6:
Local Woodlands and Community Use
(Ward Thompson et al. 2005)

The context for this investigation was the policy adopted by many local authorities in the United Kingdom to establish woodlands around urban fringes in former industrial areas. The research specifically focused upon the situation in central Scotland. The research questions were straightforward: how well are these new woodlands meeting current social and community needs, and what might be significant in making improvements?

The research strategy emphasized descriptive social survey and used a multiphased and multimethod design involving quantitative data from a large sample of respondents from the relevant communities. It included focus groups, questionnaires, and on-site observations. The focus groups involved five communities and different age groups; a series of questions moved from the general to the particular. The accounts provided were recorded and analyzed by counting the occurrence of key words. Quotes were selected to illustrate the main types of response.

The findings from the focus groups were then used to develop a questionnaire, based upon a Likert-type scale, that asked people to respond using a seven-point attitudinal scale (from "strongly agree" to "strongly disagree"). The questionnaire was administered face to face to 339 respondents in an intercept survey in a range of public settings at a range of times. The results were summarized with descriptive statistics, and correlations were drawn among key variables (see chapter 6 for correlational research strategies and a discussion of the limitations to the use of data from Likert scales for statistical analysis). The results suggested that there were distinct categories of visitors to woodlands. The key woodland sites used by respondents were then visited by the research team, and site observations were recorded.

The last part of the research drew out the main findings from the surveys and placed the results in the context of the findings of previous studies. Some earlier findings were reinforced, but the key new finding was "the overriding importance" of childhood visits to woodlands in influencing adults' subsequent attitudes and behavior. This highlighted the importance of proximity and access to urban woodlands for young people.

The research is a useful example of a complex descriptive research strategy using a design based upon multiple sources. It shows how a descriptive strategy can be used as the stepping-stone for an evaluation of the outcomes of an established landscape planning policy. It also shows how research designs for complex descriptive research strategies typically include several stages, each building on the previous stage (for example, using focus groups to derive questions for a questionnaire survey).

there are many examples where a number of comparative case studies are used to build a typology or working classification of situations that can generate further, more precise research questions (see chapter 8). It is also possible to use a case-study approach to test alternative explanations, either by selecting several case studies that provide contrasting situations, or by using a single complex case study as the basis for several contrasting modes of analysis or alternative theoretical explanations (see chapters on experimentation and evaluation).

Gerring (2007) identified four ways to select comparative case studies, based upon the spatial and temporal variation they express (Table 5.1). First, there are geographical cases that allow spatial but not temporal comparisons; second, longitudinal cases that display temporal but not spatial variation; third, dynamic cases that display both spatial and temporal variation; and fourth, counterfactual cases that are imagined (such as design scenarios) and that provide a way to test and challenge presumptions and relationships (Example 5.7). These latter types of design are typically used in strategies that are based upon design projections (chapter 12).

Example 5.7:
Village Homes: A Case Study in Community Design
(Francis 2002)

The Village Homes case study was written as an exemplar of how descriptive case studies should be prepared. It follows the method developed by Mark Francis (2001) for the Landscape Architecture Foundation (LAF) to provide a uniform way to critically evaluate landscape architecture projects and issues and to make such studies easily comparable across cases. The LAF case study method has since been widely used and adopted by ASLA's Sustainable Sites Initiative, the American Institute of Architects, and the Active Learning Program of the Robert Wood Johnson Foundation. An adapted version has been used by the Le Notre Mundus project.

The underlying aim of this type of descriptive case study is to learn from previous experience. To achieve this, the author outlines elements of the design for Village Homes, including limitations and less-successful aspects. Village Homes is a community that was designed and developed in the 1970s in Davis, California (see fig. 5.13). It was intended to be a more sustainable housing option in terms of environmental and social health. Village Homes serves as a model for community development, but it has not been duplicated.

The key research questions that Francis asked were "What makes Village Homes such a popular development, and why has it not been reproduced in subsequent developments?"

The case study design involved the collection and analysis of a wide range of data about the project, as well as responses from users. It also evaluated the success and limitations of the project. The case study presentation took the form of a narrative outlining the history of Village Homes from inception to construction and use over thirty years.

The main conclusion was that Village Homes remains a useful model from which other developments can draw inspiration and principles. The development of Village Homes has overcome numerous obstacles, and the developers suggest that it hasn't been easy or perfect, but rather an experiment from which to learn.

The value of the Village Homes as an example of a descriptive case study strategy is in showing how useful project data can be recorded in a consistent format that can subsequently be used in comparison with other projects.

Table 5.1 Case-study designs*

Case-study designs		Spatial variation	
		Yes	No
Temporal variation	Yes	Dynamic	Longitudinal
	No	Geographical	Counterfactual (imagined intervention)

*Categories and relationships drawn from Gerring 2007.

Figure 5.13 Village Homes: an aerial view

(Reprinted from Francis 2002. Reproduced by the permission of the University of Wisconsin Press. Copyright 2002 by the Board of Regents of the University of Wisconsin System.)

Case studies are particularly well suited to landscape architectural research, as the focus of interest of the discipline is typically complex, multidimensional, and embedded in a wider context, and thus hard to separate into discrete factors. There have been a number of excellent studies published in recent years in the main journals of the discipline. For example, in a theme issue of *Landscape Journal* on "Race, Space and the Destabilization of Practice," two longitudinal case studies with a strong landscape focus were included. Schneider (2007) described the evolution of African American hamlets in the Inner Bluegrass region of central Kentucky. The study uses maps, photographs, aerial photographs, and documentary sources to track the way the hamlets and their communities have changed since the Civil War in the United States (1861–65). In a complementary study, Brabec and Richardson (2007) analyzed the genesis of contemporary landscape patterns in a distinctive Gullah community on islands off the coast of South Carolina and Georgia. This study combined an analysis of existing sources in related disciplines (the area has already been much studied) with historical documentary investigation, analysis of aerial photographs, direct observation, and interviews with community members. The data presented included tables of relevant statistics and combined historical records of land tenure with contemporary aerial photos.

These two case studies illustrate a number of key features and elements of a case-study strategy. Both included a critical review of previous academic research into their topics and synthesized this knowledge with their own empirical investigations. They each used a range of complementary sources. The research in both of these cases was defined geographically and in respect to a distinctive ethnic group and its community. Both concluded by considering some implications for the future.

The example of a case study included in this chapter (Francis 2002) serves two functions. First, it illustrates the way a case study can be undertaken on a neighborhood project. Second, it tests the template for case-study research, drawing upon work undertaken for the Landscape Architecture Foundation (LAF).

Several more recent published examples of case-study research illustrate the cumulative and comparative potential for case studies. When it was launched in 2006, the European *Journal of Landscape Architecture* included a publication category called "Under the Sky," intended to "develop the critical reading of projects" in order to "bring a contribution to theory building." This has resulted in a series of project case studies that follow a broadly similar format and have been subject to peer review. Most studies have been urban infrastructure projects. Only a few have been published, and comparisons have not been drawn, but the numbers of cases are slowly building.

A similar editorial initiative in *Landscape Architecture Magazine* has established a series of critical case studies on Green Roofs (McIntyre 2009). These illustrate the potential for new knowledge created through practice to be codified in a systematic way that can begin to build a grounded theoretical understanding. The case studies have generated a vigorous debate between practitioners and academics, conducted through the letters columns, which adds further value to the process.

Another example of the way in which standard templates can be fruitful can be seen in the Web-based resources established through LAF and the Le Notre project. As was noted earlier, Le Notre is an initiative from the European Council of Landscape Architecture Schools (ECLAS) supported by the European Commission. Part of the project has involved international E-seminars with students from participating schools and building up a teaching resource. A number of case studies of urban and rural planning and design projects have been completed using a template adapted from Francis's LAF model. Such standardization should enable more systematic comparison between cases over time.

Descriptive Strategies: Summary

Descriptive strategies are well suited for:

- exploratory research into phenomena about which little is known
- building understanding about landscape characteristics and community values and activities to provide evidence in support of proposed design principles or local policy initiatives
- project-based investigations—such as predesign inventories and postoccupancy evaluations
- telling stories to raise awareness in communities about landscape character and dynamics as a basis for greater involvement
- building knowledge about the everyday practices of the discipline and profession

Descriptive strategies are also frequently part of more sophisticated research strategies that build upon the descriptive phase to undertake further investigation—for example, through evaluation. Their designs may also involve multiple methods for data collection and analysis. Overall, the variable scale and elasticity of the range of descriptive strategies typically pursued in landscape architecture makes them highly suitable for both graduate and professional research.

References

Brabec, E., and S. Richardson. 2007. A clash of cultures: The landscape of the Sea Island Gullah. *Landscape Journal* 26 (1): 151–67.

Cooper Marcus, C., and C. Francis. 1998. *People places: Design guidelines for urban open space.* 2nd ed. New York: John Wiley and Sons.

Descombes, G. 1999. Shifting Sites: The Swiss way, Geneva. In *Recovering landscape: Essays in contemporary landscape architecture,* ed. J. Corner. New York: Princeton Architectural Press.

Francis, M. 2001. A case study method for landscape architecture. *Landscape Journal* 20 (1): 15–29.

———. 2002. Village Homes: A case study in community design. *Landscape Journal* 21 (1): 23–41.

Gerring, J. 2007. *Case study research: Principles and practices*. Cambridge, U.K.: Cambridge University Press.

Goličnik B., and C. Ward Thompson. 2010. Emerging relationships between design and use of urban park spaces. *Landscape and Urban Planning* 94: 38–53.

Hooper, V. H., V. Endter-Wada, and C. W. Johnson. 2008. Theory and practice related to native plants: A case study of Utah landscape professionals. *Landscape Journal* 27 (1): 127–41.

Kim, K-H., and S. Pauleit. 2009. Woodland changes and their impacts on the landscape structure in South Korea, Kwangju Region. *Landscape Research* 34 (3): 257–77.

Mabbutt, J. A. 1968. Review of concepts of land classification. In *Land Evaluation,* ed. G. A. Stewart, 11–28. Melbourne: Macmillan.

McHarg, I. 1969. *Design with nature*. New York: Doubleday.

McIntyre, L., 2009. High maintenance superstar. *Landscape Architecture Magazine,* August, 64–77.

McIntyre, L. J. 2005. *Need to know: Social science research methods*. New York: McGraw-Hill.

McWilliam, W. J., and R. D. Brown. 2001. Effects of housing development on bird species diversity in a forest fragment in Ontario, Canada. *Landscape Research* 26 (4): 407–19.

Meyer, E. 2005. Site citations. In *Site matters: Design concepts, histories, strategies,* eds. C. Burns and A. Hahn, 93–129. New York: Routledge.

Rea, L. M., and R. A. Parker. 2005. *Designing and conducting survey research: A comprehensive guide*. 3rd ed. New York: Jossey Bass.

Relph, E. 1976. *Place and placelessness*. London: Pion.

Schneider, K. 2007. Negotiating the image of the Inner Bluegrass. *Landscape Journal* 26 (1): 134–50.

Silverman, D. 1985. *Qualitative methodology and sociology*. London: Gower.

———. 2005. *Doing qualitative research: A practical handbook*. 2nd ed. London: Sage.

Stephenson, J., M. Abbott, and J. Ruru, eds. 2009. *Beyond the scene: Landscape and identity in Aotearoa, New Zealand*. Dunedin, New Zealand: University of Otago Press.

Stobbelaar, D. J., K. Hendriks, and A. Stordtelder. 2004. Phenology of the landscape: The role of organic agriculture. *Landscape Research* 29 (2): 153–79.

Ward Thompson, C., P. Aspinall, S. Bell, and C. Findlay. 2005. "It gets you away from everyday life": Local woodlands and community use—What makes a difference? *Landscape Research* 30 (1): 109–46.

Ward Thompson, C. 2006. Patrick Geddes and the Edinburgh Zoological Garden: Expressing universal processes through local place. *Landscape Journal* 25 (1): 80–93.

Yin, R. K. 2005. *Case study research: Design and methods*. Thousand Oaks, CA: Sage.

CHAPTER 6

Modeling and Correlational Strategies

6.1 Introduction

One of the greatest challenges in understanding landscape is how to simplify its complexity and to interrelate what we observe and experience. Modeling is a research strategy based upon simplification. However, it is far from simple to describe the strategy, as there are many definitions of modeling and many typologies of models. The common feature of all these is the process of abstracting some aspect of reality and the incorporation of selected empirical data into the abstraction. In Perry's words, "Models are idealized simplifications of some phenomenon or system" (2009, 337).

Ervin (2001) identified a critical distinction in landscape models between those models that focus upon external representation (what is seen and experienced about landscape) and those that focus upon internal representation (data models of landscape process). As he notes, "In the effort to model and visualize landscape, we need to seek a balance between 'looks like' and 'acts like'" (2001, 50). Hence, models (fig. 6.1) in landscape research may take the form of an external representation—a physical construct (such as a series of cardboard layers used to represent a hill) or a graphic representation

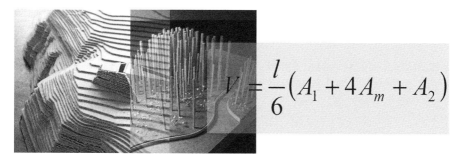

$$V = \frac{l}{6}\left(A_1 + 4A_m + A_2\right)$$

External representations 'looks like'   Internal representations 'acts like'

Figure 6.1 Types of models

(a cross-sectional drawing, for example). Alternatively, it could be an internal representation (such as a written or diagrammatic expression of the sequence by which the hill will be regraded), or a mathematical representation of the volumes of the hill expressed as formulas and a data set (see also Groat and Wang 2002).

Just as the real world is structured through relationships (for example, the angle of repose of fill material under the influence of gravity and friction), so models are based upon assumed relationships—with the type of assumptions dependent upon the nature of the model. Landscape models are also, by some definitions, spatial (Costanza and Voinov 2004, 3), although some landscape-related models—such as preference models—may not be. The process of model building may be bottom up, working from small units to build a representation of a larger reality, or top down, starting with aggregated data and breaking it into parts. In either case, as Perry notes, "parsimony is central to good modeling: we seek the simplest model that serves our purpose adequately" (2009, 337).

Modeling can be used for a range of research-related purposes, from synthesizing descriptive information to predicting and communicating the way systems operate to the exploration of possible new relationships. This range of roles prefigures how modeling techniques can be used in different ways within a number of different research strategies and designs.

As a research strategy in itself, modeling is a process in which the representation of landscape or some aspect of landscape in simplified terms enables new knowledge to be generated. This chapter highlights four related strategies in which modeling plays a fundamental role: descriptive/synthetic modeling, analytical modeling and correlation, predictive modeling, and dynamic simulation modeling.

Descriptive/synthetic modeling strategies place emphasis upon the creation of a narrative or graphic representation that displays the key conceptual features and relationships of the phenomenon or system under investigation. They may typically incorporate a range of empirical data. *Analytical* modeling strategies, including correlation, investigate and formalize sets or combinations of real-world relationships in mathematical terms. *Predictive* modeling strategies use statistical techniques to predict the nature of real-world situations based upon a selected sample of observed data. *Dynamic simulation* modeling strategies use process models that represent the dynamics of real-world situations and may be used in a number of ways, ranging from exploration of new situations to theory testing.

In each case, there is an inescapable truism that every model created is inherently false, in that it simplifies some aspect of reality, but may be said to be only approximately true (Perry 2009, 337). "Complex models fit reality to some degree, which is usually not zero, but is never perfect" (Costanza and Voinov 2004, 10). The challenge in model-based strategies is to determine the optimum level of simplification for the purpose at hand. This may not be as complex as some expect. As Perry notes, "complex problems do not necessarily require complicated answers" (2009, 337).

Davis et al. (2007, 481) situate modeling in the "sweet spot" between inductive case-study research that generates rough and basic theoretical propositions and the more logically precise theory testing using multivariate analyses. We also see modeling as a strategy that mediates between empirical description and formal explanation, and have therefore located it in our classification system within the objectivist paradigm between description and experimentation. In the following sections we describe the four variations that we have identified.

6.2 Descriptive/Synthetic Models

The most basic type of model is one that provides a simplified description of a complex situation. It may be focused upon one dimension of the situation—for example, topography—or it may synthesize different dimensions of landscape. In a sense, most descriptions of landscape are "models" in that they simplify key relationships and characteristics of a complex reality using a coherent symbolic language of representation. However, the focus in this chapter is upon situations where the construction of a defined model with clear specifications is a defining feature of the research strategy.

Example 6.1:
Environmental History of an Abandoned Mill
(Ferguson 1999)

This project was stimulated by an interest in flood protection and historic preservation, but it evolved to provide a more general demonstration of the relationship between economic development and environmental change. It focused upon a former mill site in the Piedmont region of Georgia, in the United States. In the nineteenth century the site was a major cotton mill, located at the site of a major bedrock shoal in the river and was surrounded by a significant settlement. Today, the area is abandoned, and the site of the bedrock shoal is buried under sediment. The researcher seeks to understand the development of this situation. In particular, what are the prospects for combining flood protection with conservation of the site's historic features?

The research strategy was focused upon development of a descriptive model of landscape change based upon historical records and contemporary field observation and hydrological analysis. The dynamics of the site were described in several ways. Archival records of historical observations from early settlers provided a qualitative account of changes since European colonization. A previously published geomorphological investigation described the land use and erosion history of the wider catchment area. Based on fieldwork, the author constructed an analytical model of the evolution of the longitudinal profile of the river channel at the mill site.

The historical model of the landscape dynamics of the mill site was used to speculate upon the future trajectories of the site and the prospects for flood protection and historical conservation. The research had two outcomes: it established the landscape constraints and opportunities for historical preservation of the old mill site, and at a more general level it illustrated the long-term consequences of exploitive land-use practices.

This example demonstrates the value of building a simple but effective synthetic landscape model from diverse and complementary sources.

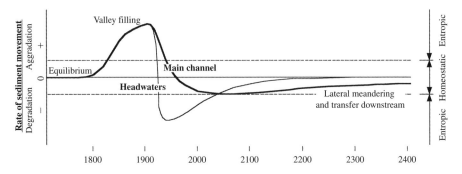

Figure 6.2 A synthetic landscape model

Descriptive/synthetic models may summarize the outcomes of empirical investigations, synthesize data from different sources, articulate a proposition that is being tested or explored, provide the base data for scholarly design interventions, provide a stimulus for social research (as in preference studies using landscape "simulacra"), or provide the basis for policy testing and evaluation (Groat and Wang 2002).

Example 6.1 of a descriptive modeling strategy (Ferguson 1999) illustrates the use of a synthetic model (fig. 6.2). It shows how different types of data—empirical observation, archival material, previously published research, and geophysical surveys—can be integrated to provide a conceptual model of sequential change of a complex landscape.

Descriptive/synthetic modeling is, therefore, a helpful strategy to investigate complex spatial and temporal relationships in landscapes where the nature of the relationships cannot be easily or clearly seen by firsthand observation. By simplifying the mass of empirical data the researcher is better able to understand the structural and functional characteristics of the landscape. Descriptive/synthetic models are often also used as a step toward landscape classification and evaluation or as a basis for other investigative strategies.

6.3 Analytical Models and Correlation

In simplifying a phenomenon, place, landscape, or practice, one of the key challenges is to understand the relationships between the attributes or characteristics that make it distinctive. Correlation is a research strategy that uses statistical models to investigate relationships. Specifically, it seeks to identify a relationship between two or more variables in a set of data. A variable is a particular characteristic—in Example 6.2 by Milburn and Brown (2003), the variables are age, gender, and education. A variable occurs in a range of categories within a scale of measurement. Variables in correlation may be reported as nominal, ordinal, interval, or ratio categories. The choice of measurement is one of the

Example 6.2:
Research Productivity in Landscape Architecture

(Milburn and Brown 2003)

Research productivity increasingly determines tenure and discipline funding in academic institutions. However, the level and amount of research being done by educators and practitioners in landscape architecture has been recognized as a constraint on the development of the discipline. There has been speculation about possible reasons for this, but there is little evidence available about the specific relationships involved. The authors of this research aimed to improve understanding of the factors influencing research productivity amongst landscape architecture faculty in North America. They focused upon the characteristics of faculty and investigated linkages between age, gender, education, and productivity.

The research strategy was based upon correlation. The research design incorporated two questionnaire surveys administered to landscape architecture faculty. The first was sent to faculty listed as members of the Council of Educators in Landscape Architecture in the 1998 CELA directory, and the follow-up survey was administered to sixty-six landscape architecture department heads at universities in North America.

Questions in the first survey sought demographic information, as well as attitudes about research. The second questionnaire was designed to measure the research culture within academic departments. Questions formulated by reference to previous research literature and responses to nine questions were reported in this article. Both surveys used a Likert-type scale (i.e., ordinal categories). Research culture was analyzed with descriptive statistics, and relationships between the key variables and research productivity were analyzed using descriptive statistics, including graphs and a basic correlation coefficient. The results indicated no statistically significant relationship between gender and research output. A negative relationship was identified between age and research productivity: that is, research output decreases as age increases after thirty-five. There is a significant relationship between education and productivity, which is higher for those with a PhD. The research concluded by considering possible explanations and relating these to the literature.

The example demonstrated an exploratory correlational strategy, seeking statistical evidence of relationships about a situation where little was known. The researchers used a research design based upon descriptive statistics and a basic correlation coefficient to investigate the relationship between two independent variables expressed as nominal data (gender and education), one independent variable expressed as ordinal data (age bands), and a single dependent variable expressed as interval data (number of publications).

The goals of the research were modest, but careful attention to the research design—in particular, the nature of the data and the analysis it could support—meant that the results were robust and the strategy effective.

key factors in the research design of correlational research as it determines the way in which relationships can be statistically analyzed. Notes on Method 6.1 explains the different categories of measurement and their significance for research strategy and design.

Correlational research is "objectivist" in terms of the classification of strategies we explained in chapter 1. The characteristics that are analyzed as variables are presumed to

Notes on Method 6.1: Measurement and Counting

Measurement of landscape phenomena is central to a number of landscape architectural research strategies and is a key consideration in research design. A measure is a description of the quantity or size or extent of something that has been determined by reference to some known or fixed standard. The most basic form of measurement is nominal: the identification of the number of items in a known category—for instance, how many oaks may be present in a given area. Ordinal measurement places categories into some sort of order based upon some recognized criterion, such as tall, medium, or small, but it may lack absolute value. In interval measurement, the steps in a sequential order are all of the same size or difference—for instance, 1, 2, 3, 4, 5. Ratio measurement is the most powerful measure, as it assigns a precise value based upon comparison with a standard unit or scale of reference that starts at 0, such as length in meters.

The type of data available determines the type and power of statistical analysis that can be undertaken and, therefore, shapes the research design. This can be a point of debate between researchers. Data that is technically ordinal (such as Likert scales) is not infrequently treated as if it were interval data and is used to calculate measures, such as averages, that are not strictly applicable in the context in which they are used. Some researchers argue that this practice is worthwhile because it enables comparison with many other studies that have made similar assumptions; others argue for a more precise use of data. Because correct application of measurement is a critical part of any research design, the type of data that is available and the way it is used are important considerations in deciding the overall strategy to adopt.

In most common forms of measurement, three useful descriptive statistics are the mode, median, and mean. The mode is the category that occurs most frequently. It is the only statistic that can be used to describe nominal data. A researcher might find that the most common tree species in a park is the red oak—this is called the modal category. The median is the category that represents the midpoint of a set of data. Half the measured phenomena will have a value that is less than this figure, and half the phenomena measured will have a value that is more. For example, the median height of a sample of fifty plants will be the height where there are as many taller plants as there are shorter. The arithmetic mean (often referred to as the average) is the "center of gravity" of the data. It can only be derived for interval or ratio measures. It may not lie in the center of the distribution—for example, if there are proportionally more tall plants in the sample, the mean (average) height will be taller than the median.

There are also a number of statistical measures—such as standard deviation—that describe the way observations or recorded phenomena are distributed across a data set. These are addressed in chapter 7.

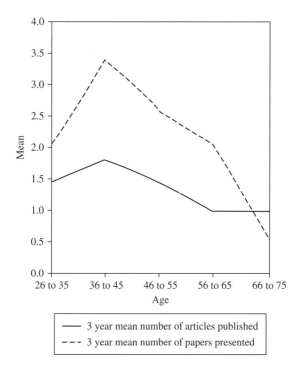

Figure 6.3 Descriptive statistics

(Reprinted from Milburn and Brown 2003. Reproduced by permission of the University of Wisconsin Press. Copyright 2003 by the Board of Regents of the University of Wisconsin System.)

be independent of the researcher, and typically considerable effort is spent ensuring that their measurement is unbiased. Correlational analysis uses both descriptive and inferential statistical techniques to identify evidence of a relationship. There is considerable overlap with methods used in experimentation (chapter 7).

Groat and Wang (2002) identified two types of correlation—one that aims to clarify and predict relationships and a hybrid approach that aims to draw provisional conclusions about causality. This highlights the relationship of correlation with a deductive approach to investigation. In this text we have placed correlational research centrally in the inductive-deductive spectrum, as a strategy that seeks relationships that may, but do not necessarily, enable formal propositions to be tested. We have also associated correlation with modeling and simulation, the common feature being an emphasis upon the creation of simplified representations of complex real-world systems, based upon mathematical and other forms of symbolic analysis of important relationships.

6.4 Simple Correlation

Simple correlation can use both descriptive and inferential statistics, but it is the latter that makes correlation a "modeling" strategy. Descriptive statistics can be very effective in establishing the likelihood of a significant relationship. However, while the research design and subsequent analysis is straightforward (and for that reason will appeal to the many nonquantitative researchers in landscape architecture), the results are limited in their application. It is impossible to assign any measure of strength or level of significance to a relationship that is suggested by descriptive statistics. Nor can any prediction be made about how a relationship identified in a data sample may relate to the real world. Most correlational research, therefore, uses a research design based on inferential statistics to establish the nature of relationships, and this introduces several new concepts and terms.

Inferential statistics are aimed at drawing conclusions about a data set that has some degree of random variation—for example, due to measurement errors or because the data set is drawn at random from a larger population. The inferential statistical techniques used in correlation are based upon the construction of mathematical models of populations (Giere 1997, 132). There are three important dimensions that must be considered in the research design: Is there a relationship between the variables in the sample that is the focus of the research; if so, how strong is the relationship; and, how can the knowledge about relationships in the sample provide knowledge about the real world from which the data has been drawn?

A variable is a measurable attribute (such as the age of a researcher or their research productivity) that can have a range of different values. In statistics, an independent variable is a value that may change independently of the relations being investigated (such as age), while a dependent variable is a value that changes (e.g., productivity) as a consequence of changes in the independent variable.

There are a number of techniques used to investigate the statistical significance of relationships between variables. The choice of technique depends upon the overall research design—in particular, the nature of the sample and the nature of the data— and, specifically, the type of measurement used (Rea and Parker 2005, 234). For example, the correlation coefficient known as Pearsons "r" can be used to analyze the relationship between two sets of interval data. Inferential statistics typically require higher order measures than basic descriptive statistics.

Given the difficulty of creating a controlled experimental setting in a landscape (chapter 7), correlational research strategies in landscape architecture typically focus upon relationships in a real-world setting involving either natural given data or data generated through a survey instrument. In Example 6.2, Milburn and Brown (2003) investigated the relationships between characteristics of the researchers and research productivity in landscape architecture faculty in the United States. The design used both descriptive and inferential statistics applied to data generated from two questionnaires.

Example 6.3 (Hands and Brown 2002) illustrates a strategy that used images as surrogates for the landscape. The research design was based upon the manipulation of images to test the effect upon people's perceptions of different approaches to planting (fig. 6.4).

Example 6.3:
Preference for Ecological Rehabilitation Sites
(Hands and Brown 2002)

Ecological rehabilitation of decommissioned industrial land can be perceived by many as "messy" and, therefore, undesirable, especially during the first stages of establishment. However, while studies have been undertaken to analyze public and residents' perceptions of a range of urban restoration settings, it is also important to consider the perceptions of people who are employed on or adjacent to brownfield sites. This project investigated the visual preferences of employees for ecological rehabilitation projects, and set out to identify which design elements had the potential to ameliorate negative perceptions.

The research adopted a correlational strategy that looked for relationships between variables that had been identified as potentially important. The research design was based upon analysis of responses to computer-generated visualizations. Thirty-two visual simulations of ecological rehabilitation landscapes shown at establishment and mature stages were used in a questionnaire format. Evidence of human intent was portrayed in the simulations by the inclusion of interventions such as a constructed bird box and by signage. Other variables in the photographs related to the appearance of vegetation used in ecological restoration.

The survey was administered to all the employees in a factory adjoining a brownfield site, who ranked photos on a "Likert-type" scale from one to seven, with one being "strongly disliked" and seven being "strongly liked." Subjects were also asked to fill in a questionnaire that included questions about their attitudes toward rehabilitation, level of participation in outdoor activities, and membership in environmentally oriented associations. Open-ended comments were also invited. The data was analyzed using SPSS software as well as Microsoft Excel 1997. Demographic information was described using descriptive statistics.

The main findings were that employees perceived ecological rehabilitation at the factory site to be messy and problematic. Apparent human intervention on the site produced mixed results. The authors concluded that the addition of designed interventions to ecological projects on factory sites can significantly improve employee preferences, without significantly affecting ecological functionality. Several suggestions to improve visual preferences were determined, including planting rapidly growing ground cover or nurse crops during establishment phases, maximizing the use of color during this stage, and using highly visible, strategically placed plantings to create the impression that the rehabilitation process is a planned procedure, rather than neglect of a site due to carelessness.

The correlational strategy uses a research design based upon visual stimuli to investigate relationships between preference and landscape design actions. The design was limited by the use of a sample of employees from only one company, which prevented formal generalization of the results to a wider population.

Appendix A: Visual Simulations

Photo Set #1

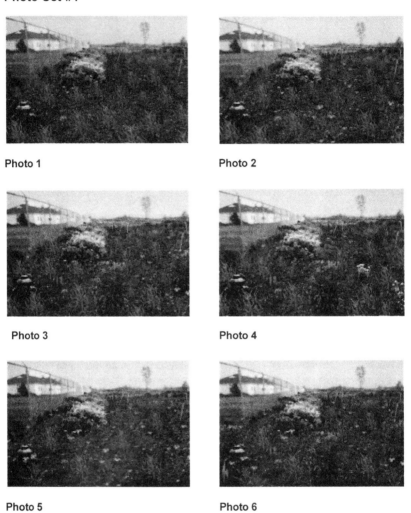

Photo 1

Photo 2

Photo 3

Photo 4

Photo 5

Photo 6

Figure 6.4 Visual landscape variables in correlational research

(Reprinted from Hands and Brown 2002. Copyright 2002, used with permission from Elsevier.)

6.5 Multiple Correlations

Relationships in landscape phenomena are seldom expressed as simple correlations of two variables. There are typically several important variables involved, and most correlational research strategies seek to identify which of a number of possible variables have

Example 6.4:
Landscape Preference and Place Attachment
(Kaltenborn and Bjerke 2002)

This research started from the recognition that while there is wide awareness of the cultural and psychological importance of place attachment, there is much less knowledge about how attachment to a particular place, or type of place, relates to landscape preference. The question is important because it affects how generic knowledge about preference might be applied in specific situations.

The investigation focused upon a small rural municipality in Norway currently undergoing significant landscape change. In a related study, the researchers had investigated the relationship between environmental orientation and preference. Here, the multiple correlation strategy investigated the relationship between reported landscape preferences and a number of indicators of place attachment. The research design used both factor analysis and multiple-regression analysis techniques.

The subjects for the study were a large (501) random representative sample of adults in the municipality who had been recruited by telephone and sent a questionnaire. Landscape preferences were analyzed by subjects rating the attractiveness of twenty-four photographs selected to provide a variety of types of rural setting in the municipality. The ratings used a seven-point Likert-type scale. The mean scores for each photo were also subject to factor analysis, which identified four key landscape categories that explained the preferences. Place attachment was measured using a questionnaire with ten statements about place; the statements were rated by participants.

The strength of place attachment was tested for each of the images using analysis of variance, and the relationship between place attachment and preference was analyzed using multiple-regression analysis. In both cases, individual landscape images as well as grouped categories were tested.

Place attachment was positively correlated with preference in all except six images that showed typically modern agriculture. Overall, place attachment predicted around fifteen percent of the variance in preferences for farm environments and twenty percent for more natural environments. It was noted, however, that only twenty-five respondents were farmers, and the relationships with modern agricultural settings might have been stronger if more farmers had participated.

The study is interesting because of the way it seeks relationships between two dimensions of landscape that are typically investigated separately. The strategy uses a design incorporating conventional survey instruments and multiple correlation techniques to explore a fundamental aspect of landscape planning. As with many examples of landscape research strategies that use correlational techniques on questionnaire surveys, however, there are detailed aspects of the research design that can be questioned. Here, correlational analysis is applied to data that has been derived from ordinal (rather than interval) measures (i.e., to the mean scores of Likert scales). As with so much applied research, it is necessary to strike a balance between practicality, utility, and the finer points of research design.

Figure 6.5 Place as a variable: Roros, Norway

(Reprinted from Kaltenborn and Bjerke 2002. Used with permission from the publisher, Taylor and Francis. Copyright 2002.)

a statistically significant relationship. To achieve this, research designs often incorporate the correlation technique called multiple regression. This allows investigation of a series of independent variables and one dependent variable, in order to identify which variables exhibit the strongest correlation with others, in time and/or space. This may or may not suggest directional cause or effect, but it narrows down the possibilities for further investigation. Another technique, known as factor analysis, allows investigation of a complex matrix of interrelated variables, seeking causal relationships among a whole set of interrelationships. Some designs use multiple analyses that are undertaken in sequence, for example, when factor analysis is used to distill significant variables from a wider set, followed by multiple regression analysis of selected variables that have been identified in the initial analysis or created by aggregating initial results.

In Example 6.4, Kaltenborn and Bjerke (2002) adopted a multiple correlation strategy to investigate the associations between preferences for landscape and attachment to place (fig. 6.5), which they applied through a research design that used multiple regression analysis.

6.6 Spatial Correlations

One of the defining characteristics of landscape as a phenomenon is its spatiality. Hence, one of the critical dimensions in which researchers may seek evidence of systematic relationships between variables is in their spatial relations. Geographers have utilized spatial correlation analyses for over fifty years to identify systematic relationships between phenomena situated in space, and they have generated a large body of research literature. The emerging science of landscape ecology is also fundamentally grounded in the investigation and understanding of spatial relationships between species, communities, and biophysical patterns within landscape and comprises a major body of research activity, with its own distinctive strategies.

In this text, we have not included detailed consideration of the wide range of spatial correlation approaches that have emerged within geography and landscape ecology, but we include an example (Mander et al. 2010) that illustrates a spatial correlation strategy located at the intersection of landscape ecology and landscape architecture (Example 6.5). The focus is upon the relationship between landscape identity and coherence.

Example 6.5:
Landscape Coherence
(Mander et al. 2010)

The context for the research is the Europe-wide effort stimulated by the European Landscape Convention and directed toward characterizing and maintaining rural landscape identity and improving its sustainability. One of the concepts that is widely used but poorly specified in landscape characterization and management is landscape coherence. This research developed a measure of landscape coherence and applied it in Estonia.

The conceptual basis for the research was the proposition that landscape coherence is the similarity between soil pattern (potential landscape) and land-use intensity (actual landscape). The research design was based upon spatial correlation models, and the relationship between soil and land-use intensity was measured using spatial correlograms (fig. 6.6), which are a graphic analytical technique that employ a well-established measure of spatial autocorrelation. The investigators argued that where the correlograms of different landscape dimensions coincided, then the landscape was coherent.

Correlograms for soil and land-use intensity were compared across a range of landscape regions. Three types of relationship were identified: situations where soil patterns were more fragmented than land-use intensity, situations where land-use intensity was more fragmented than soil patterns, and situations where the two patterns do not differ significantly and have similar measures of autocorrelation. The investigators argue that in the latter case, where patterns do not differ, human practices have closely followed landscape potentials, creating a highly coherent landscape. In contrast, in uplands, where the underlying landscape potential is highly fragmented (heterogeneous), human activity has tended to simplify landscape character, whereas in lowlands, where landscape potential is typically more homogenous, human activity has increased fragmentation.

The investigators conclude that the approach has practical potential in offering a way to measure coherence, which is an important but elusive landscape quality. The proven application is so far limited to just one country, with a particular human and environmental history.

This example shows how correlational strategies can be applied spatially. The research design created descriptive landscape models that were compared and used to interpret differences in landscape character. The correlational modeling strategy used here has some similarities to an experimental strategy, as the models were used to explore a theoretical proposition. However, the proposition was not tested formally, as would be the case in a research design based upon experimentation.

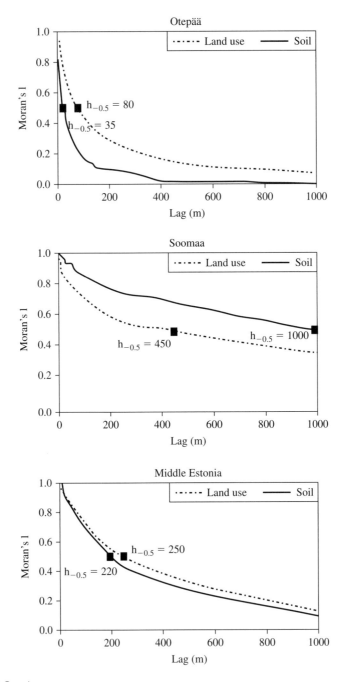

Figure 6.6 Correlograms

(Reprinted from Mander et al. 2010. Used with permission from Elsevier. Copyright 2010.)

Correlational strategies are investigative and retrospective—that is, they seek and identify relationships in data taken from the world and, hence, from past conditions and events. However, if they are based on suitable data, the statistical tools used *may* enable predictions to be generated about what future conditions might occur. For example, the Scenic Beauty Estimation approach (see chapter 7) pioneered by Daniel and Boster (1976) involved a research design that used linear regression analysis to identify the relationship between perceived scenic beauty and biophysical variables in the landscape, such as relief. The design uses empirical data derived from responses to preference surveys and analysis of the attributes of the scene represented in the photographs used in the survey to generate regression equations that best "explain" the preferences of the survey respondents. Once created, these equations can be used to predict the likely scenic beauty of other real or imagined (modeled) landscapes, based upon their biophysical attributes. This highlights the strategic connection between correlation analysis and predictive modeling.

6.7 Predictive Modeling

Predictive models generate simplified representations of some aspect of reality *as it may come to be*. The key feature of a predictive model is that the unknown state depends upon a set of assumptions about the relationships between key variables in the known (present) state. These may be derived from analysis of empirical data (such as the linear regression equations created from correlational analysis, as illustrated in the previous examples) or from idealized theoretical models (such as models of landscape connectivity or economic rationality). The relationships may be either deterministic or random. However, the dynamics of change are not actively modeled. In a predictive model (as opposed to a dynamic simulation model—see below), the predicted state is a logical extension of the currently known situation. This creates opportunity for a different type of modeling strategy (fig. 6.7).

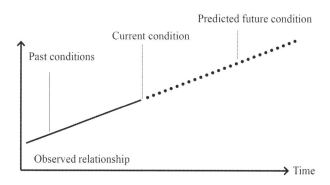

Figure 6.7 Predictive models

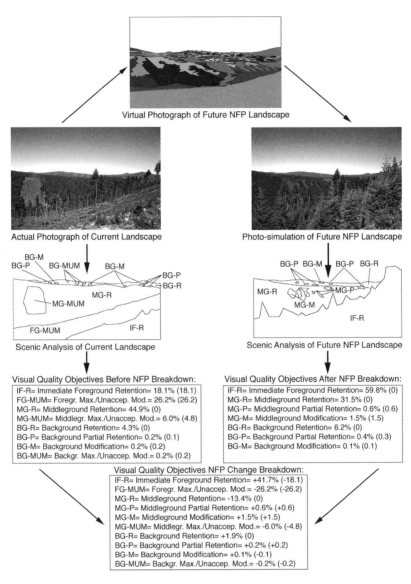

Figure 6.8 Landscape visualization for predictive modeling
(Courtesy of Ribe, Armstrong, and Gobster 2002 and the U.S. Forest Service)

Willemen et al. 2008 (Example 6.6) provides an illustration of a research strategy that uses a predictive approach to landscape modeling. The research design incorporates three complementary models in order to adapt to the different availability of landscape data.

Example 6.7 (Ribe et al. 2002) investigates the relationship between what Gobster (1999) has described as "scenic" and "ecological" aesthetics, in the context of forest

Example 6.6:
Spatial Characterization of Landscape Functions
(Willemen et al. 2008)

The context for this research is the rapidly growing policy interest in measuring and regulating landscape uses and functions as part of the wider environmental management paradigm of ecosystem services. The objective of the investigation was to develop a methodology that could show how landscape functions are distributed and vary in space.

The research strategy was based upon predictive modeling. The design featured three techniques for mapping and measurement of functions, which were demonstrated in a case-study application. The techniques used were:

- empirical observation of the spatial delineation of actual landscape functions (for example, the location and extent of residential neighborhoods), and functions delineated by policy making (e.g., zoning)

- spatial sampling of indicators of landscape function and statistical (regression) analysis and projection of their distribution (for example, tourism suitability as indicated by accommodation sites)

- deduction of the location and extent of landscape functions for which no empirical data is available, based upon selection of an indicator and development of decision rules (e.g., leisure cycling, based upon the potential leisure population)

In evaluating the methodology, the investigators noted a number of limitations, and the difficulty in validating the model, which highlighted the need for clear communication of its assumptions to any end users. Nonetheless, they considered that the maps produced by the research could have value for policy makers.

The value and interest of the example as a research strategy lies in the way in which the investigation used a design that incorporated complementary techniques to produce a spatial model of landscape function. The process shows how research is about the art of the possible—developing a strategy and design that are appropriate to both the problem and the availability of data.

management. This example is described by the authors as "simulation" modeling. However, in our organizing classification the definition of simulation limits the term to the modeling of *dynamic* relationships. This example is more accurately described in this context as a *predictive* strategy.

6.8 Dynamic Simulation Modeling

Simulations are representations of selected features or characteristics of a real-world situation. Simulation is differentiated from static representation (e.g., drawing) and predictive modeling by a focus on *dynamic* relationships, although the distinction can be blurred. There are two interlinked categories of dynamic models used as a basis for research strategies in landscape architecture: process models that represent the way that landscapes

Example 6.7:
Visualizing and Testing the Role of Visual Resources in Ecosystem Management

(Ribe, Armstrong, and Gobster 2002)

Visual forest management has been a major focus of landscape architectural research in the United States for fifty years, with a primary concern for how to better understand and manage public forest lands in response to public perceptions and preferences. Comprehensive visual management procedures have been developed and applied, but until recently there has been less of a focus on the relationship between visual and ecological management priorities.

The context for this study was the political and public controversy over the risks to endangered species—specifically, the spotted owl—as a result of forest management practices in the Pacific Northwest. One consequence of the spotted owl controversy was a change in forest-management policy, with a shift to a more biocentric orientation. This was to be made operational through a reduction in emphasis upon clear-cut forestry and a greater focus upon regeneration harvesting strategies. This research asked the question, what are the visual consequences of such a change? Specifically, will a biocentric policy approach result in less concern about the visual and scenic effects of harvesting or are visual policy and design still needed?

The research strategy was based upon the construction of a predictive model of the visual character of forests. The researchers aimed to model the visual character that might result under a revised biocentric policy and to compare preferences for these predicted scenes with the current situation. The research design (fig 6.8) involved the development of statistical models of preferences for different aspects of character. It was based upon a case-study location, which was selected to represent a typical forest area with relatively low visual quality objectives, where unfavorable public perceptions could still be a significant factor in future management. The research design involved three main phases:

function and simulation models that represent the way complete landscapes change over time under different combinations of conditions and decisions.

Landscape process models typically focus upon biophysical dynamics, such as energy flow and microclimate (Brown and Gillespie 1995), while landscape simulation models typically focus upon the dynamics of landscape patterns, such as land use or vegetation cover. Increasingly, complex regional models comprise a number of interconnected dynamic models of both process and pattern (Steinitz et al. 2003).

Landscape-simulation modeling as a research strategy thus represents in some way the dynamics of real-world interrelationships through a model and uses this to create new knowledge (fig. 6.9). However, as He points out, "most model simulations do not lead to new understandings of the modeled process themselves. The primary and subsequent results simply reflect the relationships used in building the model, which, in turn, reflect current understandings of the processes" (He 2008, 494). The exception to this is when a

First, a GIS-based terrain model was constructed that represented the visual appearance of the landscape. Photo simulations were prepared for a range of situations, including both broad vistas and closer views, under both the old and new policy settings.

Second, the researchers undertook two evaluations of the images. One used respondents from the general public sampled to represent a diversity of attitudes toward public forests. This was used to assess the scenic beauty of randomly assigned images. The other evaluation used a small panel of experts to assess the visual quality status of the existing and predicted landscapes, in terms of the categories used in the current visual-quality management system.

The third phase used multivariate analysis to identify any differences in scenic beauty scores between current and predicted scenes and to assess whether these differences could be explained by changes in visual-quality categories.

The results suggest that the change in policy would have generally positive effects on perceived scenic beauty in situations with a broad vista of forest, but that there could be significant negative effects on scenic beauty if harvesting under the new regime resulted in sharp contrasts in forest condition.

The example illustrates the way that models are necessary simplifications that should be designed according to the question under investigation. The researchers emphasized that there were a number of real-world dynamics, such as natural disturbances-that were not modeled. Furthermore, the model was only intended to predict visual consequences. This strategy of simplification enabled the researchers to achieve a high level of validity in the aspects they did model.

This example is valuable because of the way it demonstrates how a real-world policy change can be investigated with a modeling strategy based upon robust but pragmatic predictive modeling and analytical techniques. The predictive model did not model the dynamics of change—it was not a process model—but it enabled the prediction of the likely effects upon preference of changes in management priorities and forest planning policy.

simulation model generates emergent results that arise from relationships and feedbacks within the model that were not previously recognized or understood. As a general rule, therefore, simulation modeling used as a *research strategy* must apply the simulation in some way (for example, by generating new landscape possibilities based upon a change of zoning rules) that can be evaluated against higher-level policy goals.

Several strategic research functions can be identified for dynamic simulations. They include exploring, forecasting, testing, and learning. Running a simulation model can reveal aspects of the interrelationships between variables that were not known or anticipated. This is particularly likely if there is a random dimension built into the model. Emergent results might reveal the possibility of thresholds—points at which the system fails or shifts to a new state. Hence, the simulation can be the basis for an *exploratory* strategy.

A simulation model can also be used to forecast the future condition of the modeled system under a range of circumstances. Simulation can be used to test hypotheses or

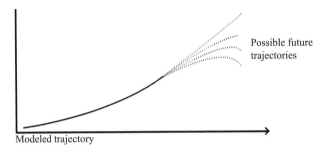

Figure 6.9 Simulation modeling

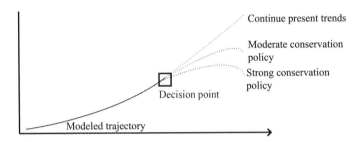

Figure 6.10 Dynamic simulation modeling expressed as alternative landscape futures

propositions about the behavior of the modeled system. Finally, simulations can be used as stimuli or agents in social and community processes and can enable researchers to learn about the effect of system behavior on social and political dynamics.

The dynamic simulation modeling approach known as Alternative Landscape Futures Modeling (Steiner 2000, Ndubisi 2002) is one of the most distinctive landscape planning contributions to environmental research. Hulse et al. (2000) noted that while predicting possible future situations has been a feature of environmental studies for over a century, the systematic analysis of future possible land uses and landscape conditions gained particular impetus in the United States from the enactment of the National Environmental Protection Act (NEPA) in 1969. NEPA introduced the requirement for the analysis of the potential environmental effects of a project as part of the decision-making process *before* it is approved and commenced. The NEPA process included "alternatives analysis"—identifying different possible ways in which the project might be undertaken, and their implications. "Alternative Futures" extended this process beyond a specific project to entire landscape scenarios (Baker et al. 2004).

Steinitz et al. (2003) identified two alternative futures strategies—design-led and decision-based. In a design-led strategy, a limited number of possible alternative futures are created through design exploration. Then they are systematically compared. The process works backward from the potential alternative future landscape configurations that have been created, such as compact or diffuse development, and assesses the implications for different dimensions of landscape health and performance.

As Steinitz et al. highlight, this strategy does not explicitly connect outcomes to different policy options. This is because the futures are not the outcome of decision-process models, but are typically combinations of linear projections (e.g., population) and imagined futures. These types of futures models were widely used in the 1960s and 1970s and are still common, as they do not require sophisticated integrated-modeling capability and enable a wide range of possibilities to be explored.

The design-led strategy does not pursue or presume correspondence between the models and scenarios generated through the research and any objective reality, as the futures are to a significant degree *imagined* or projected, rather than objectively predicted. We classify design-led scenario-based research in the "subjective" part of our classification of research strategies, in chapter 12, "Projective Design."

The second possible alternative futures strategy that was adopted by Steinitz et al. (2003) is based upon decision-choice landscape models. Here, the starting point is to identify issues and policy options, and to build dynamic landscape-simulation models that generate alternative possible futures based upon the combination of policies that are adopted. Steinitz et al. identify a range of models used at different stages in this type of strategy to generate options and model consequences. The research design can, therefore, be quite complex. The alternative futures created are also frequently described as scenarios, each of which constitutes a set of policy choices and their biophysical consequences.

Alternative futures research deals with coupled environmental and human systems (Global Land Project 2005), in which the landscape outcomes depend upon both the biophysical landscape processes and the human institutions that shape the directions of landscape change. The primary outcome is decision focused, enabling elected politicians, officials, and communities to better understand the consequences of current ways of acting and managing and to explore and test out alternative ideas and strategies. As Steinitz et al. (2003) note, the alternative futures can also highlight the consequences of *not* acting—of failure to make important decisions—and this can be a powerful message.

In many ways, landscape-based alternative futures research represents a watershed or regional scale version of the global environmental systems modeling being undertaken to investigate the nature and implications of human-induced climate change. In coming decades, landscape-scale adaptation to climate change is likely to become a critical dimension and driver of alternative futures research.

The credibility of simulation-based alternative futures research depends upon the extent to which dynamic simulation models can be shown to be valid representations of the biophysical and sociopolitical "real world" as we understand it today. Alternative futures scenarios can be feasible, plausible, or possible (Steinitz et al. 2003) and can be established for different time periods into the future, depending upon how the models in the research design are specified and upon the knowledge base and uncertainties they embody. The imperative is to create models that are fit for practical policy and planning in the "real world," and as such we place the "alternative futures" use of simulation models in the objectivist part of the classification of strategies.

Example 6.8 illustrates an alternative landscape futures strategy focused upon the consequences of population growth and development for two biophysical dimensions of landscape—water quality and biodiversity. Hulse et al. (2000) report upon the develop-

Example 6.8:
Planning Alternative Future Landscapes in Oregon
(Hulse et al. 2000)

The context for the work is the emergence of "ecosystem management" as a planning paradigm for complex watersheds under pressure from development. The research focused upon the Willamette River Basin in the state of Oregon, United States. The overall strategy involves a long-running collaborative alternative futures program aimed at adaptive learning. The research design uses a number of linked simulation models and digital representations to inform policy development, through the analysis of the landscape effects of different types of policy action (fig. 6.11).

The aspect of the program reported in the article highlighted here is structured around GIS representations of past, present, and alternative future conditions in the 320-square-kilometer Muddy Creek watershed. The investigation was organized in four phases:

- Descriptive analysis of how the landscape had changed and evolved and defined trajectories of change, based upon expert knowledge.

- Depiction of alternative futures for the year 2025, based upon stakeholder workshops. The options included a plan trend future (continuing current policies) and high and moderate conservation and development options. These addressed the question of how human activities and actions might affect future landscapes.

- Evaluation of the consequences of the alternative futures for water quality and biodiversity. Experts used GIS hydrological models and GIS biodiversity and habitat models to predict the effects of the land-use changes outlined in stage two.

- Risk assessment of the sensitivity of the hydrology and biodiversity indicators to different land-use decisions.

The outcomes were shared with regional and local communities and decision makers, and the conservation scenarios have been influential in shaping policy initiatives at the state level and within federal agencies. The example is interesting as a simulation-modeling research strategy because of the way the design uses both process models and dynamic models of landscape cover as part of a long-term collaborative research process.

ment of alternative futures scenarios in Oregon with significant stakeholder participation. Their research design exemplifies the use of landscape-process models focused upon specific dimensions that inform and are informed by a wider GIS-model of land-use change.

One of the strengths of the Willamette Basin alternative landscape futures research has been its integration within a regional community over a long period of development. This is reflected in the depth and richness of the historical analyses of landscape change, the adaptive and evolving nature of the process, and its multiple connections to a range of regional and local policy institutions within Oregon. It clearly demonstrates the benefits

Pre-EuroAmerican Scenario (PESVEG) ca. 1851

Land Use / Land Cover (LULC) ca. 1990

Plan Trend 2050

Development 2050

Conservation 2050

Figure 6.11 Alternative landscape futures: Muddy Creek, Oregon

(From Hulse, Gregory, and Baker 2002. Used by permission of Oregon State University Press.)

Example 6.9:
Alternative Futures for the Upper San Pedro River Basin
(Steinitz et al. 2003)

The Upper San Pedro River Basin covers approximately ten thousand square kilometers of semiarid landscape in southern Arizona and New Mexico. It has very high biodiversity, and in common with many sites of alternative futures research is undergoing rapid development. The basin includes a number of different categories of federal land, including a major military installation, and in this case the sponsoring agency was an environmental research branch of the U.S. Department of Defense.

The research strategy set out to use alternative futures models to identify critical landscape functions and to highlight the consequences of different possible policy decisions. The research design was iterative and comprised a framework of six sets of landscape models, each addressing a specific research question. Both stakeholders and an expert research team are involved. The six questions that structure the research, and their corresponding model model types:

How should the landscape be described?	representation models
How does the landscape operate?	process models
Is the current landscape working well?	evaluation models
How might the landscape be altered?	change models
What predictable differences might the changes cause?	impact models
How should the landscape be changed?	decision models

of combining sophisticated GIS- and landscape-modeling capability within an adaptive and grounded research strategy.

Steinitz and his team at Harvard University's Graduate School of Design developed and applied a subtly different strategy to investigate alternative landscape futures that has been applied in a number of case studies in the United States and elsewhere. The strategy is particularly notable for the clarity of the investigative structure and the way in which the research design integrates different types of landscape-related models within an overall process model (Steinitz et al 2003). Example 6.9 illustrates the strategy in a classic study situated in the Mountain Southwest region of the United States.

Modeling Strategies: Summary

- Models are simplifications of reality.
- Modeling research strategies use models to generate new knowledge. They may be based upon description, analysis, and correlation, prediction, or simulation.

These questions were addressed in three iterations. In the first, the questions are asked in sequence from top to bottom, *scoping* the research. For example, asking the initial question helps define the study area, while the final question defines who the potential stakeholders might be.

In the second iteration, *specifying the method*, the questions are addressed from the bottom upward—starting with a clarification of what types of decision might and could be made, defining the scale and nature of scenarios, and finishing with a specification of the data needed for the study.

The final iteration is *implementation*—building models that represent the current landscape, running process models to predict future possible trajectories, evaluating the effects of these trajectories upon landscape conditions, identifying possible decisions to change those trajectories to follow different pathways, assessing the possible effects of these decisions, and finally identifying which decisions should be implemented. The process is reviewed and re-iterated as required to address emerging questions and understandings and to incorporate stakeholder responses.

A key feature of the design is the suite of digital process models used to operationalize each stage and phase of the investigation—including socioeconomic development models, hydrological models, vegetation models, habitat models, and visual models. Analyses are communicated with GIS maps, graphs, tabular data, etc.

The research strategy shows how a range of landscape models can be integrated within a dynamic simulation strategy that is focused upon understanding the implications of different types of policy decisions. It highlights the value of clarity in research questions and research design and shows the strong links that can be made between research into landscape dynamics and practical policy formation.

- Specification of model structure and parameters is dependent upon the strategic purpose of the research and the practicalities of research design.

- Descriptive models are *synthetic* and focus upon integrating a range of data sources to represent a landscape. They frequently provide the basis for more extended strategies of investigation.

- Analytical models, such as correlation research, gather data from existing real-world situations and investigate *relationships* between variables.

- Predictive models focus upon understanding how the future *may be* depending upon how it *has been*.

- Dynamic simulation models integrate knowledge and assumptions about *how* landscapes change and where this may lead.

- Alternatives futures is a distinctive application of dynamic simulation modeling used to improve understanding about the landscape consequences of different policy decisions.

References

Baker, J. P., D. W. Hulse, S. V. Gregory, D. White, J. V. Sickle, P. A. Berger, D. Dole, and N. H. Schumaker. 2004. Alternative futures for the Willamette River Basin, Oregon. *Ecological Applications* 14 (2): 313–24.

Brown, R. D., and T. J. Gillespie. 1995. *Microclimatic landscape design: Creating thermal comfort and energy efficiency.* New York: John Wiley and Sons.

Costanza, R., and A. Voinov, eds. 2004. *Landscape simulation modeling: A spatially explicit, dynamic approach.* New York: Springer-Verlag.

Daniel, T. C., and R. S. Boster. 1976. *Measuring landscape esthetics: The scenic beauty estimation method.* USDA Forest Service Research Report RM167. Fort Collins, CO: Rocky Mountain Forest and Range Research Station: USDA.

Davis J. P., K. M. Eisenhardt, and C. B. Bingham. 2007. Developing theory through simulation methods. *Academy of Management Review* 32 (2): 480–99.

Ervin, S. M. 2001. Digital landscape modeling and visualization: A research agenda. *Landscape and Urban Planning* 54 (1–4): 49–62.

Ferguson, B. K. 1999. The alluvial history and environmental legacy of the abandoned Scull Shoals Mill. *Landscape Journal* 18 (2): 147–56.

Giere, R. N. 1997. *Understanding scientific reasoning.* 4th ed. Fort Worth, TX: Harcourt Brace.

Global Land Project. 2005. *Science plan and implementation strategy.* IGBP Report No. 53/IHDP Report No. 19. Stockholm: IGDP Secretariat.

Gobster, P. H. 1999. An ecological aesthetic for forest landscape management. *Landscape Journal* 18 (1): 54–64

Groat, L., and D. Wang. 2002. *Architectural research methods.* New York: John Wiley and Sons.

Hands, D. E., and R. D. Brown. 2002. Enhancing visual preference of ecological rehabilitation sites. *Landscape and Urban Planning.* 58: 57–70.

He, H. S. 2008. Forest landscape models: Definitions, characteristics, and classification. *Forest Ecology and Management* 254 (3): 484–98.

Hulse, D., J. Eilers, K. Freemark, C. Hummon, and D. White. 2000. Planning alternative future landscapes in Oregon: Evaluating effects on water quality and biodiversity *Landscape Journal* 19 (1–2): 1–19.

Hulse, D., S.V. Gregory, and J. P. Baker, eds. 2002. *Willamette River basin planning atlas: Trajectories of environmental and ecological change.* Corvallis, OR: Oregon State University Press.

Kaltenborn, B. J., and T. Bjerke. 2002. Associations between landscape preferences and place attachment: A study in Roros, Southern Norway. *Landscape Research* 27 (4): 381–96.

Mander, U., E. Uuemaa, J. Roosaare, R. Aunap, and M. Antrop. 2010. Coherence and fragmentation of landscape patterns as characterized by correlograms: A case study of Estonia. *Landscape and Urban Planning* 94: 1–37.

Milburn, L-A., and R. D. Brown. 2003. The relationship of age, gender, and education to research productivity in landscape architecture faculty in North America. *Landscape Journal* 22 (1): 54–62.

Ndubisi, F. 2002. *Ecological planning: An historical and comparative synthesis.* Baltimore, Johns Hopkins Press.

Perry, G. L. W. 2009. Modeling and simulation. In *A companion to environmental geography,* ed. N. Castree, D. Demerritt, D. Liverman, and B. Rhoads. Chichester, U.K.: Wiley-Blackwell.

Rea, L. M., and R. A. Parker. 2005. *Designing and conducting survey research: A comprehensive guide.* 3rd ed. New York: Jossey Bass.

Ribe, R. G., E. T. Armstrong, and P. H. Gobster. 2002. Scenic vistas and the changing policy landscape: Visualizing and testing the role of visual resources in ecosystem management. *Landscape Journal* 21 (1): 42–66.

Steiner, F. 2000. *The living landscape: An ecological approach to landscape planning.* New York: McGraw-Hill.

Steinitz, C. et al. 2003. *Alternative futures for changing landscapes: The Upper San Pedro River Basin in Arizona and Sonora.* Washington, DC: Island Press.

Willemen, L., P. H. Verburg, L. Hein, and M. E. F. van Mensvoort. 2008. Spatial characterization of landscape functions. *Landscape and Urban Planning* 88: 34–43.

CHAPTER 7

Experimental Strategies

7.1 Introduction

Experiments are a key part of the methodological foundation upon which modern science has been built. In its classic hypothetico-deductive form, science involves five key steps (McIntyre 2005; Giere 1997): First, carefully observing the world and the causal relationships between variables within it; second, reflecting upon the theories that have been developed to explain these relationships; third, identifying a gap or inconsistency in that understanding and formulating a research question; fourth, proposing an explanation (a hypothesis); and then finally undertaking an experiment to test the explanation to see whether it stands up against "brute facts."

Experimentation is, thus, a fundamental research strategy in science disciplines. It involves a logical process of formally testing a plausible hypothesis in a situation that has been controlled or constrained in some way in order to focus upon investigation of a causal relationship (Giere 1997; McIntyre 2005). Classic experimental design has a number of key features (Giere 1997; Grinnell 2009; Montgomery 2005; Groat and Wang 2002), summarized in Notes on Method 7.1.

As these features highlight, experimentation is a highly artificial situation, in which the investigator has imposed "a very tight grid" upon the world under observation (Crotty 1998, 27–28, after Husserl 1970). Why take so much trouble? The rationale for the strict procedures of experimentation is to maximize the *reliability* and *validity* of the findings. Experimental reliability is the achievement of consistent results over repeated investigations. Experimentation attempts to achieve this by minimizing the influence of the investigator upon the relations under investigation, by minimizing external environmental influences, and by ensuring standard techniques and measures.

Experimental validity has two dimensions—internal and external. External validity indicates the degree to which the results of an experiment can be generalized to a wider population. This is sought by random selection and assignment of subjects and treatments and by undertaking sufficient replications of treatment or involving a large enough number of subjects to enable statistical inference. Internal validity is the extent to which we can be sure the outcomes are due to the treatment applied, which depends upon the detailed design of the experiment and the conditions under which it is undertaken.

Notes on Method 7.1: Features of Experimental Design

A *causal relationship* that is being investigated (e.g., mulching soil around plants increases their growth rate).

An *independent variable* in the relationship—the causal variable—that can be manipulated (treated) in some way (e.g., the surface condition around a plant that can be changed by applying mulch).

A *dependent variable* that demonstrates the effect, and in which the outcome of the treatment can be measured (i.e., plant growth).

An *identifiable unit* in which the outcome can be observed (i.e., a plant specimen).

A *pretest* (before treatment) measurement and a *post-test* measurement

Two *discrete situations* or groups of subjects—the *experimental group*, where the treatment is applied, and a separate *control group*, where the relationship between the independent and dependent variables can be observed without the treatment.

Random selection of the units of measurement (e.g., human subjects) and random application of the treatments.

Statistical analysis of the results, in order to assess the characteristics of the observed relationship and the extent to which it is representative of a wider population.

There is a range of ways in which an experiment can be designed (Montgomery 2005). One approach is "best guess"—selecting variables based upon the best understanding of the system or situation. A more systematic strategy is to test "one factor at a time." However, this can be time consuming and does not take into account interaction between factors, so an alternative is to test several factors together in a "factorial" experiment. Most experiments in landscape architecture involve multiple factors. They fall into one of three types: classic, field, or quasi experiments (fig. 7.1).

Classic experimental conditions that have all the features described in Notes on Method 7.1 (above) are very hard to achieve in any of the fields of activity of landscape architecture. Removing the context of a landscape and all the relationships around it take us away from landscape and landscape architecture into other realms, such as materials science, plant science, and human psychology. It is not a surprise, therefore, that much of the experimental research into the elements and materials of landscape, and into human behavior in landscape settings, is undertaken in related disciplines. Nonetheless, some landscape architectural researchers have focused upon creating a controlled environment in which to undertake research. Example 7.1 (Chon and Shafer 2009) illustrates this strategy.

A second type of experimental strategy that is more often used in landscape architecture is field experimentation, where the logic of experimentation is applied in a "real-world" setting, such as a research station, where laboratory conditions are sought

Quasi experiment e.g survey   Classic experiment   Field experiment

Figure 7.1 Types of experimentation

as far as is feasible. Example 7.2 by Hitchmough (2009) illustrates a field investigation into the performance of different plant establishment techniques.

The most common experimental strategy in landscape architecture, however, is to adopt quasi-experimental research designs. These are designs in which some, but not all, aspects of classic experimentation are retained. Quasi experiments are, therefore "near" experiments, or approximations to an experiment (Hesse-Biber and Leavy 2008, 190). Examples 7.3, 7.4, and 7.5 illustrate different quasi-experimental strategies that focus upon different experimental criteria. Finally, the metaphor of experimentation has also been adopted as a way of exploring and testing an idea through design activity (Steenbergen 2008). This is reconsidered and expanded in chapter 12.

7.2 Classic Experiments

One of the most extensive bodies of experimental research in landscape architecture is associated with the investigation of landscape perception and preference. Interest in preference studies developed especially in the United States during the 1960s in response to federal legislation that required environmental-impact assessment for government-funded projects. This stimulated a sustained research effort funded by the U.S. Forest Service to develop predictive models of landscape preference that could be used in managing the extensive forestry operations undertaken on public land. The classic expressions of experimental strategies in preference research were based upon research designs, methods, and techniques drawn from cognitive psychology (Shafer et al. 1969; Shafer and Brush 1977; Daniel and Vining 1983), with the Scenic Beauty Estimation (SBE) approach (Daniel and Boster 1976) as perhaps the best-known example. SBE hypothesizes a relationship between the preference expressed for a landscape and the biophysical attributes of that landscape (fig 7.2), and it uses an experimental design to investigate the nature of that relationship.

The challenges faced by researchers who wanted to use an experimental strategy in this context were complex—in particular, they needed to measure the attributes of a

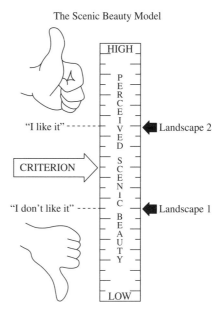

The Scenic Beauty Model

Figure 7.2 Scenic Beauty Estimation
(Courtesy of the U.S. Forest Service, Rocky
Mountain Research Station)

Perceptual Component

complex landscape and to obtain people's preferences in a standardized way. The design they adopted was to use photographs as surrogates for direct experience of landscape and to measure landscape attributes based upon the content of the photographs. The subjects of the experiment—people—were shown slides of photographs in a controlled setting—a lecture theater—and asked to rate their responses.

These preference studies illustrate one of the reasons that classic experimental strategies are seldom used in landscape architecture: it is very hard to design an experiment with a representative population sample in a controlled setting. Much early work on landscape preference used the relatively captive audience of landscape architecture students (and the example below follows that approach). This enables investigators to achieve the reliability of highly controlled conditions. However, it comes at the cost of limiting the validity of the results, as the population sample is not representative.

An alternative strategy that is more widely followed is to undertake quasi-experimental investigations. There is less control over the conditions under which subjects participate in the "experiment," but there is a greater opportunity for a representative sample of subjects. This illustrates the need for continual trade-offs between different aspects of experimental design in order to maximize the performance of the experiment in terms of the criteria that are most critical for the research question.

Example 7.1, a study by Chon and Shafer (2009), uses a virtual tour of a landscape presented in a laboratory setting to obtain landscape preferences of urban greenways (similar to fig. 7.3). It controlled the conditions under which people express their preferences

Figure 7.3 Virtual reality laboratory

(Photo courtesy of Brian Orland, Immersive Environments Lab, Pennsylvania State University)

Example 7.1:
Aesthetic Responses to Urban Greenways
(Chon and Shafer 2009)

The context for this research is the increasing use of greenways as public open space in urban environments. The focus was upon gaining a better understanding of the factors that influenced perception and preference for urban greenway trails. The investigators built upon previous research that identified the wider perceptual significance of environmental attributes such as naturalness and openness. It asked two questions. First, are these attributes important for greenway trails? Second, how do they relate to preference, expressed as "likability"? They adopted an experimental strategy with a research design that uses a laboratory-type setting to obtain the preference measures.

Two real greenway landscapes provided the basis for the creation of Web-based virtual tours that were based upon a series of viewpoints along each trail. Students were invited as subjects and were shown the virtual tours in a computer laboratory. The research design asked respondents to describe the cognitive and emotional characteristics of the trails, using a series of Likert scales. These responses were subject to factor analysis to identify five key dimensions: maintenance, distinctiveness, naturalness, pleasantness, and arousal. These dimensions were then treated as independent variables in a multiple-regression analysis of their causal relationship with the respondents' evaluation of the "likeability" of the trail.

The results indicated that there was consistency with previous work that identified the key cognitive and affective dimensions of preference for urban settings.

The research is included here because the design demonstrates the use of controlled laboratory conditions that are typically associated with experimental strategies. However, the research was not structured as a classic experiment and lacked external validity because of the nonrandom sampling of subjects.

Figure 7.4 Field experimentation, Lincoln University

(emphasizing reliability and internal validity), but at a cost in external validity, as the sample that was available did not represent the general population.

7.3 Field Experiments

Many applied sciences utilize field experiments, where experimental procedures are followed in a real-world setting. In landscape architecture, field experiments (as opposed to design experiments—see below), have most typically been undertaken in relation to the establishment and management of plants and other "soft" landscape materials in urban and industrial settings (fig. 7.4).

In Example 7.2, Hitchmough (2009) illustrates many of the key features of experimentation, other than the use of a controlled environment. In order to minimize the implications of the natural variation in field conditions, the research design includes trials across a number of different locations within the study site.

7.4 Quasi Experiments

The majority of experiment-like research in landscape architecture is based upon social scientific strategies that are generally described as quasi experiments. The focus is typically upon investigating some aspect of human relationships with landscape or within landscape architecture. The experimental conditions cannot be controlled to the same

Example 7.2:
Diversification of Grassland
(Hitchmough 2009)

Landscape architects have been involved in the design and management of urban grasslands for many years, but there is an increasing demand for improved performance of such grasslands in terms of biodiversity, human experience, and reduction of energy and carbon costs. One response has been to create species-rich grasslands that are modeled upon traditional rural meadows. However, in urban settings the establishment and management options are quite different from the original situation. This study aimed to identify species that could be successfully established and would persist in urban grasslands. The study also sought to better understand the process involved.

The research was based upon a field-experiment strategy that investigated the factors influencing the practical success of introducing new perennial herbaceous species into urban grasslands.

Specifically, the research tested the hypothesis that establishment techniques such as mulching, weed control, and mechanical cutting would have a positive effect on indicators of success such as plant weight, size, and mortality. Three separate experiments were undertaken, based upon a meadow used for field trials. There were randomized treatments of different plots, and measurements were taken of both treated and control situations. Three spatial replications were undertaken to minimize the effects of environmental variations across the site.

The investigator used the same horticultural techniques on each plant and used standardized measurement methods. The results of each experiment were analyzed using standard statistical techniques, which determined whether there was any significant difference between the treated and control situations (that is, whether the data came from the same hypothetical population or not).

The results showed that two factors were critical to successful establishment and longer term survival of introduced species in a meadow setting—the fitness of the species for the site (i.e., plant selection) and the nature of the management regime (particularly, the timing of cutting). Techniques such as mulching were less significant than the size of the gap cleared for the initial planting, and in either case the effects were of short duration. The broader implications are that landscape architects need to be familiar with the detailed ecological requirements of the species they use and to have a breadth of knowledge that enables them to select species suitable for particular sites.

The example is helpful because of the way it demonstrates the application of a classic field experimental strategy to a practical and relevant landscape architectural problem. It also shows the benefit of an established long-term field experiment. These results were based upon studies spanning seven or more years, suggesting that building useful and credible knowledge in the discipline often requires a long-term program of investigation.

Example 7.3:
Willingness to Discuss Local Landscape Development

(Höppner et al. 2008)

The context for this research is the increasing focus on participatory techniques in spatial and landscape planning, in general, and the importance of public participation in decision making in Switzerland, in particular. However, while there is considerable academic knowledge about the general factors that affect participation in political decision making, there is much less understanding of what influences the willingness of people to become involved in particular issues in landscape planning.

The researchers adopted a quasi-experimental strategy in which they tested three specific hypotheses about willingness to participate in landscape planning. They focused on the influence of place attachment, institutional trust, and efficacy (the capacity to influence decisions and the likelihood of achieving an outcome). The conceptual framework drew upon behavioral theory and communicative planning theory.

The researchers identified a municipality in which there had been a planning process aimed at producing a Landscape Development Plan. The process had included a number of events involving farmers and representatives of community organizations that had then been extended to the whole population, who had been invited to workshops and information meetings. However, the attendance by locals who were not farmers or other stakeholder representatives was poor. The researchers wanted to find out why. What influences the willingness of people to become involved?

The key features of the research design were, first, clearly specified hypotheses; second, questions based upon seven-point rating scales; third, a randomized population sample; and fourth, the statistical analysis of results. This analysis was based upon two correlation models—one that examined the influence of the main variables (institutional trust, self-efficacy, outcome-efficacy, and place attachment) upon willingness to participate and a second that analyzed the interrelationship between efficacy and trust.

The analysis of results supported some parts of their hypotheses, but not others. For example, place attachment had a direct effect upon willingness to participate. However, personal interest in the physical landscape was more significant than social belonging. On the other hand, trust in institutions had no influence. The interaction of self-efficacy (belief in being able to contribute to the process) and outcome-efficacy (belief that a positive outcome could be achieved) was a significant influence.

The investigators then drew out implications for landscape and spatial planning practice, highlighting the importance of what they called individual internal factors—or self-confidence—and their relationship with the other factors. They concluded by highlighting the need for communication strategies at an early stage in a project aimed at overcoming internal barriers to participation.

The example is interesting as a quasi-experimental strategy because of the way the hypotheses were well grounded in theory and expressed through clear and valid measures. The research design used a large random sample to ensure that the findings have external validity. The investigation generated relevant outcomes that challenge previous assumptions about participation, and stimulated further research.

degree as in a laboratory or field experiment, because the research subjects—that is, people—are sentient social organisms. Therefore, the focus is placed instead upon achieving some of the attributes of an experiment in the research design—for example, in the selection of subjects—and in the design and analysis of the survey.

Example 7.3 features a study by Höppner et al. (2008), who adopted a quasi-experimental strategy in which they tested hypotheses about community participation. In contrast to Chon and Shafer (2009), whose research design focused upon internal validity, the emphasis in this research design was upon maximizing external validity, through the use of a large randomized sample of respondents.

One of the key features of much landscape research is its focus upon particular places and small communities. This can make access to large randomized population samples difficult—the community may not be large enough or diverse enough to generate such a sample. Example 7.4 (Rogers and Sukolratanametee 2009) illustrates a different quasi-experimental strategy to investigate the effects of sense of community in four different communities. It follows the experimental method more closely in style and terminology than many other quasi-experimental studies by applying "treatments" to different communities. As the treatments were limited in their spatial application to particular communities, all households in the four different communities were surveyed.

The example is also of interest because of the way in which it explicitly uses the *null hypothesis*. The null hypothesis is used to structure the statistical analysis of the results and represents the claim that there is no difference between the effects observed in the control group and those observed in the experimental group. That is, it proposes that the experimental results do *not* demonstrate a causal relationship between the independent and dependent variables. The statistical analysis is structured to test this claim. If a statistically significant difference is observed between the effects observed in the two groups, then the null hypothesis is rejected, and the investigators conclude that there is a causal relationship between the variables under investigation. Despite the explicit experimental design, the study findings, nonetheless, must be qualified by the observation that, like Example 6.4, the study applied multiple-regression analysis to ordinal data (see discussion in chapter 6).

7.5 The Metaphor of Experimentation

A classic experimental research strategy imposes a tight discipline upon research design, which contrasts in many ways with the divergent thinking that is characteristic of much landscape architectural practice. However, the *metaphor* of experimentation has been used within a range of other types of research strategy used in the discipline. Three types of situation are briefly introduced below and are then expanded upon in chapter 12.

First, there is a potential relationship between experimentation and case studies. Gerring (2007) argued that case studies can be usefully considered as a form of quasi-experiment. The argument for this derives from a consideration of the nature of the case study as a "spatially delimited phenomenon (a unit) observed at a single point in time or

Example 7.4:
Neighborhood Design and Sense of Community
(Rogers and Sukolratanametee 2009)

The context for this research is the rapidly growing urban population in North America and the major transformations taking place in the character of urban centers. This dynamic raises questions about the factors that create a sense of community in sub-urban neighborhoods. A range of urban-design strategies have been promoted on the presumption that they will enhance community, including so-called "ecological design." However, while there is significant research on the value of "natural settings" in urban areas and upon public perceptions of ecological elements, there is only limited research evidence about the effect of ecological design as an overall factor in creating a sense of community.

This research follows a quasi-experimental strategy. It started from a formal null hypothesis that ecological design does *not* enhance sense of community in designed neighborhoods.

Four different communities of a similar size, but with differing expressions of ecological design, were investigated. The research design had several features. The urban design elements that characterized the communities were measured. These included indices of density, street design, public space, land-use mix, and edge definition. Sense of community was measured in the communities through a self-administered questionnaire with Likert-type scales relating to a number of indices such as "never feeling at home." In the analysis these measures of community (the dependent variables) were combined into three composite measures. Questionnaires were mailed to all households in the chosen communities, and a total of 210 were returned from the four communities. The data were analyzed using a multiple-regression technique called principal component analysis.

The analysis found that two of the composite measures of sense of community were positively associated with the presence of ecological design indices, thus disproving the null hypothesis. These effects are not explained by social demographic variables. The analysis also revealed that ecological designs do not seem to significantly alter the underlying social processes.

The researchers concluded that ecological designs that connect residents to the nat-ural environment and to each other enhance sense of community, but social processes have a stronger role than ecological design in creating community and are independent of ecological design. There was no evidence that residents in ecologically designed communities had different social processes than those in conventional communities. Hence, while ecological design can enhance the sense of community, it does not deter-mine the nature of community. So what are the mechanisms that lead to the positive effect? The researchers speculated on possible casual factors and argued for further investigation.

This example is valuable in the way it illustrates the use of the null hypothesis to struc-ture a quasi-experimental investigation. It also shows how a quasi-experimental design can be created by selecting different real-world cases—in this situation, the four com-munities of similar size but with different design attributes. As in the previous example, however, the design involved some compromise in data analysis.

over some period in time" (Gerring 2007, 19). This enables "the intensive study of a single case where the purpose of the study is—at least in part—to shed light on a larger class of cases (a population)" (2007, 20). Gerring goes on to argue that while case studies are conventionally regarded primarily as a way to generate hypotheses, cross-case comparisons can be used to test hypotheses, in a way similar to field experiments. This insight points the way for a much more systematic selection of case studies within landscape architectural research and to the expansion of their use to more formally test theoretical propositions.

A second line of development of the metaphor of experimentation seeks to create stronger connections between landscape architecture research and the science disciplines that also focus upon land, by framing landscape planning research as a meta-experiment. The term "meta" is typically used to describe a higher-level analysis that compares and synthesizes the results of many other more detailed studies. Nassauer and Opdam (2008) have suggested that large-scale scenario-based investigations can be undertaken in a way that tests hypotheses about land use and environmental interactions, using the cumulative results of many site- and place-based studies within a large regional study. Hence the "experimental" frame is widened to a regional scale.

Third, a number of scholars have conceptualized design explorations in a studio as experiments that "test" the effect of different design interventions (i.e., operations or "treatments") upon a particular setting or type of setting as a way to generate innovative design proposals (Steenbergen 2008, 326). These approaches are examined in chapter 12.

Experimental Strategies: Summary

Experimental and quasi-experimental strategies are used when:

- The research builds upon an established body of knowledge that is expressed in formal theories and models, and
- The aim of the research is to test hypotheses that predict relationships.
- There are clearly identified causal relationships between key variables that can be controlled and measured.
- Samples can be obtained that enable robust statistical analysis and prediction.

Within landscape architectural research, the scope for experimentation in a classic sense is limited. However, field or quasi-experimental investigations can be usefully undertaken. Further, the metaphor of experimentation can contribute insight and rigor when applied to a wider range of strategies across the discipline.

References

Chon, J., and C. S. Shafer. 2009. Aesthetic responses to urban greenway trail environments. *Landscape Research* 34 (1): 83–104.

Crotty, M. 1998. *The foundations of social research: Meaning and perspective in the research process.* St. Leonards, Australia: Allen and Unwin.

Daniel, T. C., and R. S. Boster. 1976. *Measuring landscape esthetics: The scenic beauty estimation method.* USDA Forest Service Research Report RM167. Fort Collins CO: Rocky Mountain Forest and Range Research Station, USDA.

Daniel, T. C., and J. Vining. 1983. Methodological issues in the assessment of landscape quality. In *Behavior and the natural environment.* Vol. 6 of *Human behavior and environment,* ed. I. Altman and J. Wohlwill. New York: Plenum.

Gerring, J. 2007. *Case study research: Principles and practices.* Cambridge U.K.: Cambridge University Press.

Giere, R. N. 1997. *Understanding scientific reasoning.* 4th ed. Fort Worth, TX: Harcourt Brace.

Grinnell, F. 2009. *Everyday practice of science: Where intuition and passion meet objectivity and logic.* Oxford, U. K.: Oxford University Press.

Groat, L., and D. Wang. 2002. *Architectural research methods.* New York: John Wiley and Sons.

Hesse-Biber, S. N., and P. Leavy. 2008. *Handbook of emergent methods.* New York: Guilford Press.

Hitchmough, J. 2009. Diversification of grassland in urban greenspace with planted, nursery–grown forbs. *Journal of Landscape Architecture* (Spring): 16–27.

Höppner, C., J. Frick, and M. Buchecker. 2008. What drives people's willingness to discuss local landscape development? *Landscape Research* 33 (5): 605–22.

Husserl, E. 1970. *The crisis of European sciences and transcendental phenomenology: An introduction to phenomenological philosophy.* Evanston, IL: Northwestern University Press.

McIntyre, L. J. 2005. *Need to know: Social science research methods.* New York: McGraw-Hill.

Montgomery, D. C. 2005. *Design and analysis of experiments.* 6th ed. Hoboken, NJ: John Wiley and Sons.

Nassauer, J. I., and P. Opdam. 2008. Design in science: Extending the landscape ecology paradigm. *Landscape Ecology* 23 (6): 633–44.

Rogers, G., and S. Sukolratanametee. 2009. Neighborhood design and sense of community: Comparing suburban neighborhoods in Houston, Texas. *Landscape and Urban Planning* 92 (3–4): 325–34.

Shafer, E. L., J. F. Hamilton, and E. A. Schmidt. 1969. Natural landscape preferences: A predictive model. *Journal of Leisure Research* 1 (1): 1–19.

Shafer, E. L., and R. O. Brush. 1977. How to measure preferences for photographs of natural landscapes. *Landscape Planning* 4: 237–56.

Steenbergen, C. 2008. *Composing landscapes: Analysis, typology, and experiments for design.* Basel: Birkhauser Verlag.

CHAPTER 8
Classification Schemes

8.1 Introduction

Classification strategies produce new knowledge by sorting and structuring data into a system of organization, using typical properties, patterns, behaviors, or themes. This book is an example of classification. It places examples of published research studies in the field of landscape architecture within a systematic framework based upon the nature of the research strategy, assessed on two dimensions: relationship to theory (inductive-deductive) and epistemology (objective-subjective).

Classification strategies range from obviously simple to deceptively complex. To many, classification seems so "primitive" a form of measurement and analysis that it is not recognized as research. Nevertheless, others acknowledge "it is a necessary condition for all higher levels" of analysis (Coombs 1953). In some cases, classification is synonymous with the highest level of science. Pedhazur and Schmelkin (1991) explain the constructed nature of classification more expansively:

> Simple or complex, universally accepted or highly controversial, classifications reflect concepts, variables (e.g., socioeconomic class, race, political party affiliation, religious orientation), and are thus an integral part of an implicit or explicit frame of reference . . .
>
> The question whether or not a given classification is meaningful or useful cannot be answered without considering why it is used in the first place and what has led to the specific definition of the variable. Classification is a form of measurement . . . a means, not an end. The meaningfulness or usefulness of a given measure can be assessed only within a given theoretical or practical context. (1991, 18–19).

The cumulative and consensual process of research, discussed earlier, is illustrated most vividly in classification. As "a means, not an end," classifications produce new knowledge that may be meaningful in constructing, testing, or strengthening theories about grouping or organizational structure. Certain long-established and/or received theoretical constructs (for instance, library indexing systems or taxonomic classifications) suggest that some classifications may also serve as a theoretical "end" in themselves. However, even established taxonomies or indexes depend on the constant renewal of classification procedures, whenever new data become available (new works produced; new organisms discovered), in order to validate their conceptual structure. A classification is thus never "finished."

Because classification is shaped and limited by the types, properties, and scale of data being considered, we have located this large group of research strategies in the "inductive" column of the framework. And because classification typically depends upon theoretical or practical *values* to select and organize data, classification strategies reside on the constructivist row. Classification is, therefore, one of the most fundamental and elastic of research activities and extends to nearly every discipline. Accordingly, environmental classification may also adopt the widest possible array of forms and purposes.

Many other research strategies depend implicitly or explicitly upon classification (whether preliminary or well-developed) in order to advance their own goals. This is especially true for classification/interpretation and classification/evaluation strategies, but correlation, experimentation, and logical argumentation strategies often rely on a priori classification. Because classification strategies are so often compounded with other strategies, it becomes necessary to isolate preliminary classification stages from other research goals. Such an exercise can help reveal the conceptual value or limits of classification in the context of any given study (as will become clearer in some of the examples).

At the highest level of complexity, classification may be used to reveal and refocus attention on specific, meaningful patterns and themes hiding within data. In certain circumstances classification may extend into or merge with other research strategies. This is very common in landscape architecture and urban design research. Site-based studies may be highly synthetic, typically involving multiple steps and a variety of research strategies. However, as in any other sort of classification activity, the typical first stage of investigation is to collect, organize, and understand descriptive data about the phenomena being investigated.

In many ways, the conventional three-step procedure for conducting site analyses may be compared with a compound research strategy involving stages of classification, evaluation, and interpretation, with a fourth strategy—perhaps proposition, or modeling—typically added. Imagine we are charged with the task of deciding how much land is usable for the purposes of a given program. Ideally, we also want to find the best or most suitable (least destructive) uses for the available land. The design process begins, simply enough, with an elaborate classification procedure. In normative practice, preparation for this kind of investigation usually involves a site inventory. Usually an inventory comprises data gathering—for example, empirical or secondary data sets (such as topographic maps, rainfall data, or soil analyses). Inventories may also consist of original, subjective data such as visual or spatial experiences (Lynch and Hack 1984).

The second stage of analysis also involves classification through sorting and grouping, as well as spatial correlation of certain significant patterns. Evaluation methods weigh site information along certain categorical parameters and priorities, in order to rate portions of the site according to their capacity for development (low, medium, high suitability). For instance, to evaluate a site's suitability for development, the researcher seeks data indicating depth to bedrock, or water table elevation, or soil percolation rates. "Meaningful" patterns are sought that may indicate site suitability or sensitivity for development, areas where development cost or environmental impact is lowest, or where opportunities for site interpretation, conservation, or scenic value is highest. The patterns of these conditions are isolated, highlighted, and revealed using a variety of graphic techniques with which most students of design and planning are familiar.

Finally, site synthesis offers a realignment of these data, a redefinition of site itself through describing new or existing patterns, limits, and other themes based on values and intended performance. This work belongs to simulation or scenario-testing aspects of design.

As we have previously noted, and discuss further in chapter 12, design may *become* research if it is planned and undertaken as a systematic process of inquiry, with a clear theoretical framework and research questions. Separating out the component strategies involved in conventional design practices (in this case to highlight the role of classification) helps illustrate how conventional investigations may be reframed as researchable problems. It also shows how classification as a research strategy frequently interrelates with other types of inquiry.

Any classification strategy requires a collection and understanding of preliminary descriptive data in order to choose, understand, characterize, differentiate, and arrange objects, individuals, populations, or conditions into classes. In order to differentiate and discern "belonging"—that is, to discover the qualitative and quantitative similarities and differences between things—classification relies on the development of a clear conceptual framework, a theory of organization. The important work of challenging, critiquing, and modifying classification strategies is itself a legitimate research activity.

This chapter is organised under five broad headings, each dealing with a different and distinctive set of methods for selecting and organizing data. In the next section, we examine basic methods of collecting, inventory, and cataloguing. Then, we review the creation of a typology, placing data into discrete categories. Following this, we examine taxonomy, in which categories are sorted into a hierarchy according to specified rules of association. Next, we examine the construction of indices, in which data categories are listed numerically, and, finally, we examine the process of creating a bibliography and literature review.

8.2 Collection/Inventory/Catalogue

Before anything can be sorted or classified into groups, it must be generated and/or collected. Most classification work therefore relies on prior descriptive or creative work. A whimsical published example of an unclassified collection includes the evocative essay "Un Jardin peut en cacher un autre," by Hans Obrist, in which the author generated close to five hundred alphabetically ordered titles for imaginary gardens. This poem served as a work of conceptual art for a garden exhibition (1998–2000) at the Villa Medici in Rome.

A Garden
Actual Garden
Ad-hoc Garden
African Garden
Agglomeration Garden
Aggregative Garden
Agora Garden
Agricultural Garden
Air Garden
Airport Garden
Airship Garden
Amazon Garden
Ambiguous Garden
American Garden
Analogous Garden
Angel Garden
Apocalyptic Garden
Apotheotic Garden
Arty Garden
Artisanal Garden
Asian Garden
Astral Garden
Atopic Garden
Autonomous Garden

Excerpt from "Un Jardin peut en cacher un autre," compiled by Obrist (2002).

This work illustrates a necessary first step in any classification strategy. A collection of items is identified and brought together on the basis of some shared quality (in this case, a reference to gardens) and is then sorted (in this case, alphabetically), grouping like with like (in this case a's with a's, b's with b's, and so on). It then becomes possible to take the next step in classification—to search for any patterns that might occur and that might throw further light upon the nature of the original phenomenon.

Depending on its overall strategic orientation, classification research typically needs to be designed to generate a sample that accurately represents a range of differences and similarities. This suggests that *random* sampling, the most common basis for research design in some types of research strategy (e.g., correlation, experimentation, and quasi

Notes on Method 8.1: Sampling

Because of the extraordinary complexity of most landscape phenomena, it is impossible to study every single unit of its composition. One of the most basic questions in implementing a classification strategy is to decide what data or population will be most relevant to the purpose of the research. Sampling is the process of selecting what data to gather.

> Both primary [empirical] research and research synthesis involve specifying target populations and sampling frames. In addition, both types of investigation require the researcher to consider how the target population and sampling frame may differ from one another. The trustworthiness of any claim about the population will be compromised if the elements in the sampling frame are not representative of the target population. (Cooper 1998, 41)

In our consideration of research strategies, the approach to sampling is the critical decision in shaping a research *design*. It sits at a lower level of generality than does the primary research strategy, although particular research designs (using distinctive sampling approaches) are typically associated with different types of strategy.

The link between research design and strategy is critical, because the sampling approach adopted in the design provides a key basis for making a claim to valid new knowledge—which is fundamental to the strategy. It is quite possible to draw reasonable conclusions from limited sources *if* we believe the information to be an accurate or valid sample of all available data. Frequently, however, it is not. Depending on the subject of study, therefore, the sample or target population needs to be narrow enough to make a feasible and relevant study, and yet broad enough to yield generalizable results or patterns. Although it is well beyond the scope of this book to explain the intricacies of sampling, there are many excellent methods manuals available (see below).

Four broad sampling designs can be used:

Opportunist sampling is taking whatever data come to hand. For example, someone researching landscape history may have to work from an incomplete data set—perhaps a diary, old property records, a few photographs or letters. Available data may be determined simply by what has survived or is thought to have survived from the past. One of the reasons that much historical research is interpretive is that

experimentation), may be less useful in classification than *purposive* or *representative* samples—which are more likely to show a broader range of difference, character, and pattern. For instance, this book has been created through purposive sampling. Notes on Method 8.1 offers more discussion about sampling within research design.

The next method of classification employs the techniques of an inventory of stores—that is, collecting, sorting, and (re)grouping—in order to identify belonging: "How many units do we have to consider? What is the difference between *x* and *y*? Is that difference important? Why? To what group does *x* or *y* belong? What are the chief determinants of membership? How many distinct groups exist here? What are the relationships the historical record is almost always fragmented; the researcher must therefore triangulate, draw inferences, and actively interpret the available data to construct a plausible account.

Purposive (sometimes described as theoretical) sampling seeks out data expected to be most helpful in addressing the research question. For example, in a descriptive study of the use of native plants in the landscape industry in Utah, researchers approached local professionals that had a direct role in selecting and using plants. Their findings did not reveal anything about wider attitudes towards native plants held by a larger population, nor can they be generalized to the use of native plants by landscape professionals in different regions, because that was not the purpose of the research. It was focused upon landscape professionals in one region.

Representative sampling is the process of selecting data in order to be able to draw statistical conclusions that extend beyond the actual data analyzed, most typically about a wider population from which it is drawn. Representative techniques involve careful proportional and categorical selections of respondents, sites, objects, etc., that depend very much on the conceptual constructs guiding the study. For instance, the structure of the American electoral college for national elections is a form of representative sampling, based on matching the size of voting districts with census data.

Random sampling is the selection of data where the investigator has no influence upon the choices, which are made by chance (measured arithmetically). Representative and random sampling are typically used to implement an experimental or quasi-experimental strategy.

Selection of sampling type involves both theoretical *and* pragmatic factors. The ultimate value of the research being conducted, whether that demands descriptive, interpretive, or predictive accuracy, is only as good as the type, number, and distribution of the data that are sampled.

Recommended further reading:

Pedhazur and Schmelkin (1991), chapter 15.

Zeisel (2006), chapter on sampling.

Groat and Wang (2002), chapter on data collection.

---

between groups? Why?" and so on. This resembles the process many people use when arranging the kitchen cupboards, bookshelves, or a collection of DVDs. Example 8.1 offers an inventory of published research in landscape architecture.

Catalogues resemble basic inventory in many ways, but possess slightly more complex aims—to sort examples of images, text, design work, or other data, and regroup according to specific principles and themes. A *catalogue raisonné* is a type of exalted inventory: an exhaustive list, register, or accounting of the entire oeuvre (body of work) of an artist that may organize work by medium (etchings, paintings, etc.), subject (portraits, still lives, etc.), or stylistic period (the Blue period).

Example 8.1:
Twenty-Five Years of *Landscape Journal*
(Powers and Walker 2009)

This research was undertaken as part of a review of *Landscape Journal* on the occasion of its twenty-fifth anniversary. *Landscape Journal* was established in 1982 by the North American Council of Educators in Landscape Architecture (CELA) to disseminate research and scholarship in the discipline. As the authors explained, there had been no systematic analysis of the nature of the articles published, nor of their authorship. Their goal was to produce a descriptive baseline inventory of both to support reflection upon the discipline and advancement of editorial policy. However, the more important purpose of the research was to inventory and analyze the most common types of research being used and published in *Landscape Journal*.

The investigators combined descriptive and classificatory strategies (see also chapter 5), using a range of methods. Details of authorship were categorized using an "open coding" method guided by an eleven-category rubric drawn from the current organization of CELA conference track themes (discussed in chapter 2). This provided subject areas, descriptions, and topics into which the articles could be placed.

The entire publication record was catalogued arithmetically for four seven-year periods, each corresponding to the approximate tenure of different editorial teams. Results were analyzed by categories and represented in graphic form as histograms, showing both nominal and ordinal information, as well as percentages.

The example is particularly interesting not only for the relevance of the subject to this text, but also for the clarity with which it illustrates a number of distinct steps in the implementation of a classification strategy: data collection, recording, analysis by themes, and presentation.

The card catalogue system that predates digital retrieval systems in libraries is a form of index that served to regulate book shelving and retrieval procedures. This was essentially a classification based on the theory of the organization of knowledge. The Dewey Decimal system and the American Library of Congress comprise different cataloguing theories; a bewildering variety of cataloguing schemes existed before either of these standard organizational systems was adopted.

Because catalogues are ideally suited to organizing many kinds of visual material, as well as design objects and artifacts, catalogues are quite common in landscape architecture. Catalogues typically collect evidence from a range of purposeful or representative case studies. For example, a catalogue (or finding guide) of a collection of work from Daniel Kiley's office might be organized by temporal themes (such as the chronology of the designer's oeuvre), typological themes (purpose of projects undertaken, e.g., corporate, institutional, residential), stylistic themes or motif (orchard, quincunx form in planting design; cisterns and runnels, etc.), or even collaborators (work with Eliel Saarinen, Kevin Roche, Harry Wolf).

It is apparent that if cataloguing is the primary research strategy, it is often subsequently inflected by or reciprocal to interpretive strategies. In other words, the catalogue's thematic categories emerge from basic classification processes, but the shape of classification schemes often interacts with, and is in turn modified by, those themes and concepts. This interdependency or groundedness is a special quality of more complex classifications, such as exhibition catalogues.

An example of an exhibition catalogue is *Eco-revelatory Design: Nature Constructed/ Nature Revealed,* a special issue of *Landscape Journal* (1998) that catalogued a group of fifteen works and eight essays subsequently written about those works (fig. 8.1). Curated by Brenda Brown, Terry Harkness, and Doug Johnston, the works exhibited were thematically organized into six groups: abstraction and simulation; signifying features; exposing infrastructure processes; reclaiming, remembering, reviving; and changing perspectives. Although the articulation of these themes is based on interpretation of the content and goals of each of the works, the catalogue itself is a work of classification.

Example 8.2 offers a selective catalogue of storm-water management techniques (fig. 8.2) that create urban amenities (Echols and Pennypacker 2008). Rather than a simple inventory, this article is a catalogue because of the thematic logic of the grouping.

8.3 Typology

When the logic of taxonomy is applied to a more comprehensive catalogue of phenomena such as site conditions, forms, or concepts, the principles or performances that underlie the phenomena become part of a theory of classification. Both the theory and the method for this research are called *typology*—the systematic study of types.

In essence, typology is a taxonomic classification scheme applied comprehensively to entire categories of built form, relative to cultural values and practices. Studies of patterns and precedents (whether historic, organic, industrial, or otherwise) may make valuable contributions to typologies of form, shape, structure, arrangement, association, materials, construction technique—in short, if it can be named, it can be typed.

Typology thus seeks to categorize and marshal a vast array of variant design forms and motifs, typically as a response to pragmatic cultural and environmental problems. Typological characteristics may range from size, cost, program, and use, to broad conceptual patterns and values. Identifying and describing (diagramming) specific qualities and characteristics allow the researcher to establish patterns of association that relate design elements hierarchically across scales.

Although stemming from the same root word (type) as typology and placing a similar focus on original or principal forms—*archetypes* should be considered theory, rather than a classification strategy. This can be a point of confusion. For example, Appleton's (1996) work on archetypes of human visual and spatial preference advances a theory based on ideas of evolutionary determinism. Although this and related theories have been

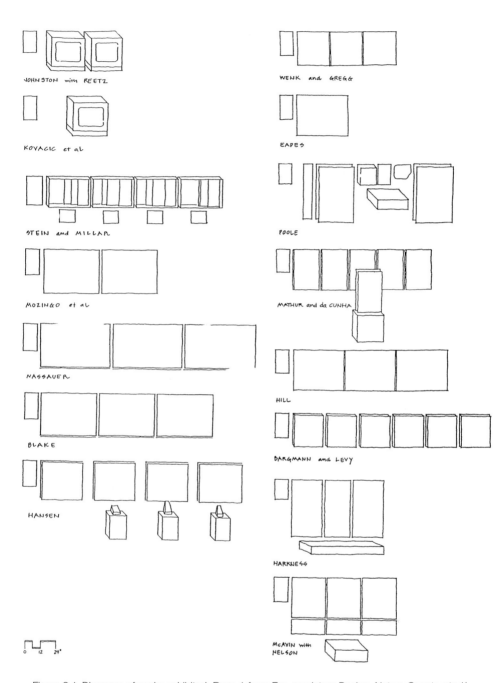

Figure 8.1 Diagrams of works exhibited. Page 1 from *Eco-revelatory Design: Nature Constructed/ Nature Revealed*

(Reprinted from *Landscape Journal*, 1998. Reproduced by permission of University of Wisconsin Press. Copyright 1998 by the Board of Regents of the University of Wisconsin System.)

Example 8.2:
Artful Rainwater Design
(Echols and Pennypacker 2008)

The investigators undertook a study of rainwater collection techniques to discover how utility and beauty might be better integrated into site-design projects. The project recognizes design opportunity in response to the growing needs of municipal governments to manage nonpoint sources of runoff with many "small, safe, integrated" site solutions (fig. 8.2). Rather than concealing heavily engineered storm-water solutions underground, at great public expense, the investigators believe they should be "celebrated on the surface as site amenities."

The project is significant because "[a]ddressing the amenity aspect provides a useful strategy for ensuring that storm water management 'starts at the source,' as so many experts have advised" (268). The investigators also identify an opportunity to demonstrate the value of landscape design in rainwater harvesting by enhancing the value of the site through enriched visual, tactile, educational, and interpretive experience.

The professional relevance of the project is that if landscape architects were not aware of this type of practice, they might lose market share to engineers. However, its wider social relevance lies in the opportunity to change public attitudes toward rainwater as a precious renewable resource, as well as in providing an experience of "near nature" that could be ubiquitous in both urban and rural settings.

The utility goals (health and safety) for storm water solutions were already well documented, but little attention was paid to understanding amenity (welfare). The investigators therefore sought to "bring specificity to amenity goals and objectives related to storm water management and to identify design techniques used to achieve those goals" (269).

An inventory of twenty rain garden exemplars was assembled and reorganized around five separate goals or concepts of amenity that were identified, described, and categorized. "Initial categorization was guided by this question: What amenity aspects of storm water management design enhance a project's attractiveness or value? Thus we developed a list of observed rainwater-based amenities, compared it to a larger list [published goals from the literature] . . . and discovered that our identified ARD amenity goals formed a clear subset" (271).

The amenity goals observed in the researchers' sample "included education, recreation, safety, public relations, and aesthetic richness" (272). Each of these categories is detailed, discussed, and illustrated by specific design techniques in several gardens, making it possible for other practitioners to apply the basic principles and techniques to other sites and situations.

This article makes its underlying logic and process very transparent and is, therefore, a great case study from which to learn. Categories chosen to organize the catalogue of projects are clearly theorized and grounded in the literature, and implications for wider applications are suggested.

discredited by many, theories of archetypes persist, finding their way into cultural and historical interpretation. Whether one may be tempted to explain a particular form with a theory of archetypes (or not), the research method used to isolate or identify that form would be called typology and would belong to the strategy of classification.

Figure 8.2 Waterworks Garden, Renton, Washington

(Project by Lorna Jordan with Jones and Jones, and Brown and Caldwell. Photograph by Eliza Pennypacker. Originally published in *Landscape Journal*, 2008. Reproduced by permission of University of Wisconsin Press. Copyright 2008 by the Board of Regents of the University of Wisconsin System.

Since the 1950s, typological studies of buildings, housing schemes, and streets have been especially important in urban planning and architecture, as well as in historic preservation for vernacular landscapes and practices. Increasingly, typologies are being developed for technical solutions to common problems including campus plans, parking lots, storm water detention, and green-roof systems. The theory of New Urbanism is associated with an emphasis on urban typologies of American small towns of the early twentieth century. Example 8.3 presents a typology of ideal planned communities (fig. 8.3).

8.4 Taxonomy

Taxonomy refers to the theory, principles, or practices of classification into provisional or established categories. The term derives from the Greek roots *taxis* (meaning arrangement or order) and *nomos* ("law" or "science"). A taxonomic scheme is typically structured as a hierarchy, beginning with broad inclusive ranks or categories (most general), and ending with the narrowest (most specialized).

Biological taxonomy, a modern development of Linnaean classification (named for the Swedish botanist Carolus Linnaeus 1707–1778), is perhaps the most easily recognized example of taxonomy. In this system, to a certain degree classification is "an end in itself"—an expression of cumulative knowledge of the world that is the final step in a rigorous process of close observation and measurement, elaborated by countless generations of scientists and naturalists over more than two centuries. It is interesting to note that despite its global acceptance as a theory of the hierarchies of life forms, relating closely to theories of biological complexity and evolutionary development, this biological classification system continues to undergo modification as new species and relationships are discovered (and lost) and as new observational techniques (such as DNA testing) are developed.

In the hierarchical relationships between supertypes (or superclass) and subtypes (or subclass), the subordinate group must always include all the basic traits of the supertype, together with enough additional, predictable distinguishing features to constitute a distinct subtype. For example, according to Table 8.1 below, the Siberian tiger is a subspecies belonging to the family of cats (*Felidae*) in the mammalian class; however, not all mammals are Siberian tigers, nor are they all cats. As a corollary to the logic of the hierarchical relationship, the population belonging to each rank in the taxonomy should always decrease as specialization increases.

Anything that conforms to this sort of hierarchical logic—anything, that is, having shared properties yet further differentiated and divisible into superimposed or "nested" scales relating from general to specialized phenomena—may, therefore, be classified according to a taxonomy. This applies to much of the world. In addition to plants and animals, other examples of physical or structural taxonomies might be applied to soil types; streams, rivers and watersheds; ecological systems; brownfields; and so on.

The development of a useful taxonomy need not be as elaborate as, say, the Linnaean system, and may extend to the hierarchical organization of a set of abstract ideas, theories, or value systems. For instance, among theoretical taxonomies developed for the fields of planning, political science, and education theory, Bloom's (1956) "taxonomy of cognitive objectives" is a well-known hierarchical classification of learning objectives established by progressive educators. Arnstein's (1969) schema for a "ladder of citizen participation" suggests how a citizenry may progress in various stages from disengagement to empowerment in community decision-making processes. The "taxonomy of scholarship" in Boyer's *Scholarship Reconsidered: Priorities of the Professoriate* (1991) is used by Kapper and Chenoweth (2000) as a paradigm for "understanding the breadth of disciplinary work that occurs in the academic sector: the scholarships of discovery, integration, application, and teaching" in landscape architecture (150). Each of these powerful theoretical taxonomies involves less than a dozen categories; each has motivated many subsequent research studies designed to test or refine the conceptual relationships that it expresses.

Example 8.3:
A Typology of Designed Communities
(Forsyth and Crewe 2009)

In essence, this study is a response to an unrealized intellectual opportunity. Many comprehensive planned communities were constructed on a metropolitan scale during the period of the United States' fastest urban growth. The authors believe that analysis of these designed communities will "provide a key window into the design, planning, and development professions' hopes about physical solutions to contemporary urban problems." However, the authors add, "due to their prominence as models of urban design they are a focus of attention," and are sometimes inappropriately admired, criticized, or copied as models for generic development schemes (56–57).

The purpose of using the classification strategy was to expose "differences and internal diversity" within these historic precedents. A particular challenge was to study their underlying social or ideological purpose, in order to call attention to its role as a separate consideration from their form. The relevance of this type of study for the discipline is didactic: it raises awareness that while community forms may be transferable, planners cannot expect to get the same result from a particular form unless the original social frameworks are also maintained.

More than two dozen model communities were analyzed, together with interviews, literature reviews, and primary archival work, in order to generate descriptive data that was then classified. A matrix (fig. 8.3) was developed that summarized and integrated several previous typologies proposed by urban historians. The components of this typology were explained, illustrated, and justified. A sample of designed communities was then sorted into groups on the basis of this matrix.

The main findings of the study were that the most widely copied examples of designed communities were not always the most "socially or ecologically idealistic models . . . while the most idealistic have remained the mainstay of courses in the history of physical planning" (74–75). The implications of this research will challenge professionals involved in urban development to think more seriously about the difficulties and the rewards of designing socially and ecologically idealistic communities.

Although the authors do not illustrate the reasoning behind their classification matrix in great detail, this article is clearly written and argued. It is a useful example of typology as a method within the classification strategy. The authors clearly explain the role of the central construct or theory of organization in the way the sample is chosen and the scheme is applied.

Place	Country or US State	Description	Date opened	Social neighborhood	Architectural villages	Diverse communities	Designed enclaves	Ecoburbs	Ecocities	Technovilles
Almere	Netherlands	New town	1970s		x			xx		
Auroville	India	New town	1960s			xx		xx		
Brasilia	Brazil	Free-standing new town	1960s	x	xx					
Civano	Arizona	New urbanist village	1990s	x				xx		
Columbia	Maryland	Satellite new town	1960s	xx		xx				
Cumbernauld	Scotland	Satellite new town	1950s			xx				
False Creek	Vancouver	Infill village/new town	1970s			xx				
Golden Grove	South Australia	Mixed-tenure village/new town	1980s	xx		xx				
Hammar by Sjöstad	Sweden	Infill village/new town	1900s/2000s					xx	xx	
Hampshire College	Massachusetts	Experimental college	1970s				xx			
Hope VI program, multiple sites	United States	Started 1990s	1990s				xx			
Irvine	California	Satellite new town	1960s			xx				x
Izumi Park Town	Japan	Satellite new town + technopolis	1970s	x						xx
Kentlands	Maryland	New urbanist village	1990s	xx	xx					
Kista	Sweden	Science city	1970s						x	xx
Leisure World	California	Retirement new town	1960s				xx			
Poundbury	England	New urbanist village	1990s		xx					
Seaside	Florida	New urbanist village	1980s		xx					
Singapore (various)	Singapore	New towns and neighborhood units	from 1950s	x					xx	
Stevenage	England	Satellite new town	1940s	xx						
Sun City	Arizona	Retirement new town	1960s				xx			
Sydney Olympics/ Newington	Australia	Infill village/new town	1900s/2000s						xx	
The Woodlands	Texas	Satellite new town	1970s	x				xx		
Tsukuba	Japan	Technopolis	1960s							xx
Vallingby	Sweden	Satellite new town/ transit-oriented	1950s	x					xx	
Village Homes	California	Village	1970s					xx		

xx = major emphasis, x = secondary emphasis

Figure 8.3 Developments analyzed. Matrix 2 in Forsyth and Crewe (2009).

(Originally published in *Landscape Journal*, 2009. Reproduced by permission of the University of Wisconsin Press. Copyright 2009 by the Board of Regents of the University of Wisconsin System.)

Table 8.1 Taxonomic classification of Siberian tigers and Romaine lettuce*

Siberian Tiger	Romaine Lettuce
Kingdom	**Kingdom**
Animalia (animals)	*Plantae (plants)*
Phylum	**Division**
Chordata	*Tracheophyta (vascular plants)*
Subphylum	
Vertebrata	
Superclass/Class	**Class**
Mammalia	*Angiospermae (flowering plants)*
	Subclass
	Dicotyledonae
Order	**Order**
Carnivora	*Campanulatae*
Family	**Family**
Felidae (cats)	*Compositae*
Genus	**Genus**
Panthera	*Lactuca (lettuce)*
Species	**Species**
Panthera tigris (tiger)	*Lactuca sativa (cultivated lettuce)*
Subspecies	**Variety**
Panthera tigris longipilis	*Lactuca sativa longifolia*

*Adapted from *American Heritage Dictionary*, ed. Morris 1978

8.5 Index

Preparing a useful index is a common form of classificatory research. According to the *American Heritage Dictionary of the English Language,* an index is "anything that serves to guide, point out or otherwise facilitate reference." Indices range from the simplest (counting up sets of identical or similar things) to the most complex (grouping or reorganizing similar things by theme or concept). They function on many levels, from a simply organized inventory of objects or events to an interactive digital finding aid for the archived drawings and private letters of a well-known figure in planning history.

An index to a scholarly book, for instance, may simply list every page where a similar name, place, or concept occurs in a text (for example, "Bias, 77, 102, 153"). Similar to the illustration below, an index is typically alphabetically arranged and then subdivided by themes.

Example of a simple index[1]

Cultural difference, 3
Cultural studies, 116
Culture of enquiry, 9
and personal style, 94–95
as family of research methods, 88
becoming a participant in, 84
definition, 83, 169
metaculture of inquiry, 171

Related to the idea of the index is the *glossary*—a select list of specialized or technical vocabulary terms, usually with extended definitions, and often used, for example, in textbooks. A glossary is typically used as an aid to understanding a text of a particular discipline, but it may also stand alone as a form of classification. For instance, a glossary of terms might be developed in describing the parts of an Italian Renaissance garden.

A *concordance* is a type of index where every occurrence of principal or significant words in a literary work is counted, located in the text, and sometimes defined. For example, using a concordance, one might be able to find every instance of the word "nature" used in the collected works of Thoreau. In itself a form of classification, concordances also potentially present interesting data sets for hermeneutic-interpretive researchers.

Similar to collections and classes of words, visual forms such as symbols, emblems, and icons may be organized into indexes. *Emblemata* are catalogues for the symbols of typical motifs in mediaeval and Renaissance insignia and decorations. As another type of systematic index, *iconography* is defined as the theoretical and historical study of symbolic imagery, pioneered by the eminent art historian Erwin Panofsky (Cosgrove and Daniels 1988). It is important to mention here that the classificatory research activity involved in *producing* an iconographic index should not be confused with the interpretive research involved in *applying* it to visual communications. Panofsky himself distinguished between the narrow sense of iconography as a classification scheme and the deeper sense of iconography (iconology) as a theory of interpretation (see chapter 9 for more on this discussion).

Classifying and organizing the structure of ideas that comprise disciplinary knowledge have obvious and important uses in landscape architecture. Simple forms of indexing languages include *subject keywords, heading lists,* and *thesauri.* In the late 1970s and early

---

[1] From Bentz and Shapiro 1998, 207.

1980s, an emerging realization of the potential of computers to assist in design problems was combined with growing consciousness of the research needs of the profession. This resulted in a period of great interest in developing computer-based indexing languages for landscape architecture. For example, having organized a standardized plant material language, Hightshoe and Niemann developed PLTSEL (Plant Selection System), a "computer-based data bank for rapidly organizing and retrieving visual, cultural, and ecological information on over 500 native plants" in the midwestern and eastern regions of the United States (1982, 23).

Facet analysis is a more sophisticated technique for classification that was developed in the 1960s by the library information scientist S. R. Ranganathan and the Classification Research Group (Spiteri 1998). As opposed to a taxonomy, in which an item or organism may only have one place to reside, facet analysis offers multiple ways to identify or locate a term or idea. Facet analysis helps to develop an indexing language for documents (indexes, abstracts, bibliographies, for example) with compound themes, so that they can be more easily and reliably retrieved.

Because of its interdisciplinarity, landscape architecture has many examples of compound themes—landscape urbanism, natural history, social ecology, and so on. Hohmann (2006) writes that the first classification scheme for landscape architectural knowledge was developed at Harvard University around 1920 by Theodora Kimball Hubbard (see chapter 9). Sixty years later, Fredericks (1982) used facet analysis to propose the development of a new indexing language structure in landscape architecture in order to update, structure, and control the retrieval of documents. It is interesting to note that Example 8.4 began as Fredericks' master's thesis in landscape architecture.

Another form of index that is peculiarly and increasingly important in academic disciplines is *citation indexing* and analysis. "Citation analysis is an important tool used to trace scholarly research, measure impact, and justify tenure and funding decisions. Web of Science, which indexes peer-reviewed journal literature, has been the major research database for citation tracking. [However, t]wo new tools are now available to count citations: Scopus and Google Scholar" (Bauer and Bakkalbasi 2005). Scopus is a large international abstract and citation database of research literature (print and web), boasting "more than fifteen thousand peer-reviewed journals from more than four thousand publishers, and more than a thousand Open Access journals," among other resources. Scopus is also recognized for its citation-indexing features and its own variant of the "impact factor."

The impact factor is a result of *citation impact analysis*; it measures two things—the number of times that an individual article is cited by others within any citation index and, as a sum of these citations, the relative weight or impact that any particular journal has on the discourse of other researchers in the field. To some, this measurement matters a great deal, while to others it simply offers evidence of the increasingly self-referential (and possibly self-serving) formation and reproduction of knowledge as a consensual and, frankly, commercial venture.

Example 8.4:
An Indexing Language for Landscape Architecture
(Fredericks 1982)

Because landscape architecture is an interdisciplinary field, the complexity of content in its subject matter can make it difficult to retrieve articles. An indexing language, specifically a keyword system that recognizes compound themes that are typical in the field, is needed.

The author believes the outdated hierarchical, enumerative scheme that had been developed by Hubbard and Kimball (1920) should be replaced by a faceted classification scheme.

Twenty of the most commonly used books in landscape architectural education were used to extract a representative list of terms for development and demonstration of the scheme. "Facet analysis involves sorting terms in a given field of knowledge into facets. Facets are terms which represent groups of other terms and have distinct characteristics such as homogeneity (uniformity) and mutual exclusivity (together they identify the scope of the field)" (50).

A computer program was developed to arrange the lists of terms alphabetically. The authors found that the following list of facets described the field of landscape architecture: "problems, components, purpose, theory, process, methods, materials, professional aspects, and history" (52).

The indexing language thus developed gives more efficiency, accuracy, and precision to retrieval systems. This would benefit future researchers in the field. The relevance of this for the field is to give work by landscape architects enhanced visibility and to benefit researchers by identifying redundancy or gaps in the field of knowledge.

Although this article is outdated, it offers an outstanding example of indexing as a research strategy utilized in landscape architecture. In this case, the researcher also had a background in library science. Today, computer programming, information science, and community informatics are of growing interest to landscape architects, as data sets and other types of reference information becomes increasingly complex. This study presents an example of a classification strategy that is so sophisticated that it borders on logical systems (chapter 13), in the sense that it seems to "invent" a language system. However, the research design used to organize the indexing language was grounded in an inventory (purposive sample) of landscape educators' most-used books, and thus it fits better in classification schemes.

Citation impact analysis is different from *structural citation analysis,* in which the relationships between research articles can be mapped out as a type of cluster analysis. In Example 8.5, Burley et al. (2009) invoke forest ecology as an analogy for structural citation analysis, where the research article is similar to a stand of trees, and the citations and reference list within it represent the species of individual trees that make up the stand.

Example 8.5:
Citation Analysis of Transportation Research Literature
(Burley et al. 2009)

The National Cooperative Highway Research Program considered whether it was necessary to update *A Guide for Transportation Landscape and Environmental Design* (1991). In particular, the researchers wanted to find out whether or not a new Federal transportation paradigm called Context Sensitive Design was reflected in the research and whether or not new thinking about transportation environments was better integrated into issues of community and culture.

In order to understand the "latent" structure of new knowledge about design of the roadside environment the authors conducted a structural citation analysis on the literature of transportation in peer-reviewed journals in landscape architecture (*Landscape Journal, Landscape Research,* and *Landscape and Urban Planning*). The principal research problem was to find structural evidence (or not) of integration or at least connectedness in the dimensions of new knowledge (fig. 8.4).

The study examined 101 source articles published since 1991, together with 1,351 references or cited articles contained within them. Evidence was analyzed using a form of multivariate cluster analysis. In other words, this study combines classification strategies with statistical correlation and modeling in order to generate its findings. Thirteen significant axes or dimensions (similar to facets, see Example 8.4) were identified that contained clusters of other terms.

"Since the dimensions in this citation universe are not widely connected," the authors accepted the hypothesis "that transportation landscape research is disjointed and fragmented" (488). This is partly explained by the breadth and complexity of the transportation landscape research, "and may be emblematic of professional practice issues in transportation planning" (489). However, it also reflected the differences between the type of research published in landscape journals, compared to other transportation research published in other sectors.

This article exemplifies methodological clarity, not only defining the terminology and limitations of the methods used, but also explaining the significance of the results. Understood as a variant within the large group of classification strategies, this study shows how citation indexing can be a practical and relevant method when applied to problems in landscape architecture.

8.6 Bibliography and Literature Review

As a general term, *literature review* is used to describe a variety of strategies of investigation. It is worth noting that reviews may be, in and of themselves, a means to an end (as when used to establish a baseline for a new study) or an end in themselves (as when a research synthesis is published). Cooper (1998) suggests a set of related terms

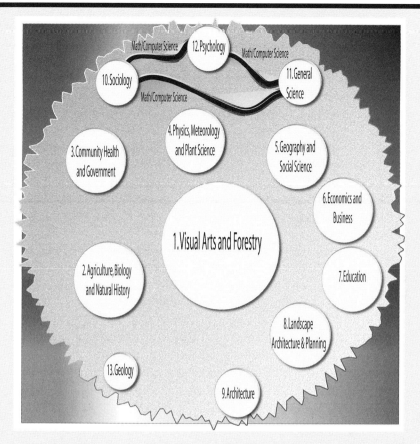

Figure 8.4 Transportation landscape and environmental design universe: a map of the road-side research universe

(Image courtesy of Jon Burley. Reprinted from *Landscape Research*, 2009, with permission from the publisher, Taylor and Francis. Copyright 2009.)

(a taxonomy) in ascending order of complexity, including literature review, theoretical review, research review, integrative research review, research synthesis, and meta-analysis. The basic building block for all of these is the literature review.

In graduate and professional research, the data for a literature review typically include peer-reviewed publications. The literature review relies on a highly focused sample generated through a *literature search*. The *target population* includes all publications relevant to a given research problem, concept, or question. The sampling frame is, therefore, generated, and limited, by keywords, databases, search engines, and other techniques.

Literature reviews are typically used by researchers (and required by virtually all peer-reviewed venues) to establish a baseline for available knowledge on any given topic. Reviews can have a number of different objectives, for instance, program impacts, measurement techniques, and theoretical frames, among other possibilities. Alternatively, whenever there is a lack of clarity or consistency in the use of a particular term or concept, literature review can be a useful strategy for initializing new inquiries or theory. Many excellent examples of literature reviews appear in environmental research publications, ranging from simple preparatory component parts of primary research articles all the way to synthetic review articles that can stand on their own. A review article may combine thematic classification with a more reflexive scheme or framework for interpretation or evaluation.

For any investigation, the "state of the question"—in other words, the synthesis of all relevant, current, available published knowledge about a specific topic—will point in the direction that new research needs to go. Spirn (2009) makes a strong case for the value of the review article in landscape architecture:

> What landscape architecture now needs is a series of review articles on particularly important or newly emerging areas of research. For many disciplines, from the humanities to the social and natural sciences, review articles are the primary mode for advancing and defining a field. A review article is a major contribution. It is usually written by a senior scholar who surveys hundreds of books and articles and presents a synthetic overview of this comprehensive bibliography, probing such questions as: What are the principle themes and threads of inquiry, and what are the key works and contributions in each area? What are the regions of agreement and disputed territories? What are the gaps in knowledge and which are potentially fertile areas of knowledge? . . . Without such [review] articles for our own discipline, how can we arrive at an understanding of the status of the many fields within landscape architecture? (2009, 121)

Spirn's challenge is inherent within two older studies condensed below, both motivated by intellectual problems in the transformation of landscape architecture into an autonomous discipline in the 1970s and 1980s. The purpose of the first study (Example 8.6) is quite simply to establish and characterize a baseline of available knowledge for a then-emerging field of visual analysis. The *subject* of the second literature review (Example 8.7) is monitoring (an evaluation strategy), but the researchers' particular "need to know" demanded the use of a classification strategy to set up the study.

Because reliable sources of new knowledge all typically undertake preliminary literature reviews like these, the evolution of thought on a subject is tacit, or implicit in both the

(Priestley 1983)

When the conference *Our National Landscape* (Elsner and Smardon, 1979) took place, it assembled the largest and most comprehensive collection of work in the field of visual analysis. This provided an opportunity to assess all citations included in the *Proceedings,* in order to "produce a generalized picture" of the field and "thereby guide further research" (52). Eighty-one of the 102 papers included bibliographic material. These references were first collected and inventoried as a single list, counting the number of times each was cited. Next, the references were categorized and reordered by frequency of citation by category, and by reference.

Bibliographic analysis found that "almost one-third of [all] the citations were works in environmental psychology and psychology," while another 25 percent of the references pertained to landscape architectural practices (inventory, analysis, visual impact, and the like). However, when only the twenty most frequently cited sources were analyzed, it showed that about 50 percent of them reflected landscape architectural practices.

The results of analysis provide an indication of the make up and distribution of the literature in the field, especially for the United States, in the late 1970s. It was also noted that citations did not necessarily signal endorsement of the work cited.

The researchers theorized that because the references came almost equally and independently from adjacent disciplines (reference disciplines), the development of this field in landscape architecture was still "young." Citing Thomas Kuhn (1970), the author believes the data showed landscape visual analysis was still in a "preparadigm period," bewildering in its diversity, lacking consensus, experiencing "competing schools of thought" (56), and needing further conceptual integration.

This makes a good teaching article for two reasons. First, it is clearly written, with an overarching classification strategy and a straightforward research design that uses easy-to-understand methods. Second, the subject matter is directly relevant to understanding the historical evolution of research strategies, as it illustrates a variety of concepts that relate to intellectual development of landscape architecture in relation to disciplines.

impact and structure of current literature (see citation analysis above). This is one of the many reasons why we say that knowledge is consensually produced. Over time, however, received and no-longer-questioned ideas or "proofs" may become so thoroughly embedded into the very fabric of our questions, assumptions, strategies, and methods that they disappear from view.

The most sophisticated of all literature reviews is the *meta-analysis,* or the analysis of analyses—in effect, "analysis squared." When seeking corroboration or inconsistencies between a group of previously executed studies, techniques of meta-analysis are often combined with correlation or evaluation strategies. A glossary for the United States

Environmental Protection Agency defines meta-analysis as "[t]he systematic analysis of a set of existing evaluations of similar programs [cases or studies] in order to draw general conclusions, develop support for hypotheses, and/or produce an estimate of overall program [study] effects" (US EPA 2010).

This pragmatic definition is consistent with the basic logic of classification developed for this chapter—inventory (gathering a data set), analysis (systematic sorting or grouping by conformity, nonconformity, or directionality of outcome or theme), and synthesis (level of consistency or support for hypotheses or overall effect). There are instances, however, where meta-analysis is not useful. Cooper (1998) writes that "the basic premise behind the use of statistics in research synthesis is that a series of studies address an identical conceptual hypothesis. If the premises of a synthesis do not include this assertion, then there is no need for cumulative statistics" (108).

Meta-analysis can also be a way of recovering "lost" or undercited studies, by finding/placing them back within the scope of other comparable research, principally studies with identical sampling techniques or hypotheses. Meta-analysis can also be very useful in the context of a very well-trodden research environment, in which multiple studies of very similar phenomena and populations have been undertaken and published. However, in meta-analytical techniques, any problems with the data sampling, flawed analyses, confounding factors, or bias cannot be discerned or eliminated. In other words, good meta-analysis of flawed studies will generate flawed results. One of the challenges to greater use of meta-analyses in landscape architecture is the inconsistency in the way statistical analyses have been applied to different types of data (see chapter 6).

Classification Strategies: Summary

This brief survey has shown that there are dozens of permutations on the way that classification strategies may be used in landscape architectural research. Classification strategies are integral to many research programs. They may be the primary focus of research, as shown in the examples in this chapter, or be combined with other research strategies in some way.

The chapter has highlighted several types of classification strategy:

- Collecting/inventory/cataloguing
- Typology
- Taxonomy
- Indexing
- Bibliography and literature review

In all cases, a clear understanding of the principles and logic of organization are essential. It is quite likely that classification strategies will not be discovered or used in isolation. Many powerful studies have resulted from staged research strategies that combine, say, classification and evaluation or classification and interpretation. It is, therefore, good practice to anticipate the many potential uses of this strategy and to look for evidence of combined studies in the literature.

References

Appleton, J. 1996. *The experience of landscape*. Rev. ed. Chichester U.K.: John Wiley and Sons.

Arnstein, S. R. 1969. A ladder of citizen participation. *Journal of the American Institute of Planners* 35 (4):216–24.

Bauer, K., and N. Bakkalbasi. 2005. An examination of citation counts in a new scholarly communication environment. *D-Lib Magazine*, September. http://www.dlib.org/dlib/september05/bauer/09bauer.html (accessed March 2010).

Bentz, V. M., and J. J. Shapiro. 1998. *Mindful inquiry in social research*. Thousand Oaks, CA: Sage.

Bloom, B., M. D. Englehart, E. J. Furst, W. H. Hill, and D. Krathwohl, eds. 1956. *The taxonomy of educational objectives: The classification of educational goals*. New York: David McKay Co.

Boyer, E. L. 1990. *Scholarship reconsidered: Priorities for the professoriate*. Princeton, NJ: The Carnegie Foundation for the Advancement of Teaching.

Brown, B., ed. 1998. Eco-revelatory design: Nature constructed/nature revealed. Special issue, *Landscape Journal* 17 (2).

Burley, J. B., V. B. P. Singhal, C. J. Burley, D. Fasser, C. Churchward, D. Hellekson, and I. Raharizafy. 2009. Citation analysis of transportation research literature: A multidimensional map of the roadside universe. *Landscape Research* 34 (4): 481–95.

Coombs. C. H. 1953. Theory and methods of social measurement. In *Research methods in the behavioral sciences*, ed. L. Festinger and D. Katz, 471–535. New York: Dryden.

Cooper, H. 1998. *Synthesizing research: A guide for literature reviews,* 3rd ed. Thousand Oaks, CA: Sage.

Cosgrove, D., and S. Daniels, eds. 1988. *The iconography of landscape: Essays on the symbolic representation, design and use of past environments*. New York: Cambridge University Press.

Echols, S., and E. Pennypacker. 2008. From storm water management to artful rainwater design. *Landscape Journal* 27 (2): 268–90.

Elsner, G. H., and R. C. Smardon, eds. 1979. *Our national landscape: A conference on applied techniques for analysis and management of the visual resource proceedings*. United States Department of Agriculture, Forest Service. Berkeley, CA: Pacific South West Forest and Range Experiment Station.

Forsyth, A. and K. Crewe. 2009. A typology of comprehensive designed communities since the Second World War. *Landscape Journal* 28 (1): 56–78.

Fredericks, R. 1982. An indexing language for landscape architecture. *Landscape Journal* 1 (1): 49–58.

Groat, L., and D. Wang. 2002. *Architectural research methods*. New York: John Wiley and Sons.

Hightshoe, G. L., and R. S. Niemann. 1982. Plant Selection System (PLTSEL): Midwestern and eastern floristic regions. *Landscape Journal* 1 (1): 23–30.

Hohmann, H. 2006. Theodora Kimball Hubbard and the "intellectualization" of landscape architecture, 1911–1935. *Landscape Journal* 25 (2): 169–86.

Kapper, T., and R. Chenoweth. 2000. Landscape architecture and societal values: Evidence from the literature. *Landscape Journal* 19 (2): 149–55.

Kuhn, T. 1970. *The structure of scientific revolutions*. Chicago: University of Chicago Press, 1970.

Lynch, K., and G. Hack. 1984. *Site planning*. 3rd ed. Cambridge, MA: MIT Press.

McCarthy, M. M., and C. B. Deans Jr. 1983. Long-term landscape monitoring: A review. *Landscape Journal* 2 (1): 60–67.

Morris, W., ed. 1978. *The American heritage dictionary*. Boston, MA: Houghton Mifflin Co.

Obrist, H. 2002. Un jardin peut au cacher un autre. *Landscape Journal* 21 (2): 15–18.

Pedhazur, E. J., and L. P. Schmelkin. 1991. *Measurement, design, and analysis: An integrated approach.* Hillsdale, NJ: Lawrence Erlbaum Assoc., Publishers.

Powers, M. N., and J. B. Walker. 2009. Twenty-five years of *Landscape Journal*: An analysis of authorship and article content. *Landscape Journal* 28 (1): 96–110.

Priestley, T. 1983. The field of visual analysis and resource management: A bibliographic analysis and perspective. *Landscape Journal* 2 (1): 52–59.

Spirn, A. 2009. In Retrospect and forecast: Remarks on the occasion of the 25th anniversary of *Landscape Journal*, ed. M. E. Deming. *Landscape Journal* 28 (1): 111–23.

Spiteri, L. 1998. A simplified model for facet analysis. *Canadian Journal of Information and Library Science* 23 (April–July): 1–30.

US EPA (United States Environmental Protection Agency). 2010. Program evaluation support web page. http://www.epa.gov/evaluate/glossary/m-esd.htm (accessed March 2010).

Zeisel, J. 1981. *Inquiry by design: Tools for environment–behavior research.* Belmont, CA: Wadsworth.

CHAPTER 9

Interpretive Strategies

9.1 Introduction

Interpretive research strategies start from the recognition that the meanings of objects, events, words, actions, and images are not always plain and obvious, and they require the investigator to actively engage in "making sense" of the phenomena they encounter. The consequence of becoming actively engaged in interpreting meaning is that conclusions can never be totally independent of the investigator. In effect, the investigator becomes a social actor within the research, and understanding is actively constructed through mediation between researcher and the data. The *interpretive* strategy, therefore, sits between the objective and subjectivist positions, midway in the classification matrix, in what we described in the introduction as a "constructionist" approach to understanding.

Interpretive strategies are also characterized by a second type of mediation, as the researcher moves reflexively between the observed data and the theoretical concepts that are brought to the investigation and used to make sense of what is found. Because the strategy sits between induction and deduction, we have located interpretive strategies in the very centre of the classification matrix.

The situations in which interpretive research strategies can be helpful vary widely, as do the research designs and detailed methods that can be used. However, interpretive strategies are most typically used when people and their social relationships are a significant or primary focus of investigation. In landscape architecture this can range from situations where information about a landscape research question comes from working with people in a particular landscape, to situations where understanding and insight is sought through analysis and interpretation of text, signs, or images that people—both past and present—have created about landscape. What is common across this range of interpretive strategies is the need for some measure of empathy with those involved, and an ability and willingness to reflect critically and actively upon the role of the researcher and the wider research community in constructing understanding.

In this chapter, four types of interpretive strategy that are commonly used in landscape architectural research are reviewed: ethnography, discourse analysis, iconography, and historiography.

9.2 Ethnography

Ethnography has been frequently described as an approach to research based upon observation, so why have we located it in the chapter on interpretation strategies, rather than in description? The answer lies in the way in which the investigator interacts with the people and their artifacts that are the subject of research. The issue goes back to the origins of sociology. One of the founders of that discipline, Emile Durkheim, argued that research into people and societies should follow the same strategies that natural scientists use to investigate the biophysical world, and should focus upon aspects that can be measured and subject to experimental and quasi-experimental methods and statistical analysis (Lukes 1973). In contrast, Max Weber, who worked at the same time, argued that research into humans had to be fundamentally different, because of the way in which we assign meaning to the world and our actions. In order to really understand meanings, a different strategy is required, which he called *interpretive*. Weber's approach to interpretation was through the concept of *Verstehen*, which implies empathy (Hamilton 1991).

Hence, the researcher becomes an actor *through whom* knowledge about the world is found. Ethnography and related forms of qualitative social research, while descriptive in the sense that they seek to provide an account of some cultural or social phenomenon, require the researcher to engage with the research as a feeling person, rather than as a detached observer. This requires different skills, especially an ability to reflect critically upon one's role, and frames the whole research strategy in a different way than "objectivist" strategies do.

The need for *active* interpretation applies to a wide range of data sources commonly used in landscape architecture—including interviews, text, and observation. The way a question is asked in a questionnaire or structured interview, for example, and the context in which it is asked, will shape and direct the nature of the answer. Many social researchers therefore encourage "respondents" (the people who are answering the question) to speak in their own words, and the researchers adopt strategies and research methods that involve active interpretation of what the respondents are saying. They also spend time investigating and reflecting upon the assumptions respondents are making and the context in which they are speaking and acting. Similarly, reading what people have written about landscape, or looking at what they said on previous occasions, involves asking questions about context, intention, and the meanings that the people involved place upon the words and phrases they have used.

Observation of people's actions can also be much enriched through an interpretive strategy. One of the main ethnographic approaches developed by anthropologists and other field social scientists is participant observation (Jorgensen 1989). Here, the investigator spends time—sometimes up to several months in a major research project—working and even living with subjects, observing their activities, participating in everyday situations and work, and building a rich account of people's lives and practices (fig. 9.1). One of the benefits of this is that not all values about landscape or landscape practices can be easily put into words, and not everyone feels comfortable or proficient in articulating their thoughts and knowledge, even in an open interview. Respondents may find it easier to talk with a researcher when both are engaged in some shared activity—say, walking or tending a garden. In other situations, for example, in landscape practice or management, what you do can be more informative than what you say.

Ethnography frequently involves conducting unstructured, open, or depth interviews, in which the investigator engages in an extended conversation with a subject or group of subjects, encouraging them to explain and expand upon their views

Figure 9.1 Participant observation

in their own words. In adopting an interpretive strategy that relies upon depth interviews, there are many issues for researchers to consider and a number of excellent texts that provide guidance. Silverman (2005) highlights a number of questions that are relevant for landscape research, several of which are addressed in Notes on Method 9.1.

A critical question in any interpretive strategy that uses ethnographic methods is whom to interview. As reviewed earlier (see Notes on Method 8.1), there are several ways to sample data that apply also to selecting respondents for depth interviews. The selection may be opportunistic—talking to someone in a community who happens to be willing and available to talk. Alternatively, respondents may be selected as representative of a wider population—chosen because they are of a particular age, gender, ethnicity, or socioeconomic status. A third option is to select by "purpose." In research related to landscape architecture, where the question is frequently related to some aspect of practice or a particular landscape or place, a researcher may seek to interview people who are well informed on the topic. These are known as "key informants." Another name for a purposive sample is "theoretical," which alerts us to the need to select key informants who are most likely to provide information that will address the question being asked. Random samples are untypical in interpretive research,

Notes on Method 9.1: Interpreting What People Say in Interviews

- *What status do you give to your data?* Do you treat what your respondents tell you as an honest and literal account of their thoughts and experience, or is it an account that is constructed to present a particular point of view they wish you to hear? This is important if you are interviewing decision makers in a planning or design situation, for example, and always vital to the way you interpret data.

- *How will you analyze the interviews?* The essential point about adopting an interpretive strategy is that it recognizes the dynamic and social nature of the relationship between the researcher and the subject matter. So analysis involves a process of working with interview data—coding, ordering, questioning, reordering, and reflecting. It is more than listing key words or themes, and it requires a commitment to actively crafting an understanding.

- *Does your approach to analysis and interpretation address your research question?* Much social science is interested in the nature of social interaction per se, whereas a landscape architectural researcher may be more likely to try to answer a question about the effect of social factors in landscape change. While it is important to be aware of the subtleties of social research, it is also essential to adopt an approach that is effective and fruitful, even if it has theoretical limitations.

- *Does interview data really help?* Undertaking and analyzing individual depth interviews can reveal rich and profound understandings, but it can be very time consuming. In a previous example, Ward Thompson (2006) used a form of group interview called a focus group (see below) to establish the main themes used to construct a questionnaire survey. This is a common technique in the initial stages of social research.

- *Are you claiming too much for your data?* It is important not to draw sweeping conclusions from a limited number of interviews or to presume that what you have found is the only "truth." It is probably just one way to "slice the cake" (Silverman 2005, 49).

as the strategy does not typically utilize inferential statistics and relies upon different tests of validity.

There are many advantages in interpretive research in adopting a research design that uses key informant interviews (fig. 9.2). In selecting people who are familiar with the topic, the likelihood is that the interviews will yield rich and relevant data. The process of identifying and contacting informants is also easier. A common approach is "snowballing": having identified an initial starting point, the researcher then asks each person they interview for the names of other people who would be well informed on the topic. Obviously, it is necessary not to take the responses naïvely (for example, if you are seeking diversity, then it is important not to just follow up one line of contact) and to cross-reference suggestions from different sources.

Depth interviews are typically undertaken one-on-one, so that they are in effect a conversation between two people, with content known only to them. Hence, it is possible to make significant commitments about confidentiality. However, open questions can also be asked in a group setting. In that case, the social dynamic between the investigator and subject(s) changes, as the exchange can be heard and witnessed by all present. Notes on Method 9.2 examines questions of ethics and confidentiality.

Focus groups (or focused group interviews) are widely used in applied research and can be a useful part of an interpretive strategy, drawing out a rich insight into a shared or common type of experience or generating ideas or strategies to resolve a problem. They are an efficient way to draw upon

Figure 9.2 Key informant interview

Notes on Method 9.2: Ethics and Confidentiality

Ethical considerations are a critical part of developing any strategy involving people (frequently described as human subjects in the research ethics literature and process). Recognition of human rights principles by organizations and in legislation, and the potential legal implications of just about any type of interaction with other people in contemporary society, mean that all universities (and most public organizations and private practices) now require researchers to meet ethics protocols while undertaking research involving people. Universities in the United States, by law, have established Institutional Review Boards (IRB), which are charged with examining and approving all research proposals involving human subjects. All graduate student researchers, as well as larger, externally funded research projects are required to seek approvals for their research programs (or to seek waivers of this requirement if not applicable to the project). A Web site developed for the Institutional Review Board at the University of Illinois (UIUC 2010) provides a wealth of historical background and procedural explanations for these protocols, but any IRB or IRB-like office will have their own, similar version.

Ethical requirements may cover confidentiality and ownership of information that is provided (see below), avoidance of physical or psychological risk or harm to the subject, obtaining consent from the subjects, respect for culturally sensitive issues or the views and knowledge of a range of people and may be used early in a research design to "scope" an issue, identifying themes that will be used in developing the detailed techniques, such as a questionnaire survey. They may also be used later in the design to tease out in more detail the findings of a larger questionnaire survey.

As the name implies, the essential points of a focus group are, first, that the group interview is focused upon a particular topic (a free-ranging discussion without a clear focus is likely to frustrate both participants and researcher); and, second, that it is in a group setting with agreed-upon protocols for interaction, so all participants can feel comfortable and be willing to express their views in front of others (frequently their peers or other members of the community). Notes on Method 9.3 offers some additional insights into focus groups.

In Example 9.1, Armstrong's (2004) investigation of the experience of being a migrant to Australia demonstrates the use of focused group depth interviews in an interpretive strategy (fig. 9.3). The researcher sought understanding of the experiences and world views of distinctive subcultures within Australia—that of Greek, Lebanese, and Vietnamese migrants—and drew together groups from within each subculture and encouraged them to share their experiences. One of the key strengths of this example is the subtle way in which the investigator draws out the experiences of people who might otherwise lie outside the mainstream of society. As an established and successful academic, Armstrong had to find a way to engage with these migrant groups, to gain their trust before they would share their experiences, and to interpret what she heard in a way that could be

places, and so on. They may mean following procedural guidelines and the submission of a formal proposal and request for approval from an ethics committee. This needs to be undertaken early in the process and before any field research is started. There may also be a requirement to seek written permission from the management of the place where interviews will be done—for example, managers of a shopping mall or the public authority responsible for a street, park, or transportation hub.

A central question in ethics reviews is the confidentiality of the material provided by people. An ethics protocol may raise questions about what happens to the information that has been collected. Can the provider of the information be identified in any way? What commitments will the researcher make about anonymity and confidentiality? How will these be implemented? It is normal in most social science research to provide a written introduction to the person being questioned explaining the purpose of the research, how the findings will be used and disseminated, and what provisions have been made in terms of confidentiality. A consent agreement form may also be included, and some protocols specify that the subject has the right to withdraw their data at any time.

Social researchers typically code all responses in a list that is kept in a secure place, and use numbers or pseudonyms to identify the data during analysis and in reporting. It is vital to ensure that you are familiar with these types of protocol before embarking on any research project involving people as subjects, and there are good standard texts in social science that expand upon all these issues and provide operational guidance.

Notes on Method 9.3: Focus Groups

Focus groups are typically made up of eight to twelve people with similar backgrounds, interests, and values, such as the migrants interviewed in Example 9.1. A group interview with a very diverse membership, each with different interests, backgrounds, and values, sets up a very different group dynamic. Although it could reveal many interesting aspects of a community, it also carries risks of conflict and may not provide a particularly coherent outcome. Even in a group with shared values, the role of the interviewer or mediator is critical to success and is even more challenging than undertaking an in-depth one-to-one interview.

In the one-to-one situation, the interviewer needs empathy with the subject and a personal manner that evokes in the subject a confidence and a willingness to talk. The interviewer needs an acute awareness of the nuances in a subject's words and actions and the ability to encourage response without leading or imposing their own values. Managing a focus group requires all these attributes, *and* an ability to keep a group discussion on task, to mediate between dissenting views, and to ensure that everyone feels included and valued. A researcher in landscape architecture with a design background may have the necessary aptitude, but he or she may not have the skills or experience in facilitating group discussion. In this case, it may be necessary either to undertake preliminary training or to work with a more experienced social researcher. It is also very helpful to have at least one other member of the research team present to manage the practical arrangements, which enables the group mediator/leader to concentrate on the interactions with and between participants.

understood by a wider audience while being true to the subjects of the research. Notes on Method 9.4 offers additional comment on cross-cultural research.

Armstrong (2004) used the idea of journey to help make sense of the experiences of the migrants she interviewed. This has much in common with biographical methods of interpretation—asking people to give an account of their *life history* and the things and events that have shaped their understanding or activities or values in landscape. Life histories are typically selected as theoretical samples. Specialists in life-history research use the term "saturation" (Berteaux 1981) to describe the situation when they keep on hearing the same story from different people with similar roles. When a researcher reaches the point at which additional interviews reveal little new generic information, they have achieved saturation. This can be a powerful approach to place-based or local landscape-based research and can be applied to a range of landscape architectural research questions.

Example 9.2 illustrates how an interpretive strategy based upon biographies is used to better understand how farmers manage their land in a rural part of southeast England, in the face of changing socioeconomic dynamics and agro-environmental policies (Bohnet et al. 2003).

Example 9.1:
Making the Unfamiliar Familiar
(Armstrong 2004)

The context for this research is the global movement of people and the growth of large multi-cultural cities with diverse migrant populations. The purpose of the research was both methodological and substantive. It was intended to explore how qualitative research methods can be used in intercultural research. It also aimed to enhance understanding of how international migrants relate to their places of origin, places in their host country, and the new places they create. The researcher argued that by using innovative methods to gather information for inter-cultural research, a more complete understanding of the attitudes of migrants can be achieved.

Why is the question of migration experiences important for landscape architecture? Armstrong argues that the effects of migration are inscribed on the landscape. Globalization and migration have changed attitudes toward design process and designed landscapes around the world. By understanding how these shifts in attitude function, the researcher reasoned, designers can better understand how to work with the meaning of places for different constituencies.

The strategy adopted was an interpretive "hermeneutic" investigation focused upon the experience of Greek, Lebanese, and Vietnamese migrants to Australia. Members of each ethnic group were interviewed in focus groups. Transcripts of the discussions were recorded, coded, and analyzed to identify what were characterized as "horizontal" and "vertical" journeys. Horizontal journeys were comparative studies that identified broad thematic experiences across migrant groups, while vertical journeys were in-depth interpretations, explorations, and reflections upon the experiences of one of the migrant groups. These were characterized as migrant "voices." In the final phase of research, distinctive metaphors and tropes of migration were identified, and the role of subjects within the research team was explored.

The study is valuable as an example of an interpretive strategy for three reasons. First, it illustrates the importance of developing empathy with, and respect for, research subjects. Second, the research deploys qualitative methods effectively to construct an overall account of a social phenomenon that would be elusive if approached with more rigid techniques. Third, the strategy shows the researcher as an active agent in the interpretation of the meanings of migration through a reflexive process of listening, analyzing, reflecting, and listening again.

The Meeting Sequence
Meeting One: Understanding Heritage Concepts
Meeting Two: Mapping Lebanese Places in Australia
Meeting Three: Heritage as Cultural Practice and Living Traditions
Meeting Four: Interpreting Heritage Significance of Lebanese Places in Australia

Figure 9.3 Discussion sequence in focus groups on migration

(Reprinted from Armstrong 2004. Used with permission from the publisher, Taylor and Francis. Copyright 2004.)

Notes on Method 9.4: Cross-cultural Research

Many cities are now multicultural, and ever increasingly so, with a wide diversity of ethnicity, each with differing sensitivities, particularly if associated with new immigrant populations. In postcolonial countries there will frequently be cross-cultural relationships and reciprocal obligations with indigenous cultures. In some these are recognized in formal treaties and implemented through a range of public statutes as well as within organizational missions. Increasingly, landscape architecture researchers may also be working in countries that are not their own and must recognize the different cultural mores of the communities in which they are working.

Cross-cultural issues may be related to the manner of interaction between people and communities, and there are likely to be either formal or informal protocols about how to make contact with communities and who to contact. Even basic landscape description using secondary sources can involve the need to consider how to engage with culturally sensitive information. In New Zealand, for example, local planning authorities now typically use a system called "silent files" to identify the general vicinity of sites that are regarded as sacred by the indigenous people (Maori), such as traditional burial sites, without revealing their exact location in the public realm. This means planners and designers are alerted to potential sensitivities that need more formal engagement with the communities concerned.

Example 9.2:
Landscape Change in the Multifunctional Countryside

(Bohnet, Potter, and Simmons 2003)

The context for this study of farmers working in the English High Weald (an area south of London) was the debate over the future of agricultural policy in Europe. Much of the debate revolved around how best to reconcile the need to reduce production subsidies, in order to comply with the global open-market agenda promoted by the World Trade Organization, while at the same time ensuring the viability of the family farming tradition that has historically maintained the identity and values of the European countryside.

This study investigated the changing nature of farming families in an area of high conservation and landscape value, where traditional farming is largely uneconomic. It probed how farming families have responded to the changing policy and economic context, and contrasted their attitudes and beliefs with those of the growing number of newcomers who are taking over as occupiers of farmland, but not necessarily as full-time farmers.

The study uses an interpretive strategy based upon life histories. The research design involved interviews with twenty-one occupiers selected to provide a wide cross-section of experiences. The interviews were guided by several themes, but were open ended in

9.3 Discourse Analysis

The examples used to illustrate ethnography used biographic methods—stories told by people about their lives—in order to better understand a larger dynamic affecting a community and its landscape. In order to understand these stories, the outcomes of the interviews and focus groups were transcribed into a linear text and analyzed using different techniques; the results were then interpreted within the wider context of the research. Discourse analysis (Potter and Wetherell 1994; Potter 2004; Paltridge 2007) is focused upon interpreting the ways that meaning is expressed through words and text. Its purpose is to seek out and better understanding the content and meaning of *discourses* within a community or in some wider part of society. That is, it looks at "patterns of language across text as well as the social and cultural context in which they occur" (Paltridge 2007, 1).

Discourse analysis starts from the premise that our knowledge and experience of landscape and landscape practice is "constructed" by the way we talk and write about it (Greider and Gardovitch 1994). From this it follows that there are distinctive patterns of discourse—that is, different ways of talking and writing (fig. 9.4). There are also different fields of discourse—sets of interrelated ways of talking and writing (such as those within the discipline of landscape architecture itself). If the patterns and fields can be identified and better understood, it is argued, they can provide insight into many of the practical issues we face, as well as into the assumptions and values that shape our responses.

format. The respondents were encouraged to tell their own story. The conversations were recorded and were later analyzed with textual analysis software to identify distinctive patterns within these narratives.

The analysis revealed some significant differences between the old families and the newcomers, but there were also differences between age cohorts of the established farmers. It highlighted how closely the history of landscape change is linked to the personal histories of those managing the land. The dynamics of change were complex, sensitive to location, and also cumulative, with actions and events resonating through successive periods. The researchers concluded that future management of this valued landscape remains problematic and would require locally specific responses.

The study shows how an interpretive strategy using a limited number of respondents can provide insight upon a global scale policy debate, and can highlight the intimate connection between landscape practices and the condition and future of the material landscape.

It should provide encouragement for landscape planners and managers to engage with land occupiers in understanding landscape change and offer a way to do this that is both fruitful and well grounded in a local landscape. This example shows how the research design (a purposive sample of key informants), the research method (ethnography, using life histories), and techniques (depth interviews) were combined to advance an interpretive research strategy.

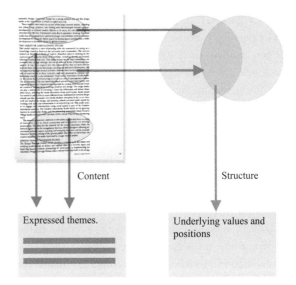

Content

Structure

Expressed themes.

Underlying values and positions

Figure 9.4 Discourse analysis

Figure 9.5 Example of literature used for discourse analysis

(Courtesy of the U.S. Forest Service, Southern Research Station)

Discourse analysis can be approached from an instrumental perspective—with a focus upon analyzing the content of a given text or texts and identification of the dominant narratives they contain. Alternatively, it can adopt a more critical perspective, seeking to reveal hidden and often "'out of sight' values, positions, and perspectives" (Paltridge 2007, 178), particularly those related to the power structures in society.

Two types of discourse analysis are particularly relevant to landscape architecture— the analysis of direct accounts (for example, depth interviews) and the analysis of secondary sources (for example, written texts in the discipline). A good recent example of the use of discourse analysis of direct accounts obtained through depth interviews is Thompson's (2000) investigation into the values that are held by landscape architects and that shape their practice (Example 9.3).

Discourse analysis can also be used to investigate the narratives about landscape that are embedded in written accounts, such as management documents (fig. 9.5).

Example 9.3:
Aesthetic, Social and Ecological Values in Landscape Architecture: A Discourse Analysis
(Thompson 2000)

This investigation is part of a larger project intended to better understand the values that underpin landscape architectural practice in the United Kingdom. The author had previously identified three broad sets of values within the literature of the profession, relating to aesthetic, social, and environmental concerns. This part of the research sought to validate this classification by analyzing the ethics and aesthetic values of practicing mid- to late-career landscape architects.

The method adopted was discourse analysis. The research design involved a purposive sample of twenty-six key informants, and the investigative technique used was the depth interview. The interviews were recorded, transcribed, and analyzed using the software tool NUDIST (Nonnumerical, Unstructured Data-Indexing, Searching, and Theory-building), which enabled the investigator to understand values held by practitioners and how strongly they were held.

The author concluded that almost all of the values identified from the interviews fell within the three fields of discourse that had been previously identified. In addition, eight major discourses and two minor ones could be identified within the three broad fields— including discourses of conservation, improvement, accommodation (of diverse social needs), artistic expression, and landscape health and integrity. The most prevalent values identified are those associated with "technocentric accommodation."

An interesting feature of this interpretive research strategy is the way it explicitly combines both inductive and deductive phases. The interview transcripts were analyzed inductively, with the investigator seeking emerging patterns of discourse. The grounded constructs were then compared against the trivalent framework of values already developed from existing theories of the discipline.

Example 9.4:
Which Nature? A Case Study
of Whitetop Mountain
(Robertson and Hull 2001)

The context for the research is that controversies about the management of natural areas appear to express a long-standing, but largely unspoken, debate about what is "natural," what counts as environmental quality, and what should be the goals of management. The researchers recognised that "naturalness" can be used to express different values and to explain many different conditions. Environmental managers therefore have to decide "which" and "whose" nature is being protected.

The interpretive strategy used discourse analysis of written reports. The research design was a case study of accounts relating to Whitetop Mountain in southern Virginia. It had three goals: first, to illustrate how different understandings of nature influence what is considered to be natural; second, to show that environmental quality is defined differently within each of these different understandings of nature and naturalness, and third, to consider the implications of alternative understandings of nature and naturalness for the design, planning, and management of natural landscapes.

The case study drew upon multiple sources of information from popular, professional, and scientific descriptions. The analysis was qualitative and relied upon the researchers' direct interpretations of the readings (compared with the use of software in the previous example).

Four initial understandings of nature were identified in the literature: ecotourism, romanticism, pastoralism, and ecologism. Bioculturalism was proposed as a fifth discourse following the analysis. Together, they provided a broad understanding of the nature of nature in this area.

This example demonstrates the way that existing literature and management documents could be used as the basis for an analysis that enhanced understanding of a continuing management problem. The discursive method enabled the researchers to raise the debate above the conflict over practical outcomes, to achieve a better overall understanding of differing values being sought by stakeholders.

Robertson and Hull 2001 (Example 9.4) investigated the way that different ideas of nature are expressed within literature about a distinctive mountain in the eastern United States, in order to better understand management issues and conflicts.

9.4 Iconology and Iconography

As a design discipline, landscape architecture is fundamentally engaged with various types of graphic representation. As Corner (1999) has argued, much of the special potential of landscape comes from its eidetic quality—its ability to evoke strong feelings through images. *Iconology* is the theoretically informed study of meaningful signs and symbols. *Iconography* is its analytical method. Like the discursive strategies discussed in the previous section, iconology/iconography involve active interpretation of meanings embedded in phenomena, in this case, graphic representations. One of the pioneers of iconography, Erwin Panofsky, distinguished between two possible approaches—a "narrower" sense that places most emphasis upon the systematic analysis of consciously made signs and symbols in a search for their intended meaning, and a "deeper," more theoretically driven interpretation of their broader social and cultural meanings and significance (Cosgrove and Daniels 1988). That deeper, theoretically driven interpretation is iconology.

Two examples reflect this distinction. Example 9.5 (Larsen and Swanbrow 2006) emphasizes the use of systematic content analysis of a large sample of images (picture postcards). The strategy was shaped around the testing of a formal proposition concerning the historical role of promotional images in urban development. The second example (Bowring 2002) places greater emphasis upon the theoretically informed interpretation of a smaller selection of images, and is aimed at identifying different cultural myths of national identity (Example 9.6).

9.5 Historiography

A review of research topics published in *Landscape Journal* (Powers and Walker 2009) identified archival research as one of the most common approaches to research published by North American landscape architecture researchers. Historiography is the interpretation of the historical record of human actions and events, and this record's representation as a recognizable narrative. The sources of data may be published writings, archived documents, other forms of written or graphic evidence (diaries, newspapers, photos, maps) and other types of ephemeral or artifactual evidence such as posters, receipts, account books, and the like. The distinguishing features are, first, the emphasis upon an evidential base, and, second, the active construction of a coherent account that is grounded in concrete evidence and relies for its structure and tone upon interpretation and inference by the researcher.

As with descriptive landscape research strategies, historical accounts can be organized in a number of ways in landscape architectural research. They can focus upon a place, a project, a wider landscape, a journey, an influential person, an institution, or type of event. All are valid ways to organize an historical interpretation of the available data, depending upon the purpose of the investigation.

Example 9.7 summarizes a landscape-based historical narrative, which uses the metaphor of landscape biography (Roymans et al. 2009). It provides an example of an interpretive research strategy used to trace and understand the socioeconomic and institutional dynamics of landscape change (see fig. 9.8).

Example 9.8 (Hohmann 2006) presents another historiography, but one focused on personal history rather than on place history. Similar to the earlier examples, it is strategically placed within a wider theoretical and disciplinary context. It examines the life and work of Theodora Kimball Hubbard, with a focus upon her role in the intellectual history of landscape architecture. The theoretical perspective adopted in this interpretation is "gendered" history, which is described by the researcher as a category of historical

Example 9.5:
Postcards of Phoenix: Images of Desert Ambivalence and Homogeneity
(Larsen and Swanbrow 2006)

This research is focused upon improving understanding of the twentieth-century growth of the Sunbelt urban areas in the southwestern United States. Images of the city of Phoenix shown in postcards appear to have been selected in order to market the city to potential investors and visitors. Phoenix is located deep in the Arizona desert, yet, over time, postcard images of its landscape have changed. Given the historical context of American urban development trends, the researchers presumed that, prior to World War II, the content of the postcard images would emphasize "Midwestern"-style cityscapes and landscapes, while after World War II they would feature lush vegetation and resort scenes, reflecting a shift in the socioeconomic drivers of development and the availability of residential air-conditioning.

The research method was iconographic content analysis. The research design used an opportune sample of postcards from a public collection of images ranging in date from 1901 to 1978 (at which time the company printing the postcards closed operations). Content-analysis techniques were used to determine the quantities of different landscape elements present in 357 postcards of the city over time. Special attention was paid to comparing pre– and post–World War II images. These differences were used to test the initial presumption concerning changes in content (see fig. 9.6).

The categories for the content analysis were derived from a review of the city's history and included both specific landscape elements and spatial configurations. The categories were pilot tested on a selection of ten postcards, after which the content list was revised. Two researchers coded the images independently. The codes were entered into SPSS software and subjected to basic statistical analysis.

The main conclusions were that, as predicted by the initial presumption, the images found on postcards of Phoenix changed in emphasis over time. However, in order for the purveyors of the images to project their intended message, they neglected important historical and cultural characteristics of the area. Native American and Mexican influences on the culture of the place, as well as water and agricultural images and transportation infrastructure, all critical for the development of Phoenix, were absent from the images. As a result, the postcards illustrate a marked disconnection between the reality of Phoenix's desert landscape and the way the city was marketed. The researchers conclude that the content of the postcards was driven more by the interests of urban development than by any intrinsic character of the city.

This study illustrates the use of content-analysis techniques as part of an iconographic method. It shows how an interpretive research strategy can be given structure by the establishment of an opening presumption or speculative proposition that can be systematically examined, but, nonetheless, remains interpretive in its overall character and approach.

	1945 and Earlier	1946 and after
Number of Images	(220)	(147)
Dominant Vegetation Type		
Non-native	51% (114)	78% (112)
Native	19% (42)	10% (15)
No vegetation	30% (67)	12% (17)
Dominant Ground Cover		
Pavement	54% (115)	48% (66)
Lawn	24% (51)	38% (52)
Desert Pan	22% (48)	14% (19)
Palm Tree Present	31% (68)	64% (92)
Saguaro Cactus Present	9% (19)	15% (22)
Dominant Water Feature	9% (19)	15% (22)
Mountain Background	24% (54)	49% (70)

Figure 9.6 Analysis of the content of postcards

(Extract from Larsen and Swanbrow 2006. Reproduced by permission of the University of Wisconsin Press. Copyright 2006 by the Board of Regents of the University of Wisconsin System.)

Example 9.6:
Reading the Phone Book: Cultural Landscape Myths in Public Art
(Bowring 2002)

This research investigated regional and urban identities of New Zealand. As a post-colonial nation with both bicultural (Maori-British) and multicultural dynamics, New Zealand has a complex and evolving sense of national identity. This identity is widely used in promoting the major economic sectors of tourism and food export. Landscape imagery and experience is a central feature, but it is frequently taken for granted. By investigating a nationwide source of cultural commentary on perceptions of regional identity, the study aimed to critique the relationship between culture, landscape, and representation.

The interpretive research strategy deployed iconographic methods and an opportunistic sample in its research design. It was based upon an analysis of the winning entries in regional competitions for the covers of telephone directories that have been held throughout the country for the last ten years. These competitions include work by both professional and amateur artists, creating a body of popular art representing regional identities. Seventeen covers were analyzed.

The theoretical foundation was Roland Barthes' concepts of connotation and denotation and the idea of cultural myth, which were made operational through an "L-diagram" that linked denotation, representation, and connotation into a logical format. Using the diagram (fig. 9.7), the telephone book covers were analyzed to identify four broad myths of identity: "landscape as identity," "everything is beautiful," an "unpopulated paradise," and "New Zealand as Arcadia." The revealed myths were so pervasive that they appeared to override other aspects of regional and national culture. The author argued that the competition mirrored society's values and at the same time "projects the ideals," due to the high public profile of the book covers.

The research is a valuable example for several reasons. It provides a clear account of an explicitly interpretive strategy applied to everyday icons that are rich in meaning. The researcher acknowledges the ability of readers to contribute their judgment to the topic, highlighting the point that there is no single "correct" reading of the icons and that meaning must be constructed through thoughtful engagement. The development of the diagrams provides a good example of the way that interpretation needs to be informed by theoretical concepts that can be practically applied.

Denotation: this is the landscape we live in	
Representation: beautiful, unflawed images of landscape	**Connotation**: this is the landscape we want to live in

Figure 9.7. The L diagram: A theoretical tool for analysis of images

(Reprinted from Bowring 2002. Used with permission from the publisher, Taylor and Francis. Copyright 2002.)

Example 9.7:
Landscape Biography
(Roymans et al. 2009)

The context for this research is the rapid urbanization of rural areas of the Netherlands and the need to better understand the relationships between spatial transformation of the landscape, social and economic dynamics, and landscape identity. The study synthesized multidisciplinary investigations of an area study in southern Netherlands. It aimed to develop landscape biography as a research strategy, elaborate the history of the study area, and explore applications to heritage management, landscape design, and spatial planning. Landscape biography is increasingly used in Europe and has received impetus from the adoption of the European Landscape Convention.

The theoretical basis for landscape biography draws upon geography, social anthropology, and archaeology, and places emphasis upon the role of landscape in the construction of community and cultural identity. The biography presented in this research highlighted three periods of critical transformation in the heathland landscapes of the region—the shifting farmsteads but stable burial grounds of the prehistoric era from 700 to 400 BC, the influence of Christianity in the High Middle Ages, and the agricultural reclamation of heathland from the mid-nineteenth century.

The research draws upon a range of data sources and presented the results as a subregional biography on an interactive Web site in order to engage designers and planners, as well as through a participatory planning process. The aim was to highlight landscape as a long-term story that is a layered palimpsest, which provides the basis for sustainable spatial transformations of landscape into the future.

This example of landscape biography emphasizes the way that interpretive research can create opportunity for creative future transformation of landscapes based upon an understanding of their transformations in the past. The research design was based upon an area case study and used a range of methods and techniques within an historiographic interpretive strategy.

analysis that seeks to place the work of men and women in the wider context of politics and power.

The final example (Example 9.9) in this chapter is a hybrid of a biography and a project narrative, investigating the way that a particular project—The Edinburgh Zoo—expressed the analytical and pedagogical thinking of the Scottish planner Patrick Geddes (Ward Thompson 2006).

Interpretive Strategies: Summary

Interpretive strategies are well suited to:

- investigating landscape issues that involve communities or social interrelationships
- making sense of the way people represent, write, or talk about landscape and the values they express

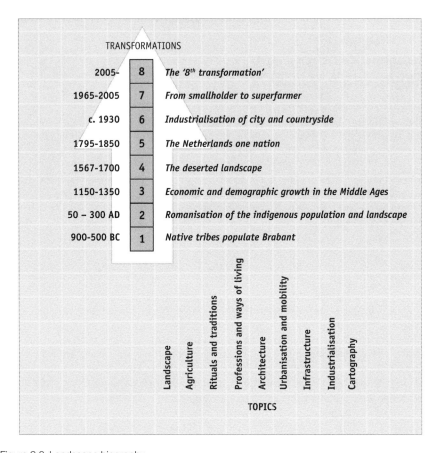

TRANSFORMATIONS

2005-	8	The '8ᵗʰ transformation'
1965-2005	7	From smallholder to superfarmer
c. 1930	6	Industrialisation of city and countryside
1795-1850	5	The Netherlands one nation
1567-1700	4	The deserted landscape
1150-1350	3	Economic and demographic growth in the Middle Ages
50 – 300 AD	2	Romanisation of the indigenous population and landscape
900-500 BC	1	Native tribes populate Brabant

Landscape · Agriculture · Rituals and traditions · Professions and ways of living · Architecture · Urbanisation and mobility · Infrastructure · Industrialisation · Cartography

TOPICS

Figure 9.8 Landscape biography

(Reprinted from Roymans et al. 2009. Used with permission from the publisher, Taylor and Francis. Copyright 2009.)

Example 9.8:
Theodora Kimball Hubbard
(Hohmann 2006)

The aim of the research was to extend the understanding of the role of women in landscape architecture beyond the conventional feminist "herstory" to a wider, more complete understanding of the construction of landscape architectural history. Its focus is the life and work of Theodora Kimball Hubbard, who began her career as the librarian to Harvard University's Department of Landscape Architecture and she developed a subsequent career as writer, editor, and critic.

The strategy was interpretive historiography. The research design used a range of sources—the subject's own published writings, other authors' accounts, and extensive archival material, including personal letters, diaries, and institutional records. The story

Example 9.9:
Patrick Geddes and the Edinburgh Zoological Garden

(Ward Thompson 2006)

Patrick Geddes was a landscape architect and planner practicing at the beginning of the twentieth century who is credited with introducing the concept of "region" to town planning. One of the few designs ever completed by Geddes and brought to fruition in the United Kingdom was the Edinburgh Zoo. It illustrates the analytical technique known as "the valley section" that he developed in order to understand the relationship between people and their environments during the course of a region's development.

This research aimed to answer how and what Geddes had contributed to the development of design and planning theory and to assess its contemporary relevance in promoting "joined-up thinking" at the landscape scale.

The strategy was an interpretive historiography that took the form of an historical account of Geddes's life, showing how his experiences and philosophy of education shaped his understanding of urban planning and people's interaction with the landscape. This relationship was then investigated and expanded vis-à-vis analysis of primary and secondary sources concerning the development of Edinburgh Zoo.

The value of this example is to illustrate how historiography can be used to better reveal and explain the emergence of important concepts in the discipline. It shows how situated knowledge and particular designs can be interpreted and related to more universal issues and processes.

of Kimball's work is constructed carefully from this material, with significant events and developments referenced, and the researcher's interpretations are supported by extracts. Basic numerical data is included—for example, numbers of library acquisitions during the subject's tenure—and extracts from archives were used to illustrate Kimball's work on classification, editing, and writing.

The researcher concluded by arguing that the account of Kimball Hubbard's life and work makes a number of contributions: It forces an expansion of understanding of landscape architectural history and of the experiences of women. It requires a reconsideration of the way in which landscape architectural history is written and who it credits, and it highlights the historical role of research and scholarship alongside that of design.

The example provides a model for the way in which detailed archival research and development of an historical biography can make a wider contribution to the knowledge and understanding of the discipline through the insights it offers into our intellectual and social formation. The interpretive strategy used a wide range of opportunistic sources and constructed a theoretically informed narrative.

- investigating situations where the historical evidence is incomplete, fragmented, or contested

- undertaking research where the relationships between evidence and theoretical understandings are not well understood

- opening up lines of inquiry that have previously been overlooked

As a strategy that lies between objectivist and subjectivist orientations, and typically includes elements of both inductive and deductive theorizing, interpretation is a diverse, hybrid category. These examples show a range of ways of designing and implementing interpretive research. Common to all, however, is the fact that the researcher is actively engaged in making sense of evidence within a social and cultural context.

References

Armstrong, H. 2004. Making the unfamiliar familiar: Research journeys towards understanding migration and place. *Landscape Research* 29 (3): 237–60.

Bertaux, D. 1981. *Biography and society: The life history approach in the social sciences.* London: Sage.

Bohnet, I., C. Potter, and E. Simmons. 2003. Landscape change in the multifunctional countryside: A biographical analysis of farmer decision making in the English High Weald. *Landscape Research* 28 (4): 349–64.

Bowring, J. 2002. Reading the phone book: Cultural landscape myths in public art. *Landscape Research* 27 (4): 343–58.

Corner, J. 1999. *Recovering landscape: Essays in contemporary landscape architecture.* New York: Princeton Architectural Press.

Cosgrove, D., and S. Daniels, eds. 1988. *The iconography of landscape: Essays on the symbolic representation, design and use of past environments.* New York: Cambridge University Press.

Greider, T., and L. Gardovich. 1994. Landscapes: The social construction of nature and the environment. *Rural Sociology* 59 (1): 1–24.

Hamilton, P., ed. 1991. *Max Weber: Critical asessments.* London: Routledge.

Hohmann, H. 2006. Theodora Kimball Hubbard and the "intellectualization" of landscape architecture, 1911–1935. *Landscape Journal* 25 (2): 169–86.

Jorgensen, D. L. 1989. *Participant observation: A methodology for human studies.* Thousand Oaks, CA: Sage.

Larsen, L., and L. Swanbrow. 2006. Postcards of Phoenix: Images of desert ambivalence and homogeneity. *Landscape Journal* 25 (2): 205–16.

Lukes, S. 1973. On the social determination of truth. In *Modes of thought: Essays in thinking in western and nonwestern societies,* ed. R. Horton and R. Finnegan, 138–153. London: Faber and Faber.

Paltridge, B. 2007. *Discourse analysis: An introduction.* London: Continuum.

Potter, J. 2004. Discourse analysis. In *A handbook of data analysis,* ed. M. Hardy and A. Bryman, 607–24. London: Sage.

Potter, J., and M. Wetherell. 1994. Analysing discourse. In *Analysing qualitative data,* ed. A. Bryman and R. G. Burgess, 47–66. London: Routledge.

Powers, M. N., and J. B. Walker. 2009. Twenty-five years of *Landscape Journal*: An analysis of authorship and article content. *Landscape Journal* 28 (1): 96–110.

Robertson, D., and R. Hull. 2001. Which nature? A case study of Whitetop Mountain. *Landscape Journal* 20 (2): 176–85.

Roymans, N., F. Gerritsen, C. Van der Heijden, K. Bosma, and J. Kolen. 2009. Landscape biography as research strategy: The case of the south Netherlands project. *Landscape Research* 34 (3): 337–59.

Silverman, D. 2005. *Doing qualitative research: A practical handbook.* 2nd ed. London: Sage.

Thompson, I. 2000. Aesthetic, social, and ecological values in landscape architecture: A discourse analysis. *Ethics, Place and Environment* 3 (30): 269–87.

UIUC Institutional Review Board for the Protection of Human Subjects. 2010. *Investigator Handbook.* Web training module. University of Illinois at Urbana-Champaign. http://irb.illinois.edu/?q=investigator-handbook/index.html (accessed March 2010).

Ward Thompson, C. 2006. Patrick Geddes and the Edinburgh Zoological Garden: Expressing universal processes through local place. *Landscape Journal* 25 (1): 80–93.

CHAPTER 10

Evaluation and Diagnosis

10.1 Introduction

Evaluation is one of the most widely used and productive groups of research strategies in environmental design. Humans live in a constantly changing social and physical environment and must continuously evaluate and reevaluate its condition and performance against human needs and values. Examples of evaluation abound in our everyday lives. Is it time to paint the house? Should we try a shade lighter this time? Would there be any long-term benefit to buying higher-priced paint? In landscape architecture, evaluation may be used critically to rank specific designs or to award commissions to design practitioners. It might also measure success or failure of public investment in community programs, to justify new water collection systems, or to advocate for change in the way that open space is configured and furnished.

Evaluation always involves a process of discrimination and comparison between alternatives. Comparison (which of these things is not like the other?) and the discernment of difference are also active components in classification. However, there is a crucial difference. In evaluation, a comparison is made between a real phenomenon or practice and an ideal or abstract condition—a perfect pitch, a balanced sweetness in wine, or a slope of less than 10 percent. Thus, evaluations are typically used to measure current conditions or outcomes (of an action, form, program, or practice) against a predetermined standard.

Evaluation research differs from description and classification in its relationship to theory. Rather than theory emerging inductively or reflexively from research activity, in evaluation research theory is already accepted and embedded within the normative/critical standards or parameters used for measurement. We have, therefore, placed evaluation in the deductive column of the classification matrix. We have placed it in the constructivist row, together with classification and interpretive strategies, because even when taking "objective" measurements of natural phenomena, evaluation applies values that are always situational and socially constructed.

There is a fine line between evaluation strategies and related scholarly practices that employ informed judgment, such as connoisseurship or critique. Peer review is a form of informed critique, a rigorous, qualitative evaluation. Is it considered evaluation research? Not at all. Evaluations, appraisals, or judgments may indeed be important forms of scholarly practice, but if they simply exercise a received standard, they do not contribute to new knowledge. For evaluation to be considered a strategy for research, *some form of normative theory must be tested and/or constructed.* Evaluation involves judgment that is both theoretically informed (like critique) and, more important, extends our understanding of that theory.

In this chapter we examine a range of examples of research strategies associated with the process of evaluation. First, we consider the development of parameters, norms, and rubrics by which the values of an evaluation are formalized. Next, we consider design evaluation, especially the role of case studies and postoccupancy evaluation. The section following that deals with various forms of diagnostic evaluation, such as feasibility studies. Finally, we consider the status of landscape assessment as a research strategy.

10.2 Parameters, Norms, and Rubrics

Ultimately, evaluation research is used in order to improve decision making for best practice or policy, in which specific theories of value will reside in a relatively stable form. Evaluation strategies may be used for the purposes of normative critique and research, for diagnosis, and for valuation—such as identifying preference and other ratings. Evaluation research thus starts with some kind of rubric, or norm, that has capacity for measurement, for example, a set of guidelines, principles, or categories drawn out from a critical/theoretical position.

Typically, parameters and norms for evaluation are socially constructed and reproduced. This makes it all the more important to select and apply parameters carefully, always keeping in mind whose values or interests are privileged in any given framework for evaluation, and whose are excluded. Normative parameters are usually disciplinary and/or professional standards that help to define or legitimize a field of practice. For instance, in landscape architecture, the fundamental professional norms for evaluating any design include "health, safety, and welfare." Other parameters may be applied, of course, but health, safety, and welfare are professionally irreducible.

Social norms, on the other hand, may be understood more broadly as a set of received conventions that govern social practices such as deportment, dress, or speech. Rousseau's notion of the social contract is a theory that explains why we might conform to social norms at all—ultimately agreeing to trade the unlimited exercise of our personal liberty for even greater social benefits of order, peace, and cooperation, among other things. Lewis (1969) explains this in a slightly different way: "Social norms are customary rules of behavior that coordinate our interactions with others. Once a particular way of doing things becomes established as a rule, it continues in force because we prefer to conform to the rule given the expectation that others are going to conform."

Received ideas that undeveloped nature is "beautiful," that cultural artifacts "spoil" our view, and that there are certain behavioral expectations for nature areas are all examples of social norms. In the fields of park management, or recreation and leisure studies, normative standards for evaluating behavior under certain social/environmental conditions and in certain contexts may be defined differently for different groups in different places at different times. It may be fine to play loud music and drink beer at the beach on a Saturday afternoon, but quite unacceptable to do so in a Japanese garden in an arboretum on a Sunday morning.

Evaluation research may rely on descriptive data in order to assess, say, recreational activity and its social consequences against norms that are expressed in similar terms (such as the amount of open space available per person). However, evaluative researchers are also frequently challenged to measure and compare qualitative experiences, judgments, or emotions. This may create a tension between different styles of evaluation and the theoretical frameworks upon which they are based (Manning and Morrissey 2005).

The precise way a research question is formed and the context in which it is asked will, therefore, limit and guide the appropriate choice of evaluative research paradigm. The role of the researcher is to select appropriate evaluation dimensions or parameters, decide on the terms for comparison or measurement, and shape a particular line of analysis. Terms for evaluation may be applied to conditions that simply will not yield simple yes-or-no dichotomies. Clarifying and justifying the limitations and presumptions is thus a critical part of developing a strategy.

Standards, codes, rubrics, ranks—all have embedded theoretical assumptions built into the relationships, or choices, between values. What kind of trade-offs are implied in choosing a research strategy and in its detailed design, and why? For instance, if asked by a researcher to rank five flowers in order of preference, you would probably not be permitted to rank a rose, tulip, and lilac together at the top of the list. A classroom quiz tests students' comprehension of material provided in a lecture, but not just *any* comprehension: it measures specific categories of knowledge that have been determined in advance as the pedagogic goals for this particular class and this particular level.

An instrument that guides such evaluation is called a rubric—a set of desired or expected answers or, in the case of a more complex qualitative evaluation, an illustrative continuum of the properties of "good," "better," or "best" answers. The excerpt (below) illustrates the structure of a learning-outcomes-assessment rubric, in this case one that was developed for an introductory course in landscape architectural history. The rubric is written according to a theory of general education that presumes all students of landscape architecture should be familiar with world cultures in order to relate events and monuments within the discipline to world geopolitical history. The evaluation instrument is structured according to educational values, expressed through specific activities and criteria that were developed to measure student mastery of information and concepts. Variable levels of student mastery are, in turn, expressed as the students' grades.

General Education Learning Assessment Guidelines

Learning outcomes (general course goals)
Students will:

1. Demonstrate knowledge of the development of the distinctive features of the history (institutions, economy, society, culture, etc.) of western civilization

2. Relate the development of western civilization to that of other regions of the world both synchronically and diachronically

Course-specific objectives (directly support learning outcomes)
By the end of this course, students should be able to:

1. (a) Identify major movements in landscape architecture and (b) relate each to its cultural, intellectual, political, economic, technological, and environmental context

2. (a) Describe the main concepts of a number of designed landscapes and (b) explain the processes by which human will invested capital resources and artistic expression into making meaningful places

3. Diagram or outline a clear framework of processes, ideas, elements, periods, and geographic regions

Direct measures of student learning (in ascending order of mastery)
Preassessment and follow-up questions, question-and-answer discussions in (and after) class, image identification and objective questions on exams, written essays explaining concepts, open-ended questions to apply concepts, reasoned interpretation of unfamiliar but typical images, informed analysis and critique of monuments using historically contemporary concepts and paradigms

Assessment criteria (grading)

Level 4 (A)
Clear and confident explanation of major cultural paradigms of western history; secure comprehension of forces and conditions that brought paradigms into focus; acute awareness of complex factors impacting the historical periods; ability to make comparisons between periods

Level 3 (B)
Developing understanding of major cultural paradigms; basic comprehension of historical forces and conditions; awareness of complexity of historical cycles; basic recognition of design and cultural theories as translated into designed landscapes

Level 2 (C)
Some comprehension of major cultural paradigms; some comprehension of context of historic forces and conditions

Level 1 (F)
Flawed or incomplete comprehension of major cultural paradigms; inability to distinguish one period from another; no appreciation of context in historic forces and conditions

Rubrics are commonly used in all forms of program evaluation as well as in research. Evaluation requires the investigator to perform an analysis (an examination) that compares the phenomena under study (in this case, student performance) with a previously identified parameter in order to assess its conformity or nonconformity to the standard. Typically, rubrics and norms will have been created in an autonomous or generic study, probably using other research strategies, such as classification (chapter 8) or logical argumentation (chapter 13). However, the key feature of evaluation *research* lies in the interaction between, on the one hand, the application of such rubrics and, on the other hand, the development of new understanding about the nature of the values within the rubric and their expression in different contexts. In other words, an evaluation strategy should simultaneously apply *and* test understanding of theory.

Example 10.1 (below) describes research conducted for the refinement of a rubric for evaluating community extension initiatives (Thering 2009). It is a highly complex study that begins by identifying a weakness in the application of existing program evaluation rubrics, given specific social contexts. As Weiss (1995) has noted, many "social programs are based on explicit or implicit assumptions (theories) about how and why they will work. Thus, the evaluation of any program should identify the underlying assumptions and then

Example 10.1:
Evaluating Transdisciplinary Collaborations
with Diversity in Mind
(Thering 2009)

Extension professionals in public universities face the challenge of devising meaningful program evaluation in the context of complex community issues and, increasingly, working across the boundaries of many different professional disciplines and players. Based on a synthetic review of the literature (a research strategy described in chapter 8), this evaluation research proposes a new rubric for the purposes of assessing outreach and engagement programs that require sensitivity to community diversity.

The author compares these types of extension services, especially those facilitating complex collaborations, to paradigms in action research:

> When these collaborations iteratively identify issues, develop strategies, then implement and evaluate the effectiveness of these strategies, this approach fits the description of "action-research" . . . When these collaborations transcend not only disciplinary boundaries, but civilian and cultural boundaries as well, to include multiple agencies and a diversity of community members, this approach fits the definition of "trans-disciplinary action-research." (1)

Quantitative documentation of empirical outcomes of extension programs may seem relatively straightforward, but there are few reliable instruments for measuring less tangible claims of value added through transformative education, partnership building, trust, develop methods for data collection and analysis to track the "unfolding of the assumptions" (67, cited in Thering 2009).

10.3 Design Evaluation

Design evaluation refers to the work of considering, measuring, and judging the merit and value of a range of competing design options. "The ability to rapidly evaluate design ideas, throughout their development within the design process, is an essential element in the goal to increase design productivity," not to mention design impact, quality, and value. (Frezza et al. 1995, in Green 2000, 122).

Design evaluation is closely related to, but different from, design critique, as they differ in their relationship to theory. When based on broad but unspecified concepts, such as "taste" or connoisseurship, design critique is essentially pretheoretical or normative. Critique should, however, be informed by theory (McAvin 1991; Swaffield 2006) and can, through the articulation and application of theoretical ideas within a particular design context, raise questions about theory. However, the focus of much that is presented as critique is typically not the development of theory per se—rather, it is aimed at better understanding the project in question. On the other hand, design evaluation may be considered

and community-capacity building. Thus, a new rubric is needed that may be applied to assessing these qualitative changes and conditions. It should have specific criteria that offer cogent guidance, draw on relevant theory, and are flexible enough to be iterative and responsive as the program unfolds.

The research design is based upon a specific case study—the Green Community Development in Indian Country Initiative. The development of the proposed rubric merged two theoretical frameworks from the existing literature on program evaluation. One framing concept is community capacity. Of ten possible dimensions useful for recognizing community capacity, the author deemed that four were particularly useful in the context of diversity issues: receptivity to prudent innovations, ability to access external resources, cooperative decision-making processes among leaders and organizations, and analytical/critical reflection on assumptions underlying ideas, and actions. The second framing concept is the so-called Logic Model based on the *Theories of Change Approach* from an Aspen Institute symposium (Weiss 1995). From this the author and her associates developed a more articulated rubric that suggests specific measures for evaluating three different phases, or levels, of overcoming obstacles to diversity.

This is a particularly complex investigation. The main research question clearly seeks to develop a better rubric for evaluating community-based initiatives. It begins with classification (a review of what is currently known and practiced) and then selects and refines specific theoretical elements (community capacity theory) within an improved rubric that is grounded in a "real-world" application (the case study). The study highlights the degree to which theories of teaching and assessment can prove useful in evaluating the effectiveness of community-based programs. The relevance of this study for landscape architects is to increase awareness and sensitivity to community responses to the provision of "expert" services by outsiders or where there may be social barriers to forming a trustful or respectful relationship.

research when it *both* applies a theory embedded in measurable criteria or standards (i.e., a rubric) *and* generates new knowledge about a situation or phenomenon. Having said that, there is a growing volume of what we might term critical design evaluation that is presented as critique.

As we have already seen, a case study is defined as a method for comprehensive learning based on extensive, "thick" description of a "complex instance," taken in context and as a whole. Indeed, to produce a case study one must first collect rich data (about a place, process, or practice) and document its particular details according to a specific organization. Now, if knowing about one case study is good, it becomes even more valuable with multiple cases or with one case that has developed over time. When multiple "instances" of similar events or places are available, it becomes possible to perform more complex analyses or compare multiple cases—in other words, to query the data in more interesting ways.

For instance, a case study may be evaluated over time according to the original values and standards of the site, program, or user. Has the design performed as the designer promised or the client expected? Has satisfaction among users of this space increased because of design decisions or practices? Has the value of the property investment remained steady or increased? Was the basic framework for this design expanded, copied, or adapted elsewhere?

Two basic types of evaluation research with case studies can be performed, but only if and when baseline site, program, or user values and standards can be measured and compared. Comparative (or synchronic) case studies examine multiple instances of similar types. For example, one might compare the cost of construction for high density, neotraditional housing schemes in Florida with those in New York or Tennessee. Evolutionary or longitudinal (diachronic) case studies examine change over time within a single case study that has already been clearly documented at a baseline level. These terms are also used in social research, where longitudinal refers to a long-term study of a single group of people.

Postoccupancy evaluation (POE) is a type of case-study evaluation in landscape architecture and planning that would benefit from more frequent use. However, a meaningful POE cannot be produced unless specific standards or criteria are available for comparison. This suggests that as early as possible in the life cycle of a project (perhaps even before design and construction takes place), baseline data should be collected and repeated at significant intervals. Ideally, these data should be compared with a set of purposeful standards and norms accepted (by designers, clients, or both) as goals for the project. Unfortunately, because most designers do not imagine the eventual research uses of design projects, many of the necessary benchmarks for a POE (predesign and post design data collection, as well as design process and construction) often go unrecorded in any rigorous or comprehensive way.

Groat and Wang (2002) cite Preiser et al. (1988) in grouping the methods and procedures of POE into three levels of increasing complexity:

An *indicative* POE is one that analyzes as-built drawings, indexing them to such factors as safety and security records. It conducts interviews of building occupants with a view toward understanding the performance of the building. An *investigative* POE goes one step further by comparing an existing situation with comparable facilities, as well as with a summary of what the current literature prescribes. Both lead to more focused recommendations for consideration and change. A *diagnostic* POE involves multimethod tactics (surveys, observations, physical measurements, etc.) all conducted in comparison to other "state of the art" facilities.

The following example (Francis 2002) revisits an example of a larger, longitudinal case study that has already been featured in chapter 5 as an example of a case-study template. However, the case study also had two postoccupancy evaluations embedded within it, including a diagnostic POE using multimethod techniques. This aspect is highlighted in Example 10.2.

The data for these POE were collected after ten and fourteen years (respectively) in the life cycle of the project, Village Homes of Davis, California. At the time of this writing, however, it has been thirty-three years since the project was initiated. A more current POE might better reveal how well the initial design concepts concerning space, program, and sociality are faring. A new evaluation, for example, might be able to query the baseline and longitudinal data to find out about other dimensions of this place that respond to contemporary issues that the original designers may never have anticipated: for example, the impact of telecommuting on measures of sustainability, how social networking sites have impacted face-to-face social activities, or whether food-production patterns have been maintained as the demographic composition of the neighborhood has shifted.

10.4 Diagnostics

Diagnostic studies are a useful form of evaluation frequently utilized by landscape architects and planners working in professional and government offices. They include feasibility studies (evaluating the carrying capacity of a site for a certain program), suitability studies (evaluating the optimization of a site for a particular program), environmental-impact analysis (evaluating the environmental trade-offs between specific interventions or even different levels of development), and cost-benefit analyses (financial trade-offs of different programs or designs).

Can such diagnostics be engaged as a form of research? It depends. While the methods used for performing site and programmatic diagnostics may be rigorous, the main determinant for its status as research is what motivates the study and how it contributes to the discipline. If a diagnostic study is undertaken solely to perform a professional service for a client, it is probably not research; if diagnostics are developed for onetime use on a unique site for a specific program, it is also probably not research. However, if a diagnostic study develops new procedures and understandings that extend the systematic knowledge

Example 10.2:
Village Homes: A Case Study in Community Design
(Francis 2002)

Although the innovative and popular planned community of Village Homes in Davis, California, has been studied by many, literature about it was scattered and inaccessible. A case study was prepared (see chapter 5, "Descriptive Strategies") that collected much of the relevant data together in a single report. Data reported in this case study included two separate postoccupancy evaluations (POE) performed by students.

The first was undertaken in late 1988 and early 1989 (when the project was about ten years old), as part of a student's master's degree work at the Technical University of Munich (Lenz 1990). "According to Lenz, his research goals were to find out how Village Homes "functioned as a neighborhood, whether the design goals as stated by the developers were met, and whether residents were satisfied with their neighborhood" (32). In order to do this, Lenz evaluated specific qualitative factors (such as attitudes, happiness, satisfaction) and quantitative measures (such as energy used, hours spent in social activity, fruits and vegetables eaten) against an ordinary (control) neighborhood nearby and compared the results. In general, Lenz found that Village Homes residents maintained more environmentally sustainable and socially active lifestyles than their peers in other neighborhoods.

A follow-up POE was conducted a few years later by Owens (1993), as part of a university class exercise. This study confirmed many of Lenz's findings. General resident satisfaction with specific measures of physical landscape amenities and conveniences (paths, landscape appeal, etc.) was very high, except for inadequate parking. In general, the authors conclude, "this mirrors the strong sense of attachment to place felt by the residents" (34). However, it is not clear if these patterns are a result of the design of Village Homes or of the social composition of those who choose to live there.

This study provides baseline data for a community that maintains its appeal for today's issues. As a model for environmentally and socially sustainable lifestyles (local food production, energy independence, zero waste, and other paradigms), POE serves as a "reality check" for others considering similar developments for other communities around the world.

This example illustrates how postoccupancy evaluations both rely upon and contribute to case studies. It also points out the very real value of student work, since both studies were performed by university students—in geography and landscape architecture programs, respectively.

---

of the discipline, then it may well constitute research. Reference to the standards explained earlier (chapter 4) for evaluating research quality explains the difference.

For instance, using scenario projections, a feasibility study might test whether a site can accommodate a housing development of one hundred units. This is a practical evaluation undertaken for the purpose of maximizing a developer's profit. If, on the other hand, a cost-benefit analysis is undertaken to observe a new phenomena, practice, or innovation that either tests or builds theory, or results in generalizable principles that may be applied in a new way to other sites or programs, then it can claim to be research.

In *Design with Nature* (1969), McHarg explained that suitability analysis begins with an understanding of embodied landscape values: "These can be ranked—the most valuable land and the least, the most valuable water resources and the least, the most and least productive agricultural land, the richest wildlife habitats and those of no value, the areas of great or little scenic beauty, historic buildings and their absence and so on" (1969, 34). Overlay analysis, a graphic technique for discerning and assigning the scale of values, as well as the evaluation of spatial correlation and conflict among these values, has already been explained (chapter 6 on correlation and modeling). However, by linking suitability analysis with a theory of value, McHarg's approach results in the development of a kind of environmental rubric that could respond to different programs or values, or dialectical trade-offs between development and conservation, or agriculture and urbanization. Within their subtle shadings of light and dark values, these composite map transparencies "illustrated intrinsic suitabilities for land-use classifications, such as conservation, urbanization, and recreation . . . McHarg's inventory process provides one of the first examples of methodological documentation of the overlay technique" (McHarg and Steiner 1998, 203). Although these hand-drawn overlays were soon replaced by computer-generated patterns, and later by geographic information systems (GIS), the basic logic for suitability evaluation has been maintained.

The uses of value-laden suitability matrices for decision making at site and regional scales may extend to other values and purposes. The benefits of environmental goods and services can be valued in dollars; the loss of these good and services can be measured in the same way, as costs to society. The value of land development may be valued on a money scale just as other qualities (beauty, recreation, water) may be valued. The trade-offs between conflicting or correlating values may be studied in terms of benefits and costs. By comparing the present values of all environmental benefits, less those of related or supporting costs, a cost-benefit analysis may be performed in order to select the alternative that maximizes the benefits of a program. As in other forms of evaluation, a routine cost-benefit is not research, but an application of cost-benefit that extends knowledge of the process and its relationship to value may constitute research if analyzed and presented appropriately.

The following two studies present cost-benefit analyses at two different scales. Example 10.3 (Sandhu and Foster 1982) demonstrates some of the advantages of landscape sensitive planning policies; Example 10.4 (MacPherson 1990) examines the unintended costs of local water codes in the desert southwest.

As theories of sustainability have become popular among researchers, interest has also grown in favor of developing best practices based upon evidence-based design evaluations. Measurement parameters for most sustainable theories demand longitudinal evidence—high performance over time. Theories of life-cycle costs and benefits, such as carbon footprint, require baseline data and long-term monitoring to take place.

Exemplar 10.3:
Landscape Sensitive Planning: A Benefit/Cost Assessment
(Sandhu and Foster 1982)

Two agricultural economists observed that urban planners, policy makers, and developers rarely take the overall costs of development into account when calculating capital or social benefits of development policies. The term *resource value loss* comprises both landscape services lost and extra costs associated with development.

This research is focused on a demonstration study undertaken for a town in northwestern Massachusetts, United States, to calculate the resource value loss for both a conventional development pattern and a landscape-sensitive pattern.

The research was designed to find out whether the benefits of a landscape-sensitive approach (conservation of land value) would outweigh its costs (professional services or accommodation for inefficient patterns, etc.). The secondary planning objective of this study was to show how trade-offs might occur: how resource value loss might be minimized while meeting the goals for population growth. The research design uses modeling and simulation of alternative and use decisions, followed by evaluation of costs and benefits.

To complete this study, researchers applied a theoretical construct called METLAND— a computer model developed at the University of Massachusetts, Amherst. METLAND "offers a framework for increasing the economic efficiency of lands in urbanizing areas" (67). Money is a stable measure of landscape use value and/or the loss of its productivity or services if developed for another use. If monetary value were assigned to units of land, the researchers reasoned, planners could more wisely and accurately understand impacts of land-use decisions. Monetary values assigned to model components were based on a variety of economic valuation models (willingness to pay, capitalization, economic rent costs impact and value reduction supply and demand).

The research finds that METLAND "avoids losses much more effectively than its alternative" (72). The significance of this study is to provide a potentially useful tool to more accurately and swiftly evaluate potential trade-offs in planning decisions.

This classic study demonstrates a compound strategy for cost-benefit analysis, using a computer model to generate alternative conditions for measurement.

Life-cycle monitoring can represent a significant investment of time and resources. Instead of measuring actual sites and landscape practices, many evaluation research projects have been undertaken through scenario-testing, using simulations that project design via controlled plan drawings or digital representations. Example 10.5 (Girling and Kellett 2002) presents such an instance.

10.5 Landscape Assessment

Landscape assessment studies are often undertaken to aid in planning processes, in order to engage public sentiment and affirm constituency values. There is a large volume of published research on landscape assessment theory, systems, and applications,

Example 10.4:
Modeling Residential Landscape
Water and Energy Use
(McPherson 1990)

In order to conserve municipal water use for human purposes, urban areas in the American Desert Southwest have enacted local ordinances that restrict use of water for domestic landscape. However, because homeowners receive a credit for removing water-thirsty plants and because of a general lack of understanding and/or investment in desert vegetation, a current trend is to entirely remove all vegetation, replacing it with rock or inorganic mulch (*zeroscapes*).

The authors argue that these water-conservation policies have unintended environmental consequences because the lack of shade in domestic environments increases the costs of cooling energy, exacerbates the urban heat-island effect, and increases desertification and air pollution as a long-term result. The question asked is "whether what is gained in water savings from existing policies that reward zeroscapes is negated by increased cooling costs" (124).

To calculate the benefits and costs of domestic landscape paradigms, three discrete design scenarios (zeroscape, xeriscape, and mesiscape) were projected. Variables for water, shade, and energy use/loss were calculated and measured using computer models. Computer modeling was thus combined with evaluation in this study.

One important assumption made in framing this study was that costs for both water and electricity (cooling) would remain in relative stasis over time. A number of technical assumptions were made about the thermal properties and energy performance of houses, as well as domestic consumption of water per capita. Researchers pointed out limitations of the model (i.e., lack of empirical data on vegetation shade effects made it difficult to identify error in analysis or to verify simulation results).

Evaluation of the three models suggests that "projected energy-water savings for xeriscapes ranged from . . . (15 to 22 percent) in Phoenix and from . . . (8 to 15 percent) in Tucson compared with respective zeroscapes . . . The mesiscape designs were more costly than zeroscapes in all cases except one" (131). Despite potential errors in the study, the data "do indicate that xeriscape designs can be cost-effective compared with the increasingly popular zeroscapes" (133).

This finding is significant for these communities because the "one-dimensional" policies intended to conserve water may also increase energy consumption, an unintended negative consequence. Because xeriscapes will require professional services to design, install, and maintain, this study is also significant because it provides a larger financial and environmental rationale for ordering those services—"to judiciously select and locate plants to meet conservation goals" (134).

This article shows that design simulation and evaluation may be engaged for a variety of purposes, depending on underlying assumptions and parameters for measurement.

Example 10.5:
Comparing Storm Water Impacts and Costs
(Girling and Kellett 2002)

This study was designed to reveal important trade-offs between compact development and environmental protection that often must be engaged in the design of new neighborhoods. The researchers compared specific metrics of neighborhood design across three different neighborhood design scenarios for a three-hundred-acre site in Oregon. Having this knowledge could significantly influence the policies of municipalities and the implementation of designers or developers in creating or meeting performance guidelines for new development.

The three schemes modeled represent common neighborhood planning paradigms and were called *status quo, neighborhood village,* and *open space.* To evaluate the scenarios, the researchers compared performance by measuring common indicators of development, such as land-use mix, density, and street network. Indicator measures of environmental performance, such as land cover and storm-water runoff, and indicator costs of development, were also compared for each scheme.

Metrics for comparison included residential density (du/acre); land-use mix and allocation (in acres); dwelling diversity (types as percentages); circulation infrastructure (e.g., streets, alleys, and sidewalks, in acres); pervious and impervious surfaces (as percentages); types of open space (in acres); tree-canopy coverage (in acres); storm-water peak flows (as cubic feet per second) and increase over existing conditions (as a percentage); storm-water nutrient pollutant loads (in pounds per year); overall costs of infrastructure per dwelling (in dollars). These data were represented as simple side-by-side graphic comparisons. Conclusions drawn from this study were nuanced:

> Comparing neighborhood development patterns from a storm water perspective, these findings suggest that the higher densities, mixed uses, and greater vehicular and pedestrian connectivity now encouraged in Oregon and elsewhere . . . can either compete with or complement goals of water resource protection . . . To become complementary, strategic trade-offs must be made (108).

In the clarity of its structure, scope, and method, this compound study is a good model for many graduate design theses, as well as research studies commissioned from professional offices. The power of scenario generation followed by diagnostic evaluation clearly demonstrates the capacity for tight focus (in selection of parameters and measures) and flexibility at the same time.

both in the landscape architecture journals and in related disciplines such as geography and landscape ecology—too much to adequately review in part of a chapter. However, much landscape assessment is undertaken using research strategies described elsewhere in this book—for example, using various modeling, quasi-experimental, classification, or logical systems approaches. The most frequent focus of landscape-assessment studies in landscape architecture is visual landscape, or scenic-quality assessment, but increasing attention is being focused upon how to better integrate visual assessment with other dimensions of landscape—for example with ecological values (Fry et al. 2009). In this section, we highlight the use of evaluative research in relation to visual landscape assessment.

In the late 1960s and early 1970s, the field of visual assessment developed in response to public outcry against industrial forestry practices that seemed to threaten the "unspoiled" character of many federal and state wild lands. In the United States, the Bureau of Land Management (BLM) and U.S. Forest Service standards on visual quality are among the most important and oft-cited of these studies, drawing particularly on work by R. Burton Litton (1968) and his associates (Litton et al. 1974), who pioneered an evaluative system that was based on visual elements of landscape composition for forest and range lands. These classic studies have formed the analytical basis for subsequent generations of visual assessment researchers, who have developed and tested visual assessment methods for a range of regional landscape types, including sometimes smaller sites, with settlements, farms, or other cultural attributes.

Much theoretical and practical debate has focused upon the research dilemma of performing an objective measurement of an inherently subjective or emotional response to visual and sensory cues. Some have theorized that beauty is the result of "informational patterns" in landscape that engage human perceptual and cognitive capacities (Lynch 1960; Kaplan 1975; Kaplan and Kaplan 1982; Elsner and Smardon 1979; Zube, Brush, and Fabos 1975, among others). Whitmore, Cook, and Steiner (1995) explain that "according to Zube et al. (1982), there are four primary paradigms of visual assessment":

- The expert paradigm, which involves evaluation of visual quality by a trained expert incorporating knowledge from design, ecology, or resource management
- The psychophysical paradigm, which focuses on a population's preference for specific landscape qualities based primarily on physical characteristics in the landscape
- The cognitive paradigm, which emphasizes human meaning associated with landscape properties based on past experience, future expectation, and sociocultural conditioning of the observer
- The experiential paradigm, which considers landscape values based on interaction of people with the landscape

Further, these authors point out, "[v]isual perception . . . is a continuum without boundaries" (29), and so there is frequent overlap between one or more of these paradigms, both in practice and in the development of new research paradigms. The following example provides a case study in comparative visual assessment that explores the relationships between these different paradigms for evaluation.

Evaluation and Diagnosis Strategies: Summary

Evaluations are among the most important research that landscape architects can do in the environmental design fields. Evidence-based design demands increasingly rigorous

Example 10.6:
Public Involvement in Visual Assessment
(Whitmore, Cook, and Steiner 1995)

The Verde River Corridor Project (VRCP) was formed in response to citizen concern about changes to and degradation of the Verde River corridor north of Phoenix, Arizona. The challenge was to engage citizens and public officials in decision making that balanced economic activity and environmental values in a way that was meaningful and rational.

In support of VRCP, researchers from Arizona State University were commissioned to conduct a special visual assessment "to identify and evaluate the perceived scenic quality of the river corridor" from multiple social perspectives (28). They needed to learn which landscapes were considered the most and least preferred scenic reaches in order to protect/manage them and also to engage public opinion in developing a rationale and support for a larger river-management framework.

The theoretical framework used by the researchers synthesized a number of precedent studies and theories developed by other researchers in the field of visual assessment. Three parallel stages of assessment were designed: expert evaluation (rated by trained professionals using criteria from the Bureau of Land Management), public valuation (a combination of trained observers, who preselected representative views, and public review to assign scenic value), and public nomination (100 percent citizen input of both the scenic reaches and the reasons for scenic preference).

Because of the complexity of visual assessments, three-stage assessment was initially designed to be combined to average or triangulate (validate) the assignment of scenic values if possible. However, researchers found that each protocol generated slightly different results, each worthy of analysis and discussion. Expert evaluation rated 84 percent of the scenic reaches (those with no cultural modifications) as highest quality. Public valuation respondents preferred scenic reaches with visible geologic structure in combination with riparian edges (see fig. 10.1), where no cultural modifications were visible. The public nomination process seemed to "transcend visual concerns" and "reflect on the river corridor as a whole" (43).

This study is significant to landscape planning because "management decisions are often dramatically influenced by popular opinion," and "can aid in predicting certain

measurements that "prove" (or at least promise) the likelihood of adequate long-term performance and value of capital investments, especially when compared to the environmental services and other resource values that may be lost in development.

- Evaluation always involves techniques of discernment or measurement.
- Comparison is made between a real phenomenon or practice and an ideal or abstract standard.
- Theory is already assumed and embedded within the normative/critical standards or parameters used for measurement.

aspects of popular sentiment" and support (43). Also, involving citizens in visual assessment may also help empower them and raise awareness of the complexity, connections, and value of the larger landscape.

The literature review for this article explains the theoretical construct and methods very clearly. The article has implications for ways that assessment/evaluation studies may be linked to action research strategies for citizen involvement.

Figure 10.1 Example of most preferred landscape—limestone bluffs along the Verde River, Arizona
(From Whitmore, Cook, and Steiner 1995. Reproduced by permission of the University of Wisconsin Press. Copyright 1995 by the Board of Regents of the University of Wisconsin System.)

- Evaluation research is utilized in order to improve decision making for best practices or policy.

- To become research, the evaluation needs to reveal new understandings or insights about the underlying theory and its application.

Evaluation is frequently associated or compounded with other research strategies. Because any evaluation scheme already has theoretical values embedded within it, evaluation can complement, confirm, or explain patterns and phenomena that emerge inductively. For this reason, evaluation is frequently partnered with modeling, as well as with description, classification, and engaged action, all categories in the inductive category.

References

Elsner, G. H., and R. C. Smardon, eds. 1979. *Our national landscape: A conference on applied techniques for analysis and management of the visual resource—Proceedings.* United States Department of Agriculture, Forest Service. Berkeley, CA: Pacific Southwest Forest and Range Experiment Station.

Francis, M. 2002. Village Homes: A case study in community design. *Landscape Journal* 21 (1): 23–41.

Frezza, S. T., S. P. Levitan, and P. K. Chrysanthis. 1995. *Requirements-based design evaluation. Proceedings of IEEE 32nd design automation conference.* Piscataway, NJ: IEEE.

Fry, G., M. S. Tveit, A. Ode, M. D. Velarde. 2009. The ecology of visual landscapes: Exploring the conceptual common ground of visual and ecological landscape indicators. *Ecological Indicators* 9 (5): 933–47.

Girling, C., and R. Kellett. 2002. Comparing storm water impacts and costs on three neighborhood plan types. *Landscape Journal* 21 (1): 100–109.

Green, G. 2000. Towards integrated design evaluation: Validation of models. *Journal of Engineering Design* 11 (2): 121–32.

Groat, L. and D. Wang. 2002. *Architectural Research Methods.* New York: John Wiley and Sons.

Kaplan, R. 1975. Some methods and strategies in the prediction of preference. In *Landscape assessment: Values, perceptions and resources*, ed. E. H. Zube, R. O. Brush, and J. G. Fabos. Stroudsburg, PA: Dowden, Hutchinson and Ross.

Kaplan, S., and R. Kaplan, eds. 1982. *Humanscape: Environments for people.* Ann Arbor, MI: Ulrich's Books.

Lenz, T. 1990. *A postoccupancy evaluation of Village Homes, Davis, California.* Unpublished master's thesis. Munich: Technical University of Munich.

Lewis, D. 1969. *Convention: A philosophical study.* Cambridge, MA: Harvard University Press.

Litton, R. B. 1968. Forest landscape description and inventories: A basis for land planning and design. *United States Department of Agriculture, Forest Service Research paper PSW-49.* Berkeley, CA: Pacific Southwest Forest and Range Experiment Station.

Litton, R. B., R. J. Tetlow, J. Sorenson, and R. Beatty. 1974. *Water and landscape: An aesthetic overview of the role of water in the landscape.* Port Washington, NY: Water Information Center.

Lynch, K. 1960. *The image of the city.* Cambridge, MA: MIT Press.

Manning, R., and J. Morrissey. 2005. What's behind the numbers? Qualitative insights into normative research in outdoor recreation. *Leisure Sciences* 27:205–24.

McAvin, M., E. K. Meyer, J. Corner, H. Shirvani, K. Helphand, R. B. Riley, and R. Scarfo. 1991. Landscape architecture as critical inquiry. *Landscape Journal* 10 (1): 155–72.

McHarg, I. 1969. *Design with nature.* New York: Doubleday.

McHarg, I., and F. Steiner, eds. 1998. *To heal the earth: Selected writings of Ian L McHarg.* Washington, DC: Island Press.

MacPherson, E. G. 1990. Modeling residential landscape water and energy use to evaluate water conservation policies. *Landscape Journal* 9 (2): 122–34.

Owens, P. 1993. *A postoccupancy evaluation of Village Homes.* Davis CA: Center for Design Research.

Preiser, W. F. E., H. Z. Rabinowitz, and E. T. White. 1988. *Postoccupancy evaluation.* New York: Van Nostrand Reinhold.

Sandhu, H., and J. H. Foster. 1982. Landscape-sensitive planning: A benefit/cost assessment. *Landscape Journal* 1 (1): 67–75.

Swaffield, S. R. 2006. Theory and critique in landscape architecture. *Journal of Landscape Architecture* 1:22–29.

Thering, S. 2009. A methodology for evaluating transdisciplinary collaborations with diversity in mind: An example from the Green Community Development in Indian Country Initiative. *Journal of Extension* 47(3): online article #3FEA2. www.joe.org.

Weiss, C. 1995. Nothing as practical as good theory: Exploring theory-based evaluations for comprehensive community initiatives for children and families. In *New approaches to evaluating community initiatives: Concepts, methods and contexts.* ed. J. Connell, A. Kubisch, and L. Schorr, and C. Weiss. Washington, DC: Aspen Institute.

Whitmore, W., E. Cook, and F. Steiner. 1995. Public involvement in visual assessment: The Verde River Corridor Study. *Landscape Journal* 14 (1): 26–45.

Zube, E. H., R. O. Brush, and J. G. Fabos, eds. 1975. *Landscape assessment: Values, perceptions and resources.* Stroudsburg, PA: Dowden, Hutchinson and Ross.

Zube, E. H., J. L. Sell, and J. G. Taylor. 1982. Landscape perception: Research, application and theory. *Landscape Planning* 9:1–33.

CHAPTER 11

Engaged Action Research

11.1 Introduction

Action research produces new knowledge based on processes of direct engagement, cognition, and social change. Its motives are simultaneously *pragmatic* and *emancipatory*. As such, action research is one of the newest and most controversial of research strategies. Indeed, it is in some ways the essential postmodern research strategy, in that the subjectivity of all experience, including the experiences of learning and knowing, is accepted and acknowledged. Accordingly, we have placed this strategy in the subjectivist row and the inductive column of the classification matrix. Not only does engaged action deal with methods and theories that are still emergent, but also with emergence itself as a phenomenon under investigation.

The paradigm of action research was initiated by Kurt Lewin's work at the Massachusetts Institute of Technology's Center for Group Dynamics "translating psychological research into community problem-solving strategies. Implicit in Lewin's formulation is the importance of achieving effective collaboration among behavioral researchers, community members, and policy makers" (Stokols 2006, 63). Lewin defines action research as "comparative research on the conditions and effects of various forms of social action. Research that produces nothing but books will not suffice" (1946). Procedurally, action research uses "a spiral of steps, 'each of which is composed of a circle of planning, action, and fact-finding about the result of the action'" (Lewin, cited in Smith 2007).

Smith (2007) has characterized two "camps" of action researchers. The British model is understood to be more closely linked to educational practices, pragmatic reflection, and "research oriented to the enhancement of direct practice," while the American model is more closely linked to the fields of social welfare, community organizing, and justice movements (Carr and Kemmis 1986; Bogdan and Biklen 1992). Both camps share the sense that action research is strategic rather than procedural: action research comprises a "series of commitments to observe and problematize through practice a series of principles for conducting social enquiry" (McTaggart 1996, 248–49). Because these "commitments" are essentially interpersonal, they are quite different from the objectivist strategies observed in earlier chapters (chapters 5, 6, and 7).

Under some circumstances, the potential for engaged action research to generate new knowledge might be challenged as underrealized, because generalizable research goals and questions are often not made sufficiently explicit. This defies the standards of research quality discussed earlier (chapter 4). However, if we acknowledge that the goal of this strategy is to generate self-knowledge, beginning with personal and interpersonal transformations, then generalizability itself needs to be reframed in terms of a series of possible individual transformations, each with its own nuances and adaptations. Riel (2010) puts it another way:

> Action [r]esearch is a way of learning from and through one's practice by working through a series of reflective stages that facilitate the development of a form of "adaptive" expertise. Over time, action researchers develop a deep understanding of the ways in which a variety of social and environmental forces interact to create complex patterns. Since these forces are dynamic, action research is a process of living one's theory into practice. (Riel 2010, n.p.)

Concepts of action research have radically influenced research within some schools of psychology and related social science disciplines. By emphasizing the necessity for community partnerships in engaged research aimed at the resolution of community social problems, including environmental design and programming, many researchers in landscape architecture had also begun to embrace action-research strategies by the late 1980s.

The emancipatory dimensions of action research originated, in part, in the American civil rights movements and in the social revolutions of the 1960s in Europe and the United States. Action research also draws upon critical theory, in the sense used by the Frankfurt School, along with associated theories of unequal political power, racial privilege, and mediations of dominant culture. Empowerment is a key concept within the emancipatory paradigm, "facilitating a politics of the possible by confronting social oppression at whatever levels it occurs" (Oliver 1992, 110).

There is historical evidence that forms of social oppression have been caused by researchers as well. Over several decades, advocates for people with disabilities or mental health problems had critiqued the apparent "objectivity" of questionable medical-research and social-service practices that were seemingly justified on the basis of neutral scientific paradigms (Hanley 2005). Partly in response to this criticism, the US Department of Health, Education, and Welfare prepared *The Belmont Report* (US DHEW, 1979), a landmark policy governing research practices involving human subjects that has served as the basis for many institutional research policies (see Notes on Method 9.2, Ethics and Confidentiality, chapter 9). *The Belmont Report* is, therefore, relevant to any discipline, including landscape architecture, which develops new knowledge through social practices such as engaged action research and pedagogy.

One of the most important ethical principles contained in *The Belmont Report* is the maintenance of an intellectual "firewall" between professional practice and research practice. In other words, in order to protect subjects and clients, it is important to establish clear differences between activities designed for the generation of new knowledge and activities used for the provision of normative therapies or services, including landscape architectural services. This may have implications for how research may be engaged with practice (chapter 14).

In this chapter we use the term engaged action to include both action and emancipatory research. Both paradigms reject the positivist/objectivist paradigm (putatively unbiased, objective, and neutral) in favor of a position that is more sensitive to power relationships and to subsequent abuses or oversights that may reveal themselves in both the production and privileges of knowledge. The term participatory (when applied to action research) is basically synonymous with collaborative engagement. This chapter begins with the application of action research ideas to teaching, as a background to the following sections. It then considers examples of participatory design in service learning situations, participatory action research, and concludes with a discussion of transdisciplinary action research.

11.2 Action Dimensions in Pedagogical Research

Etymologically, the Greek roots of the word pedagogy derive from *pais* (child) and *ago* (to lead): thus, it has been argued that "child education is inherently directive and must always be transformative" (Macedo, in Freire 2000). To teach, in large part, is to transform and build capacity for continued growth in an individual. At its core, therefore, pedagogical theory has strong affinities to engaged action research, in its efforts to develop individual capacity for identity, socialization, problem solving, and culture.

In *Pedagogy of the Oppressed,* Freire envisions a classroom "as a site where new knowledge, grounded in the experiences of students and teachers alike, is produced through meaningful dialogue" (Freire 2000, 75). This shows how both education and engaged action may be understood as linked research strategies. First, improved practices (learning and teaching, considering and deciding, designing and building, etc.) emerge when there is an equitable dialogue between researcher and participants. Second, the empowerment of participants as active partners or even leaders in the research involves an important shift in the symmetry of the process (fig. 11.1).

Related to such shifts in educational partnerships and processes, Huba and Freed (2000) describe two models for education: the dominant one being teacher-centered and the emergent one being learner-centered. In the second, emergent model, "the faculty member's role is that of a coach or facilitator: students and faculty are both responsible for delivering content, and students are actively involved in their learning" (Wagner and Gansemer-Topf 2005, 199). Evidence in support of active learning thus has broad implications for engaged research in teaching and learning, as well as for forms of design practice.

Figure 11.1 A collaborative teaching and learning environment

(Image courtesy of Laura Lawson)

In landscape architecture and other fields of environmental design, learning-by-doing, teamwork, self-reflection, and learning-by-teaching are all signature pedagogical concepts. There are a myriad of formats and approaches to creating mutual learning environments, from studio to seminars, including active learning, collaborative learning, and peer teaching (example 11.1). In addition, certain types of service learning (Examples 11.2 and 11.3) allow students to facilitate community learning and capacity-building simultaneously with their own growth. These are distinct but related approaches to engaged research aimed at collaborative or communal learning.

Example 11.1 uses a compound research strategy, combining engaged action (direct teaching and learning) with interpretive research strategies. What is very interesting is that the students at the center of this study are engaging an action research strategy on themselves and their peers. They, in turn, are the subjects of a more traditional interpretive study by the faculty/researchers, although the faculty, too, play a role as participants and facilitators in the engaged action. This layered effect—of the subject being in two places at once, in a study within another study—is typical of many academic accounts of action research in educational environments.

Example 11.1:
Learning By Teaching Others: A Qualitative Study Exploring the Benefits of Peer Teaching

(Wagner and Gansemer-Topf 2005)

This study reports on the benefits of peer teaching by students in landscape architecture. Peer teaching is a type of collaborative learning process that gives students a teaching role, and, therefore, they have to become responsible for their own learning and the learning of others in the class.

The authors cite previous research suggesting that opportunities for enhanced teaching and learning experiences would improve learning outcomes in complex fields of study, especially in the context of an experiential model of education—what the authors characterize as "learning by doing." The researchers, therefore, started from the proposition that landscape architecture would be an appropriate field to explore the impact of "mutual learning activities" on student comprehension and mastery of concepts.

The research was based upon an action strategy and followed a research design based upon two case studies of tertiary learning. Two courses were investigated: both were "elective, three-credit, upper-level courses. . . [that] focused on the application of social and behavioral factors to ecological landscape restoration" (201). Each course had different learning objectives. Using a purposive sample in which students were selected because they were representative of the diversity of a larger population, authors analyzed the students' own perception of the peer teaching technique and its impact on their learning. To accomplish this, students' expectations were recorded at the beginning of the semester, as well as at the end. Evidence from three sources (student journals, self-evaluation papers, and focus group discussions) was then analyzed in order to determine whether or not: (a) mastery of course content or (b) interpersonal skill development was enhanced by the peer teaching experience. During analysis, great care was taken to ensure the trustworthiness of the research findings: multiple reviewers, triangulation of data, student checking of findings.

The results show that by internalizing and processing new subject matter so that it became intelligible to someone else, the students felt they mastered new concepts better, were more motivated to learn, and to a certain extent, identified with other landscape architects more strongly. Because collaborative or interactive learning requires students to work with others in solving problems or performing tasks, important learning outcomes include interpersonal and listening skills, dialogue, articulating knowledge, learning management, and critical self-reflection. "Because learners are constructing their learning experience together, they have a responsibility to be engaged and active in the learning process" (Wagner and Gansemer-Topf 2005, 199).

The researchers point out that as "this is a relatively new pedagogical approach," it would benefit from additional investigations (198). In terms of the hierarchy of information presented (e.g., problem definition, literature review, research design, and analysis) and the rationale behind the researchers' decisions, this article is well structured and transparent. What is potentially confusing is the nested relationship between the methods used for analysis (content analysis) and the phenomenon under investigation (peer teaching/learning outcomes as a method within the strategy of engaged action). That is, the relationship between the researchers and their human subjects (students) is interpersonal and transformative. The students were changed as a result of this study. However, the study is reported to a wider academic community using the terminology of interpretive social research.

11.3 Participatory Design in Service Learning

Participatory design is an approach that actively involves end users and neighbors in visioning, programming, and design processes, in order to improve design quality, gain support, and help ensure that design outcomes adequately meet their needs. Participatory design is very often engaged in service learning—a type of community engagement or partnership (whether temporary or long term) that brings students and communities together to study real-world projects.

> In the service learning studio model, the teacher guides the students' work with multiple publics. . . . The students are responsible for finding out about the communities and their needs . . . [as well as] the impact of local politics on planning and design, such as competing viewpoints on community problems and methods of implementation. In this way, students acquire many skills necessary for working in urban communities. (Forsyth et al. 1999, 169)

Service learning thus applies complex pedagogical methods for engaged and active learning. Until the 1980s, many students and faculty members were familiar with only one teaching style for design studios—the traditional master-apprentice studio that "emphasizes student learning from a single master, sometimes promoting the cult-like status of individual artistic designers." The "star system" has been criticized as "wrongly authoritarian and judgmental. . . for undermining students' confidence in their design abilities" and making them dependent on a single source of knowledge (Forsyth et al. 1999, 168).

Hester pioneered service learning studios in the 1970s at North Carolina State University and the University of California, Berkeley, but they did not become widespread until the early 1990s. Today service learning studios are almost ubiquitous, and landscape architecture and urban-design curricula at the university level include at least one and often more service learning studios. In effect, service learning partnerships change the power relationships between teachers and learners and establish four new roles: the university, the community, the faculty, and the students, each of whom stands to benefit in some way. Example 11.2 below presents an account of three service learning urban-design studios that took place in 1996–97, at the University of Massachusetts, Amherst.

The popularity of service learning studios has become all but ubiquitous in public university programs in landscape architecture. "Similar to engagement in education, [community] participation in planning and design can be construed as both means and end. When considered as an end, it runs the risk of becoming routine and uninspired, but it can also be used as a means to promote cross-cultural dialogue that can result in larger visionary thinking" (Lawson 2005, 169).

The East St. Louis Action Research Project (ESLARP) is a long-term multidisciplinary engagement between design faculty and students at the University of Illinois and several neighborhoods of East St. Louis—the less affluent of these twin cities straddling the Mississippi River. Example 11.3 illustrates both service learning and participatory design strategies within the ESLARP project (fig. 11.2).

Example 11.2:
Inside the Service Learning Studio in Urban Design
(Forsyth, Lu, and McGirr 1999)

Service learning studios afford an opportunity for engaged learning and service to community simultaneously. They are increasingly used as a setting for participatory action research, because of the flexibility they provide and the way in which the different strands of activity—student learning, community service, and action research—complement each other. This service learning model was augmented at the University of Massachusetts by a new, more emancipatory and engaged service learning studio. Service learning supports the outreach and service missions of public universities, as it exposes students to complex concepts, problems, and skills in settings charged with a different sense of social priorities.

Two key questions motivated this study: a pedagogical question—how well might service learning prepare students to work with disadvantaged communities, and an outreach question—how to build "long-term relationships with communities that do not run on academic calendars" (1999, 167).

The research design was based on case studies and involved systematic surveys of student experiences of the studio to gauge student reactions and learning. The Urban Places Project (UPP) at UMass ran three service learning studios in the nearby city of Holyoke. Basic objectives for the studios were "to introduce students to socially responsible design; to teach students to value the opinions and needs of multiple publics; to teach students to collaborate; and to introduce students to the complexities of and politics of real urban design problems" in low-income urban communities where many "came face to face with illiteracy and poverty" for the first time (1999, 169–70). Following the studio experience, students were surveyed with both close-ended and open-ended questions about the perceived value of the studio experience.

For the most part, students believed the studios had been beneficial to their learning and the major objectives of the studio appear to have been met. There was significant disagreement among class members that "an emphasis on cultural issues is compatible with high artistic merit." However there was also agreement on the statement that "I have created designs and drawings that I will be proud to put in my portfolio" (1999, 173).

The authors argue that "[s]ervice learning is attractive to the university as a whole for reasons that go beyond individual student gains," e.g., helping universities become more responsible community partners, hosting local community organizations, and helping to fulfill organizational missions (1999, 175).

This example illustrates the complexity of context and approach that often characterizes action research strategies. In terms of theory and research strategy, it relates closely to the discussion of engaged action and illustrates PAR as a research strategy. As in Example 11.1, however, this is a nested study, in which service learning was engaged as the primary strategy of action research (to benefit students and community directly), about which a descriptive case study was prepared later. Another smaller study within this article uses evaluation techniques to assess learning outcomes for the studio.

Example 11.3:
Dialogue through Design: East St. Louis Neighborhood Design

(Lawson 2005)

Landscape architecture studios are challenged to provide students with real-world experiences, including issues of race, privilege, and ethnic difference. Current methodologies such as participatory action and service learning begin to facilitate discussion, but techniques are needed that transcend social barriers and facilitate cross-cultural design dialogue between students and communities.

This article describes a participatory action research (PAR) course involving students at the University of Illinois and community members in East St. Louis. It has "implications for educational goals of cross-cultural learning and efficacy of participatory design" (Lawson 2005, 168). The design studio was based on service learning and participatory design theory, and methods that also utilized reflective and interactive design techniques.

The goal of the course was to develop a neighborhood plan, but as work faltered, new techniques, such as quick-paced charrettes and development of alternative neighborhood visions, needed to be engaged. These activities helped students and residents overcome their cultural and economic differences.

The studio began typically, with an inventory of physical and social information, shifting to analysis (sharing information with residents), then developing appropriate design schema. However, because new approaches were needed to help the two constituencies communicate, partial design development was combined with community visioning. For example, in the scenario planning charrettes, multiple design alternatives and feedback techniques were used to mitigate feelings of student "ownership" of designs and to encourage dialogue between the residents and students.

The author notes, "The course became more experimental [sic] as faculty consciously addressed the need for cross-cultural dialogue. The challenge was to get students and residents talking at a level that would inspire a shared vision that could guide design and planning" (2005, 162).

The author evaluated the success of the studio based on observations, feedback received from students, and subsequent conversations. "This experience challenged students in how to use their design training in a different cultural context than their own [and] ...opportunities to interact with residents proved to be one of the most influential experiences in their understanding of how race and economic concerns affect both conditions and perspectives of the neighborhood landscape" (2005, 168).

This study is relevant to PAR in both teaching and in professional practice. Traditional community participatory action and service learning frequently include techniques (such as cognitive mapping exercises and interviews) that may be generalizable for many different communities. In this study, the program was adapted as it progressed, and more interactive techniques were introduced to engage the participants more effectively. Hence, in contrast to more conventional strategies, the research design changed significantly as the project progressed, and this was compatible with the overall "action" strategy.

Figure 11.2 East St. Louis Action Research Project (ESLARP)

(Image courtesy of Laura Lawson)

11.4 Participatory Action Research (PAR)

By synthesizing Lewin's action research paradigm with concepts advanced by Freire, participatory action research (PAR) combines critical pedagogy and active learning with community-generated activism, research outcomes, and service.

> Participatory Action Research (PAR) is research which involves all relevant parties in actively examining together current action (which they experience as problematic) in order to change and improve it. They do this by critically reflecting on the historical, political, cultural, economic, geographic and other contexts which [*sic*] make sense of it. (Wadsworth 1998)

Most PAR projects are guided by three principles: collective investigation of a problem, reliance on indigenous knowledge to better understand that problem, and a desire to take individual and/or collective action to deal with the stated problem. Example 11.4 shows how these aims are achieved through shared investigation, education, and action (McIntyre 2000, 128).

Example 11.4:
Participatory Action Research with Urban Youth
(McIntyre 2000)

This article challenges many underlying assumptions of mainstream psychological research in which the study of young people from low-income and violent neighborhoods usually fails to take into account the complex interconnections between individuals and their sociohistorical context. The author draws upon recent literature on social resilience that reports strategies for academic success achieved by inner-city youth, in order to understand better how urban young people negotiate their everyday lives in the urban environment.

The research adopted the assumption that when urban youth have "the opportunity to speak about their lives, and [we collaborate] with them in designing plans of action to address their concerns, we can more effectively frame research questions and teaching pedagogies around *their* understanding of violence and urban life" (McIntyre 2000, 125). The project, therefore, engaged community members in a PAR process to articulate how violence is experienced on a daily basis. The conceptual framework for this study was to empower youth not as "subjects" of study, but rather as "agents of inquiry and as 'experts' about their own lives" (2000, 125).

The participatory action strategy was implemented through a single complex case study design, which used a community resource inventory as a technique for "gathering information about people, identifying community concerns as well as individuals' gifts and skills, and generating knowledge about how assets can be tapped and utilized within schools and communities" (2000, 129). Other techniques included engagement of creative and interactive techniques such as collage, photovoice, and storytelling in order to cocreate student-initiated action programs. Researchers used detailed field notes, as well as personal journals, to record observations and reactions.

Grounded (inductive) techniques were used to analyze the information gathered from the creative activities, taped group discussions, photographs, and the community inventories. Findings reveal (1) the normality of violence in the participants' lives, (2) the sense of impending doom they experience, (3) how participants become both victims and perpetrators of violence, and (4) ways the community is perceived by those who live outside it.

In addition to interviews and group conversations, this particular study used creative spatial and environmental techniques, including photography and collage, and shows how techniques familiar to landscape architects can be used in a sophisticated community research project. The "next steps" of the project are action plans being developed by the participants. One response to the participants' sense of powerlessness in urban society is to enable more direct involvement in the improvement of their own urban landscape. Currently, the participants—in collaboration with city officials, businesses, and other local residents—are developing a school community clean-up project to be maintained and sustained by the community.

This study suggests how participatory action research design can be broadly applied to many situations in landscape architecture where the landscape "problem" lies amidst complex social conditions. It demonstrates a strategy that acknowledges all people (including clients and users) as researchers, as agents of change, and as coconstructors of landscape knowledge.

11.5 Transdisciplinary Action Research (TDAR)

The term "transdisciplinary" was added to action research in 2006 by Daniel Stokols. It was a response to a growing awareness in the late 1970s and 1980s of the need for wider disciplinary collaboration in community projects. As partnerships formed around increasingly complicated social and environmental problems, both researchers and community members found themselves stymied by ineffectual collaborations "strained by a mutual lack of understanding of each other's goals and expectations" (Stokols 2006, 2). Built upon a parent tradition of action research, TDAR is distinguished by the way it addresses the contemporary complexities of multimember teams. Interdisciplinary teams may work on massive projects in research networks and institutes without ever having an adequate understanding of the "circumstances that either facilitate or hinder the processes and outcomes of the[ir] endeavors" (Stokols 2006, 3).

One of the central challenges in TDAR is to develop "processes for cultivating and sustaining collaborations across multiple disciplines," somewhat analogous to community capacity building. Capacity building means the ability to do what is necessary in order to meet one's goals or mission over the long run. The concept implies a form of internal skill, organization, integrity, resourcefulness, and sustainability that pertains both to organizations and individuals. Capacity building can operate at any scale. According to *Agenda 21*, a program resulting from the United Nation's Rio Summit on sustainable environment and developmental issues, the national level of capacity building:

> encompasses the country's human, scientific, technological, organizational, institutional and resource capabilities. A fundamental goal of capacity building is to enhance the ability to evaluate and address the crucial questions related to policy choices and modes of implementation among development options, based on an understanding of environment potentials and limits and of needs perceived by the people of the country concerned. (UNCED 1992)

Engaged action research strategies are, therefore, highly relevant to practice-related research in landscape architecture at a variety of scales, from the local to the global (Castills 1983). Recently, Thering and Chanse (2011) have coedited a theme issue of *Landscape Journal* called "The Scholarship of Transciplinary Action Research." It features a collection of articles and case studies addressing the uses of TDAR in landscape architecture and community-capacity research.

Engaged Action Research Strategies: Summary

The group of research strategies collectively known as engaged action research has a number of features in common. It

- originates from a desire to empower communities
- rejects objectivist research protocols
- engages directly with communities and individuals who in other paradigms would be regarded as research subjects
- aims to empower participants with ability to steer and shape research questions and outcomes
- seeks to maintain a distinction between research aimed at understanding practice and research aimed at improving practice outcomes
- challenges researchers to work in unfamiliar ways and places
- is typically based upon case studies, although the research design can evolve as project needs become more evident

As noted above, engaged action is synonymous with collaborative action. The Center for Collaborative Action Research describes its compass as:

> the systematic, reflective study of one's actions and the effects of these actions in a workplace context. As such, it involves deep inquiry into one's professional action. The researchers examine their work and look for opportunities to improve. As designers and stakeholders, they work with others to propose a new course of action to help their community improve its work practices. As researchers, they seek evidence from multiple sources to help them analyze reactions to the action taken. They recognize their own view as subjective and seek to develop their understanding of the events from multiple perspectives. (Riel 2010, n.p.)

This passage and the processes that it describes bears a strong resemblance to the more familiar concept of the reflective, scholarly practitioner who also learns from past mistakes, seeks to constantly improve performance and service, and works to synthesize the results of his or her practical knowledge as best, or at least *better,* practices.

There is both need and opportunity to strengthen the research contribution of engaged action within landscape architecture by identifying broader research questions and implications beyond the specifics of the particular case. As with descriptive case studies, some basis for comparison and cumulative advancement of knowledge is needed in order to make a wider contribution. When framed as a research strategy, engaged action can contribute to the wider knowledge base of the discipline, as well as to the practitioner's own professional development.

References

Bogdan, R., and S. K. Biklen. 1992. *Qualitative research for education*. Boston: Allyn and Bacon.

Carr, W., and S. Kemmis. 1986. *Becoming critical: Education, knowledge and action research*. Lewes, U.K.: Falmer.

Castills, M. 1983. *The city and the grassroots*. Berkeley: University of California Press.

Forsyth, A., H. Lu, and P. McGirr. 1999. Inside the service learning studio in urban design. *Landscape Journal* 18 (2): 166–78.

Freire, P. 2000. *Pedagogy of the oppressed*. 30th anniversary ed. Introduction by Donaldo Pereira Macedo, trans. by Myra Bergman Ramos. New York: Continuum.

Hanley, B. 2005. *User involvement in research: Building on experience and developing standards for the Toronto Seminar Group*. York, UK: Joseph Rowntree Foundation. http://www.jrf .org.uk/node/1332 (accessed August 2009).

Huba, M. E., and J. E. Freed. 2000. *Learner–centered assessment on college campuses*. Boston, MA: Allyn and Bacon.

Lawson, L. 2005. Dialogue through design: The East St. Louis neighborhood design workshop and South End neighbourhood plan. *Landscape Journal* 24 (2):157–71.

Lewin, K. 1946. Action research and minority problems. *Journal of Social Issues* 2 (4): 34–46.

McLutyre, A. 2000. Constructing meaning about violence, school, and community: Participatory action research with urban youth. *Urban Review* 32 (2): 124–54.

McTaggart, R. 1996. Issues for participatory action researchers. In *New Directions in Action Research*, ed. O. Zuber-Skerritt. London: Falmer Press.

Oliver, M. 1992. Changing the social relations of research production. *Disability, Handicap, and Society* 7 (2): 101–15.

Riel, M. 2010. *Understanding action research*. Center for Collaborative Action Research, Pepperdine University. http://cadres.pepperdine.edu/ccar/define.html (accessed August 2010).

Smith, M. K. 2007. Action research. *The encyclopedia of informal education*. www.infed .org/research/b-actres.htm (accessed July 2010).

Stokols, D. 2006. Toward a science of transdisciplinary action research. *American Journal of Community Psychology* 38 (1–2): 63–77.

Thering, S., and V. Chanse, eds. 2011. The scholarship of transdisciplinary action research. *Landscape Journal* 30 (1).

UNCED. 1992. *United Nations Conference on Environment and Development*. New York: The United Nations.

US DHEW (US Department of Health, Education, and Welfare). 1979. *The Belmont Report*. Washington, DC: USDHEW.

Wadsworth, Y. 1998. What is participatory action research? Action research international. http://www.scu.edu.au/schools/gcm/ar/ari/p-ywadsworth98.html (accessed August 2009).

Wagner, M., and A. Gansemer-Topf. 2005. Learning by teaching others: A qualitative study exploring the benefits of peer teaching. *Landscape Journal* 24 (2): 198–208.

CHAPTER 12
Projective Design

12.1 Design as Research

In the introductory chapters of this book, we noted the debates about the relationship of research to scholarship, and scholarship to practice. Nowhere are these exchanges more charged than in the discourse surrounding design investigations and creative research. Increasingly, synthetic or generative design itself is being framed as a strategy for research. However, design as an investigative strategy remains poorly understood and inconsistently applied, even if frequently invoked.

As we have outlined, design theorists and educators have increasingly argued that the core activities of the field—including design, critical thinking, and critique—are valid forms of research. However, it is also widely acknowledged, by proponents and critics, that using the term *research* in an undisciplined or vernacular way threatens to undermine the credibility and impact of legitimate research. LaGro (1999), for example, argued that the field of landscape architecture needed to expand its research capacity, in part as a way of achieving its other goals as a profession. He acknowledged that the design process "involves" research tasks (inventory, analysis, evaluation, etc.), yet he concluded: "Although these analytical activities are important, they are not equivalent to either qualitative or quantitative research—at least as these activities are understood by scholars in other disciplines" (1999, 181). There is a key difference, he argued, between informed personal responses to a specific design problem and formulating a research problem that is more broadly defined, systematic, and generalizable.

The distinction is vital and quite correct. However, the significant question is whether design has the *potential* to be framed as a research strategy, and if so, how. That is to say, could a designlike process of synthetic, critical, or pragmatic investigation become research, *if* it tests or builds theory, *and* uses a protocol that satisfies the fundamentals of research quality? Chapter 8 drew parallels between predesign procedures (inventory and analysis) and classification as a research strategy. This chapter returns to the issue and explores the proposition that design-based investigations can meet the different criteria of research quality, if appropriately structured.

As a number of commentators have noted, it is easy to understand that design processes may employ or *be informed by* other research strategies (e.g., inventory, interpretation, engaged action) and may directly apply, test, or extend the results of empirical evidence, case precedents, and design guidelines produced in other studies. Design may also become the *subject* or *investigative problem* of those other research strategies (e.g., descriptive case studies, design ethnography, evaluation, typology, etc.). In either case, it is vital and essential to control or discipline the effort. It is also essential to maintain distinct boundaries between professional service and more formal research investigations for both intellectual and ethical reasons (see Notes on Method 9.2 and section 11.1).

Design only becomes an autonomous research strategy when it produces new generalizable knowledge about the world through its purposes, protocols, and outcomes. In using the term *projective design,* therefore, this chapter focuses on the unique agency of design process for research outcomes—that is, on projective design guided by research intent. It is, perhaps, helpful to briefly revisit the criteria for research quality we outlined in the first part of this book. Taking these criteria in turn, we highlight the questions that need to be considered in shaping design as research and consider how a design research strategy might be found to address them:

1. Truth value—can knowledge created through design make claims of validity or credibility? That is, do the procedures do what they purport to do? A useful indicator for the potential truth value of design research is to ask whether the process and its outcomes have a comparable degree of internal validity to that achieved in inductive strategies, such as description, classification, or action research. Is the process set up in a way that observations and evaluations are systematically examined and checked for their congruence with the research objectives and methodology? Do the research measures or observations address the phenomena that are the focus of the investigation? Are the reported outcomes consistent with the process that was undertaken?

2. Applicability—is the knowledge created generalizable or transferable? That is, can other designers can apply the findings? Here the question relates to the nature of design research settings as samples from a larger realm or population of examples. Steenbergen (2008) argues that the object of study in research by design is always variable, while the context may be either determined or variable (see Table 12.1). Hence, research by design

Table 12.1 **Design research and research by design***

	Design research	Research by design
	Object (design expression) is determined	Object is variable
Context is determined	Design evaluation	Design experiment
Context is variable	Design classification and typology	Experimental design

*Reproduced from Steenbergen 2008. By permission of the publisher, Birkhauser Verlag.

is a type of case-study research, and the extension of its findings are subject to the same opportunities and limitations of all case-study research (see chapter 5).

3. Consistency—can the knowledge created through design research be considered reliable or dependable? That is, if the process is repeated by the investigator or by others will it generate broadly consistent or equivalent outcomes? This depends upon both its internal validity (above) and the transparency of the process (see below). The results of a design process can never be *exactly* reproducible—it is not a classic experiment—but then neither can interpretive research or various other forms of inductive research be exactly reproduced time after time. The key issue is that the investigators make their procedures, presuppositions, and analyses explicit. The question of reliability in design research relates not to the specific details of every step in a process, but to the overall logic and structure of the investigation.

4. Transparency—is the new knowledge free of hidden bias, and are its assumptions open and transparent? No design research is objectively neutral—precisely because it incorporates human creative agency—but, then, neither is any research in the humanities objectively neutral. Rather, the test is whether the process and its outcomes are clearly documented and the positions of the researchers made explicit. In research by design, the research "instrument" is typically drawing, or more broadly graphic representation (Steenbergen 2008). The application of the instrument can be documented through diagramming the process and its outcomes (Bowring and Swaffield 2010).

5. Significance—does the research address questions that are of wider relevance to the discipline? This has to be answered on a case by case basis, but it is necessary to always ground research by design within a wider theoretical context, so that the questions asked and the outcomes generated can be seen to contribute to the systematic knowledge of the discipline.

6. Efficiency—does design research offer a way to achieve high-quality results without wasting resources (i.e., fitness-to-purpose and thrift, as in saving time, money, energy, and materials)? Potentially, the imaginative phase in design research can be a very efficient way of generating a wide range of possibilities, as shown in several examples below. Like other strategies, however, it can be ineffective if the goals and process are not carefully planned.

7. Organization—is the process well structured and disciplined? This does not mean mechanical, but whether the creative phases are framed within a wider research process, and are their outcomes systematically evaluated?

8. Originality—does the process go beyond the applied procedures of the discipline and develop/test some new value, idea, paradigm, or theory? Again, the test is always case by case. The critical question is not whether the setting is original—it usually will be—but are the theoretical questions and insights created during the research original?

In reviewing the ways in which design research might address quality criteria, we do not suggest that there is an inflexible "checklist"—rather, we have used the eight criteria as a suite of measures that can and should guide the development of any research project. The balance of how well the criteria are achieved will differ in each case. Design research is no different in this respect to other strategies, each of which offers different strengths and limitations. There will inevitably be methodological trade-offs. The acid test is whether the new knowledge that a researcher may claim advances the discipline in a systematic way.

Steenbergen (2008) uses the terms *design experiment* and *experimental design* to describe research by design, and the distinctions he makes are helpful in drawing out the character of the process of generalization. Design experiments are set within a given context, and the investigation applies different design-based strategies to investigate the possibilities. These may relate specifically to the context—for example, how might a particular design strategy, such as a process of ecological interventions, transform a type of site such as an abandoned suburban airfield (e.g., Downsview Park, Toronto). Or, it might relate to different types of design transformation—for example, how might new types of formal relationship be generated for a particular inner-ring urban factory site (e.g., Parc de la Villette, Paris). Hence, in design experiments the research questions will typically explore how new knowledge, values, or priorities might emerge from the creative transformation of familiar design contexts.

Experimental design, on the other hand, is the projection of new landscape compositions that may be applied in many different settings—that is, both the context and the design intervention are variable. Here, the research questions are typically driven by a desire to generate new types of conceptual design solution. Explorations of ways to sustainably house the maximum number of people in a given volume, such as the KM3 project by MVRDV referred to by Weller (2008b), fall into the category of experimental design.

Despite the frequent use of the term experimentation as a metaphor, research by design has much in common with the types of research strategies used in the humanities, fine arts, and the emergent social sciences—perhaps more so than with the strategies of the traditional natural sciences. In discussing projective design as a separate research strategy, we have placed it with the "subjectivist" strategies, along with engaged action and logical systems. This is because the strategy is centered within individual or synergistic team-based creativity and is inherently pragmatic, reflective, and synthetic (Moore 2010). Projective design has strong ties, in fact, to the development of logical, rules-based systems and is very often the proving ground, so to speak, where more abstract paradigms are made operational.

We have placed projective design in the reflexive column, between inductive and deductive modes, because theoretical understanding emerges as research is underway. Insight emerges inductively from the design setting or context and deductively from the testing and challenging of established concepts. As a projection of alternative, often theoretically informed parameters and scenarios, design belongs in the same column with modeling strategies. However, the mechanism for generating those scenarios is the creativity of the individual designer or design team.

Research by design, thus, corresponds with the processes of "abduction" (chapter 1)—an investigation of what *might* be. De Landa and Ellingsen (2007) described the creative use of design models in the exploration of the "possibility spaces" of the world. In research by design, this exploration is undertaken in a systematic way, so that the investigations enhance our understanding of the relationships between the world as it is and the possibility of what it might become. In so doing, they address the transformational processes that lie at the heart of our discipline.

In the remainder of this chapter we explore various propositional and projective design-based investigations that can be applied in a case-based, systematic, formally expressed, and reflective way. First, we examine some of the researchlike processes within design. We then review ways in which emerging design methodologies have been structured to generate new understandings, and we contrast developmental strategies (landscape urbanism), with more interpretive and reflective (phenomenological) strategies.

12.2 Design Operations

Groat and Wang (2002) distinguish between generative design, which they regard as an essentially subjective (intuitive) process related to artistic production, and more analytical or rules-based propositions used for research. They justified this distinction by arguing that "[r]esearch activity tends to be defined by propositional components: strategy, tactic, hypotheses, 'the literature,' measuring instruments, data, and so forth" (2002, 105). Increasingly, these very terms are characteristic of design experiments emerging at the intersection of landscape architecture and urban planning. In a number of recent competitions, large sites (e.g., Downsview Park in Toronto, Canada, or Fresh Kills Landfill in Staten Island, New York) are no longer treated as formal compositions, but as propositions about design process—they are more akin to an experimental field station where contingent programs may be treated or controlled over time. Hence, design operations (Corner 1999) may become used as research methods.

There are a wide variety of ways of "finding out" embedded in the design process. Designers commonly use researchlike methods, techniques, and terminology: to observe, describe, measure, count, organize, categorize, test, discover, look for influence, evaluate, diagnose, understand—all of these in order to frame and/or respond (in part or in whole) to the problem. It is helpful to reflect on the fact that these are all action verbs—they are all operations. The combination of operations one chooses to address a problem will depend upon the way that a projective design research strategy is expressed.

Normative design operations involve familiar stages—inventory, analysis, synthesis—each of which may be used as a research method, if deployed as part of a wider strategy and design. Inventory is a classificatory procedure for gathering and organizing information (see chapter 8). Analysis is the procedure by which we generally divide a whole into its component parts or variables. Synthesis is a reciprocal procedure: to reconstitute components back into a coherent whole, but, in so doing, to transform it in significant ways. As a number of contemporary theorists (Berger, Corner, and Meyer, among them) have demonstrated, potential for new transformative or operational knowledge resides in the procedural tensions and thresholds between inventory and analysis, and analysis and synthesis.

One feature of landscape transformations that makes them particularly potent is the way they frequently address ecological process, and, hence, connect the transformational role of design directly with the emergent qualities of vegetative and hydrological systems. For example, in the compound study described below (Example 12.1), a design studio investigated certain principles of urban resilience in order to develop and project a new conceptual approach for urban ecological design. The refinement of these methods was supported by a descriptive survey (inventory) of the phenomenon of resilience in "feral landscapes" in Los Angeles; these predesign studies had been conducted independently

---

Example 12.1:
Envisioning Resilience
(Woodward 2008)

This article is a complex report on a series of research activities that took place both inside and outside a design studio at the California State Polytechnic University at Pomona. The study responds to the emerging paradigm of nonlinear systems thinking in urban design and planning: "understanding that systems are not in equilibrium, that disturbance is a constant part of any system, and that succession is at best a probabilistic pathway" (97). This paradigm demands consideration of the effects of global climate change, in expectation of increasing instances of long-term drought, and diminishing capital resources. The author supposes that conditions in the urban landscape of Los Angeles will become increasingly unpredictable and unmaintained over time.

The questions raised by the study address design methods in urban design and landscape architecture. Specifically, in the developing methodologies of ecological design, landscape architects seek to foster and support characteristics of resilience to unexpected and changing conditions. This approach offers an alternative to normative urban-design and planning values, in which sociocultural and economic objectives of the landowner are primary. "Ecological design, also known as green building, seeks to reduce resource use and pollution, protect or restore ecological processes, and minimize overall impacts" (Calkins 2005, cited by Woodward 2008, 97). The purpose of this study is to refine objectives for methods in ecological design in a way that encourages resilience—that is, design that maintains functional integrity while also adapting to volatile conditions (Gunderson and Holling 2002).

Three questions were used to frame the study and to guide its design as a series of stages. First, what are the characteristics of resilient urban landscapes in Los Angeles?

Station Seed-Ball Machine
Adaptive Plant Seed Distribution System

Figure 12.1 Vectors for seed dispersal

(Reprinted from Woodward 2008. Reproduced by permission of the University of Wisconsin Press. Copyright 2008 by the Board of Regents of the University of Wisconsin System.)

To answer this, the author conducted a descriptive survey and analysis of exemplary resilient landscapes in the region. Second, assuming profound disruptions to maintenance regimes, what techniques or principles do landscape architects need to know for designing resilience? To answer this, the author adapted four basic principles (based on survey/observations) for the design of resilient landscapes. Third, what priorities should be set? This was the question addressed in the design studio.

The first stage of the study was a multimethod descriptive survey. The second phase developed four sets of design principles and procedures: establish diverse structural conditions to support ecological processes, utilize ambient processes for self-maintaining structure (e.g., propagation), optimize conditions when establishing new designs (get a head start), and utilize strategic communications to engage community acceptance.

In the third stage, these principles were put into operation in the design studio by students projecting and analyzing various scenarios at different scales of the city and modeling expected change over time, failure regimes, and recovery. A list of research agenda items was also developed to guide future questions and investigations.

Similar to many of the examples we have selected, this article combines several stages of investigation and mixes its methods. Ultimately, the purpose of both the descriptive research and scenario projection/modeling is developmental—new understandings are "captured" in improved methods for ecological design. Hence, we have described this study as primarily based upon a projective design strategy—what kind of place might the future city become? The research design for this study involved a number of ways of gathering evidence—both systematic and opportunist surveys and case study. Analytical methods were similarly diverse. However, the integrity of the process revolved around a clearly defined research agenda of interconnected questions, a systematic reporting of outcomes, and the possibility for repeat iterations and extensions of what was learned.

of the studio. In this sense, the synthetic purpose of the studio was to "test" the usability and generalizability of these concepts in the form of design operations (fig. 12.1).

The Australian landscape architect Richard Weller further extends the developmental logic of research by design. Writing that landscape urbanists "argue for and develop design tactics to garner more significant structural influence," he cites designers like Chris Reed (Stoss Landscape Urbanism), who "position themselves as 'urbanistic system builders whose interests now encompass the research, framing, design and implementation' of public works and infrastructure" (2008a, 247).

Examples 12.2 and 12.3 below feature two reports on Weller's own work. Example 12.2 opens by presenting a comparative review of landscape urbanism and other contemporary planning paradigms (e.g., new urbanism, smart growth, green urbanism, critical regionalism, and critical pragmatism) that summarizes the respective strengths and weaknesses of these theories. This first part of his study basically uses a form of classification strategy (literature review) to compare established approaches to urban design. However, for the purposes of this chapter, we are most interested in the second part of his study, in which Weller demonstrates the efficacy of landscape urbanism to inform projective design—in this case, for planning a new community in Perth, Australia (fig. 12.2). Appropriate to the

Example 12.2:
Landscape (Sub)Urbanism in Theory and Practice (Part Two)
(Weller 2008a)

The author characterizes the work of his team on the Wungong Urban Water (WUW) Landscape Structure Plan (2004–2007), on the outskirts of Perth, Australia, as both a professional consultancy as well as research on methods. This case study takes as its point of departure the assumption that best practices in suburban planning depend on sensitivity to site conditions. In so doing, the designer articulates a methodical procedure that reconciles "the industrial logic of suburbia and the eco-logic of the land" at different scales.

The 1,500-hectare project (see fig. 12.2) was framed as an opportunity to adapt landscape urbanist principles to ordinary suburban master planning. The author argues that this methodology improved the planning outcome and simultaneously "identified the need for landscape urbanism to draw on other urban theory" to address this type of project more effectively.

Several design principles for the project were developed, including protecting existing vegetation, creating a matrix of open space, integrating a storm-water system with the open space, maximizing passive solar orientation, and using endemic plant material to create local image. The study generated maps, drawings, vignettes, diagrams, and sections to illustrate the way that cultural and ecological systems intersected.

The overall organization of the plan was described as "formally resolute," dominated by the requirements of "a comprehensive storm water filtration system, orthogonal solar theory of landscape urbanism, the design scheme applies large-scale principles of landscape infrastructure. The principal value of his study is to translate, articulate, and demonstrate how the methods of landscape urbanism may be applied to new kinds of social context—arguably resulting in a smarter, more sustainable form of market housing.

Experimental design in the landscape urbanist paradigm typically involves extensive use of mapped overlays and other spatial representations of place and possibility. In a collection of essays examining the meaning and dimensions of cartography, Cosgrove (1999) uses the term "mapping" to refer to the practice of interpretive readings of existing landscapes—both as a means to understand the nondesign processes that produce landscapes, and to generate new forms and ideas. Corner (1999) amplifies the importance of mapping and other investigative strategies as a way of reconstituting landscape through "rethinking what landscape actually is—or might yet become—as both idea and artifact. In the first case, recollection; in the second, invention. In both, landscape is understood as an ongoing project, an enterprising venture that enriches the cultural world" (1999, 1). This strategy of "reconstituting landscape" through mapping is demonstrated, for example, in "Sediment," Tom Leader's work in Rome during his time at the American Academy (Leader 2002).

orientation, and the interconnected matrix of public open space" (263). Because of this the project was criticized by some as inflexible, but the overall disposition of the open space and storm-water system also gave the scheme legibility. "In these ways, the landscape architecture of this project embodies an emerging landscape urbanist 'ethos' . . . commensurate with that of a system builder" (263). It merges infrastructure with design and "appreciates the contemporary city as a hybridized, denatured ecology."

The designer concludes that in further articulation of this method what might be needed are greater constraints and regulation at the scale of the overall plan, combined with greater liberty at the scale of private property. Further, in testing the adaptability of landscape urbanism for a more developmental methodology, the author compares it to the "parent" methods of Ian McHarg.

> For instance, both landscape urbanism and McHargian planning operate at an urban scale, both are driven by the meta-narrative of ecology, and both prefer to ground the design process in empirical data. Together they form powerful theoretical and practical tools that could relate equally to smart growth, new urbanism, and green urbanism and thus position landscape architects to more forcefully negotiate the conditions of contemporary sprawl. (265)

This example merges theory and process, as well as professional practice and methodical investigation, in ways that are somewhat difficult to tease apart. What identifies it as a projective design strategy is the fact that paradigmatic goals and objectives, as well as procedures and steps, are framed around a theoretically grounded research agenda, are clearly documented and evaluated and, further, have methodological implications for the discipline that are fully explicated.

Example 12.3:
Planning by Design
(Weller 2008b)

This project responds to the dramatic population growth projections for Western Australia over the next forty years. Current development patterns would result in an extended dysfunctional sprawl of suburbia across a range of landscapes, some of significance to biodiversity, some critical for water supplies. The present urban strategy is to develop a network city, but this is limited in a number of ways.

The goal of the research is to "transcend" the existing urban development strategy, creating, over a longer time frame, a range of possible scenarios that are intended to open up public debate over new policies.

The study first establishes the region's landscape resources and the limits to growth that these constrictions impose. Then the research generates two types of scenario—the

Figure 12.2 Dreamscape: West Australia suburb. Photomontage by Andrew Thomas

(Reprinted from Weller 2008a. Reproduced by permission of the University of Wisconsin Press. Copyright 2008 by the Board of Regents of the University of Wisconsin System.)

first type includes four schemes that offer different types of land-use relationships—food city, garden city, sea-change city, and tree-change city. The second scenario features three schemes developed to project particular concentrations of urban development— sky city, river city, and surf city.

A critical feature of the project was the use of bold and accessible graphic modeling techniques to represent the alternative futures in ways that could be easily understood by public stakeholders and citizens.

This example offers a useful contrast to the alternative futures models featured in chapter 6. Those models focus upon projecting the consequences of different public policy regimes—their parameters were driven by political decisions and regulatory frameworks. By contrast, Example 12.2 is design driven, establishing alternative futures based upon the author's analysis of theoretical precedents and contemporary conceptual thinking. It generates a variety of possibilities for a region based upon ideas and imagination, and it analyzes their relationships. It is, thus, active research by design, rather than objective scenario modeling.

In the previous example (12.2), Weller uses a range of representational and mapping techniques to generate and communicate alternative scenarios for a single site. In other related work (Example 12.3) he applies the research process across the whole of the greater Perth region. This combination of a McHarg-like analysis (descriptive modeling) of landscape capacity and potential with theoretically driven projections of alternative urban typologies, establishes a range of possible landscape futures for the region.

12.3 Design Interpretations

Design transformation articulated as a research process takes place operationally— through conjecture, proposition, projection, and other tactics, but its consequences and outcomes are expressed in landscape experience. A number of theorists and designers have argued that it is necessary to counterpoise the instrumentality of the typically broad scale, horizontal explorations of possible landscape structure associated with landscape urbanist investigations with a more firmly situated phenomenological and revelatory focus. French practitioner/theorists such as Christophe Girot and Sebastien Marot have articulated a radically different sense of the nature (and thus method) of design research. Their focus is on thickness, the vertical dimension of landscape possibility. Based on reading and writing the historical layering and accumulation of site narratives, they have adopted a discursive rather than an instrumentalist approach. Marot writes: "Such a view is less focused on the program of a proposed building project than on exploring the possibilities of site characteristics and hidden phenomena. As such, it outlines a critical and reflective approach to making new landscapes" (cited in Corner 1999, 48).

To that end, both Girot and Marot describe a series of stages in the design process that are intended to generate new understandings of the depth of possibility in landscape.

Girot (1999) suggests a four-step process: Landing (a direct first encounter with place), Grounding (inventory/data collection and secondary investigation), Finding (discovery of a propositional or operative strategy) and Founding (generative design). For Marot (1999) these steps are described differently: Anamnesis (remembering the past), Preparation ("staging or setting up future conditions"), Three-dimensional sequencing (qualitative engagement with place), and Relational structuring (design in terms of spatial syntax). That these two schema are slightly different from each other, but are still roughly equivalent to a conventional site-design process, is no deterrent to our appreciation. Because these designers demand different sorts of "interpretive knowing" about their sites, they have articulated new procedural approaches to "finding out," and as a result, new understandings of how landscapes may be transformed.

In developing a mindful (rather than formulaic) protocol, these Continental theorists believe a designer is more likely to be attentive to different experiences and encounters on-site. The procedural strategy thus expands, if not actually directs, the range of possible findings. In other words, to design deliberately, at a microscale, and to systematically analyze the possibilities and relationships thus created, is a complementary research strategy to the large-scale exploration of structural landscape possibilities and relationships. In the terms proposed by Steenbergen (2008), this could be considered a parallel to experimental design.

The following example illustrates a way in which "deep" interpretative analysis of particular situations and contexts can be used to generate a richer understanding of contemporary design challenges. It comprises a set of design investigations undertaken in a studio setting, which taken together provide insight into one of Australia's most profound formal design challenges—how to create memorials for a deeply conflicted past.

Example 12.4:
Research by Design: Honoring the Stolen Generation
(Ware 1999)

This project investigated changing understandings, relationships, and formal expressions of memorial design in Australia, in the context of honoring the "Stolen Generation."

The Stolen Generation is the term used in Australia for indigenous Aboriginal children who were forcibly removed by the government from their families and communities during the nineteenth and twentieth centuries. At the time it was deemed that this intervention was in the best interest of the children, but this position has now been reevaluated.

The objective of this project was to better understand the relationship between the formal and conceptual dimensions of memorial design and, in particular, to explore the

A key feature of the Stolen Generation investigation was its attention to the multiple and frequently contested meanings and understandings of memorials and their role in shaping personal and national identity. Critical visual studies are an emerging form of design investigation that is informed by theories of identity politics. Dee (2009) has suggested "that images can have a range of critical functions including dialogic, hermeneutical, polemical, rhetorical and analytical, and therefore can contribute to theoretical understanding" (14). A critical visual study in this context is "one in which imagery is employed both as method to investigate and as form to communicate a research study" (14). In Example 12.5, Dee and Fine use this method, belonging to the projective design strategy, to explore, interpret, and synthesize alternative ways of encountering and, thus, knowing an urban site (fig. 12.3).

12.4 Design Reflections

The types of interpretive investigation at the interface of phenomenology and critical studies described above are on the frontiers of design research. They draw upon emergent methods and conceptual frameworks of investigation (such as feminist methodology), which they apply to the tactile phenomena of landscape. Other forms of design exploration do not clearly comprise research, although they are intellectually important undertakings for producing new critical directions in disciplinary thought and value.

Investigative up to a point, exploratory research is rarely disciplined or theorized enough to satisfy the parameters of research quality. However, we think of exploratory methods as important protoresearch that can be vital to design and theory formation. Both subjective and pragmatic exploratory methods may produce new conjectural knowledge—i.e., potential questions—by direct reflection upon phenomena. However, exploratory methods

---

nature of "antimemorials," progressive designs that celebrate the changing nature of memories.

The investigation was structured as a studio design project that involved several phases. These included development of a typology of memorial design, a critique of design precedents, interviews with members of the Stolen Generation, and a series of design exercises that explored the relationship between different concepts of memorial, their formal expression, and different contexts.

The author drew a number of procedural and theoretical conclusions about the evolving nature of memorials. She highlights the multiple readings of memorials and the way in which "memory exists, changes and dies within a constructed spatial realm" (Ware 1999, 57).

This example illustrates how design experiments can generate improved understandings of formal design strategies and their reflexive relationship with changing social phenomena. The generation of new design possibilities drew out critical relationships and provided an empirical basis for critical reflection upon the concept of "anti-memorial."

Example 12.5:
Indoors Outdoors at Brightside:
A Critical Visual Study
(Dee and Fine 2005)

This study was motivated by the authors' sense of the inadequacy of conventional use of images for interpretive site investigations in landscape architecture. They sought to engage the potential of an emerging technique in fine art practices and theories of visual studies called critical visual studies. "A critical visual study aims to explore the potential of image-making as a theoretical and investigative tool in and of itself" (Dee and Fine 2005, 75).

The particular objective of this study, as informed by critical visual studies, is to develop a feminist methodology to guide interpretive (hermeneutic) treatments for a postindustrial steel production site in Brightside, Sheffield, in the United Kingdom. There are many such derelict sites in this region of England. "Interpretation of cultures of the steel industry has been, on the whole, clichéd, generally consisting of either commercial sculptures of steel workers or stainless steel abstract pieces placed in sanitized landscapes" (78).

The question that guided the research was how a "greater understanding of gendered interpretations of postindustrial sites might influence their reclamation and regeneration." The authors, therefore, adapted the principles and goals of critical visual studies to "invent" a procedure that would help them understand the site differently. Their assumption was that following this procedure would result in a different hermeneutic than if they had, for instance, employed the normative conventions of site analysis that rely on remote sensing methods (such as maps, aerial photographs, or analytical data collected by others).

In particular, the authors sought to discover a nonhierarchical conception of difference between the feminine and the masculine condition in the spaces and materials they encountered on the site.

To focus on "revisiting embodied ways of knowing a landscape," the authors chose to use haptic explorations. These included visiting the site, taking time to rest in reflection there, object making, tactile installations, and micronarratives as a way of understanding site-based possibilities for feminist themes. The authors used found objects on site to produce collages and created material installations as "fictional-material readings" of the site (fig. 12.3).

The article itself is a self-reflection on the process that they used and the experience of making these places and objects. The objects made during the process and the fictional and reflective narratives are granted equal weight to the scholarly text in which they are embedded.

Although this article describes an exploratory procedure that is highly theoretical and closely situated in subjective experience, the methodology of critical visual studies is adaptable for other sites and interpretive problems. It is also possible to recreate the steps the authors pursued, in an equivalent way, for other places and researchers.

Figure 12.3 The Brashy Table

(Image courtesy of Cathy Dee. Reproduced by permission of the University of Wisconsin Press. Copyright 2005 by the Board of Regents of the University of Wisconsin System.)

cannot be considered an autonomous research strategy in the same way that more developed, reliable, and theoretically informed models are.

Moore believes the philosophy of pragmatism offers potential for a "radical redefinition of the relationship between the senses and intelligence" (2010, 1). Pragmatic research can be exploratory, fundamental to the beginnings of many important theories—a kind of "reality check" that aims to investigate phenomena without explicit expectations:

> to see "what's going on" and to describe the observations. . . No specific variables are isolated and manipulated (as in an experiment), nor is a systematic study of naturally occurring variables carried out in order to determine what the precise relationship between them is (as in a correlational study) . . . Exploratory research is particularly valuable in situations where too little is known to formulate a specific hypothesis or to plan and experiment. (Louw et al. 2005)

For instance, direct engagement and manipulation of design materials, through investigative exercises and/or construction projects is a valuable way to approach new personal knowledge and may help to frame more rigorous studies later. Other techniques for direct, pragmatic engagement include haptic encounters, drawing, and journaling (fig. 12.4).

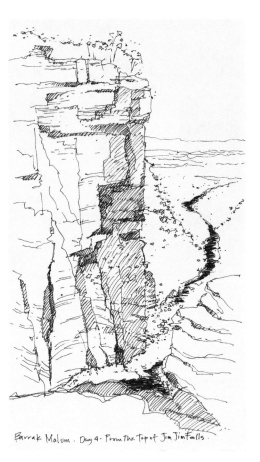

Figure 12.4 From the Top of Jim Jim Falls, Kakadu National Park, Australia

(Image courtesy of Caroline Lavoie. Originally published in *Landscape Journal*, 2005. Reproduced by permission of the University of Wisconsin Press. Copyright 2005 by the Board of Regents of the University of Wisconsin System.)

In teaching and learning environments, for example, this has long been an accepted way of improving a student's personal knowledge. Haptic techniques are also applied in support of action research strategies as a way for community members to share their own situated knowledge of memories, places, and situations.

In special circumstances, when haptic exploration is systematically or professionally conducted, self-observation may also be considered protoresearch. Kondrat (1999) explains that there are three approaches to professional self-awareness: (a) simple conscious awareness (awareness of whatever is being experienced), (b) reflective awareness (awareness of a self who is experiencing something), and (c) reflexive awareness (the self's awareness of how his or her awareness is constituted in direct experience).

Thus, the borderlands of design research may merge into the everyday activity of the scholarly practitioner discussed in chapter 3. In presenting these examples of design research, we have argued that the liminal regions between research and scholarship extend rather further into the realm of design than some commentators would accept. However, in opening with a discussion of research quality criteria, we have attempted to signal that, in our view, the determination of the location of the border itself is not a matter of forceful assertion, but of negotiation based upon established diplomatic protocols.

Projective Design Strategies: Summary

To most landscape architects, projective design is among the most familiar and well-rehearsed of creative processes, but its acceptance and use as a research strategy is contested. Just as for the other research strategies along the subjectivist "bottom row" of the framework, advocates for design as research who seek wider recognition for its legitimacy will be obliged to present their case in terms that are familiar to other parts of the academy. That being said, clearer principles that guide better integration of the synthetic and creative processes of projective design with the processes of investigation are beginning to emerge.

- Design research has great potential to address the established criteria of research quality, but the process requires effort. It is not self-evident.
- Projective design strategies may be operational, interpretive, or reflective (developmental).
- Design research can usefully be framed as a case-study approach.
- If considered systematically and structurally, the metaphor of design experiments and experimental design can be applied.

Finally, we tend to support the view expressed by Moore in *Overlooking the Visual: Demystifying the Art of Design* (2010). In making design seem more mysterious than it is, Moore explains, we do our discipline (and the wider world) a disservice. This does not mandate the necessity of turning design into a science. Rather, it is important to accept design for what it is—a mediated way of engaging the world based on situated knowing *and imagining.*

References

Bowring, J., and S. R. Swaffield. 2010. Diagrams in landscape architecture. In *The diagrams of architecture,* ed. M. Garcia, 142–51. London: John Wiley and Sons.

Calkins, M. 2005. Strategy, use and challenges of ecological design in landscape architecture. *Landscape and Urban Planning* 73 (1): 29–48.

Corner, J., ed. 1999. *Recovering landscape: Essays in contemporary landscape architecture.* New York: Princeton Architectural Press.

Cosgrove, D., ed. 1999. *Mappings.* London: Reaktion Books.

Dee. C. 2009. "The imaginary texture of the real . . .": Critical visual studies in landscape architecture: Contexts, foundations and approaches. *Landscape Research* 29 (1): 13–30.

Dee. C., and R. Fine. 2005. Indoors outdoors at Brightside: A critical visual study reclaiming landscape architecture in the feminine. *Landscape Journal* 24 (1): 70–84.

De Landa, M., and E. Ellingsen. 2007. Possibility spaces. *Models 306090* 11:214–17.

Girot, C. Four trace concepts in landscape architecture. In *Recovering landscape: Essays in contemporary landscape architecture,* ed. J. Corner, 58–67. New York: Princeton Architectural Press, 1999.

Groat, L., and D. Wang. 2002. *Architectural research methods.* New York: John Wiley and Sons.

Gunderson, L. H., and C. S. Holling, eds. 2002. *Panarchy: Understanding transformations in human and natural systems.* Washington, DC: Island Press.

Kondrat, M. E. 1999. Who is the "self" in self-aware: Professional self-awareness from a critical theory perspective. *Social Service Review* 73 (4): 451–77.

LaGro, J. A. 1999. Research capacity: A matter of semantics? *Landscape Journal* 18 (2): 179–86.

Lavoie, C. 2005. Sketching the landscape: Exploring a sense of place. *Landscape Journal* 24 (1): 13–31.

Leader, T. 2002. Sediment. *Landscape Journal* 21 (2): 75–81.

Louw, D. A., D. M. van Ede, and A. E. Louw. 2005. *Human development.* 2nd ed. Cape Town, South Africa: Kagiso Tertiary.

Marot, S. 1999. The reclaiming of sites. In *Recovering landscape: Essays in contemporary landscape architecture,* ed. J. Corner, 44–57. New York: Princeton Architectural Press.

Moore, K. 2010. *Overlooking the visual: Demystifying the art of design.* Abingdon, U.K.: Routledge.

Steenbergen, C. 2008. *Composing landscapes: Analysis, typology and experiments for design.* Basel: Birkhauser Verlag.

Ware, S-A. 1999. Research by design: Honoring the stolen generation—A theoretical anti-memorial. *Landscape Review* 5 (2): 43–58.

Weller, R. 2008a. Landscape (sub) urbanism in theory and practice. *Landscape Journal* 27 (2): 247–67.

———. 2008b. Planning by design: Landscape architectural scenarios for a rapidly growing city. *Journal of Landscape Architecture,* Autumn, 18–29.

Woodward, J. H. 2008. Envisioning resilience in volatile Los Angeles landscapes. *Landscape Journal* 27 (1): 97–113.

CHAPTER 13
Logical Systems (Axioms, Rules, and Argumentation)

13.1 Introduction

Logical systems are strategies that attempt to make sense of phenomena and ideas and to place them within a coherent system or order. If a coherent system does not yet exist, the researcher will attempt to recognize or synthesize one. As such, logical systems are related to, but go far beyond classification strategies (chapter 8). They "tend to be ends in themselves; their entire mission seems to be to frame logical conceptual systems that... interconnect previously unknown or unappreciated factors in relevant ways" (Groat and Wang 2002, 301–2).

In practical terms, this hybrid category defies the singular term strategy. It is essentially synthetic and metatheoretical. Of all the strategies we identify in this book, it is the least developed in the literature of landscape architecture. This strategic bundle includes the development and dynamics of self-contained language structures such as grammars, codes, programming languages, mathematics, virtual realities, and games of many kinds. It is important to emphasize that although other research strategies use such codes for, say, evaluation or classification studies, the intellectual strategy of building the code in the first place belongs to the logical systems of axioms, rules, and argumentation.

The lack of clear identity for this category—that is, the difficulty in naming and evaluating it—may be partly explained by its large scope and ambition, as well as its many connections with other research strategies. For instance, this category overlaps with complex classification strategies, especially at the level of pattern languages and indexing languages. It also relates closely to evaluation (which applies the codes and rubrics developed in logical systems). Research in logical systems also frequently interacts with both design and modeling strategies, especially in the development of spatial models, decision models, and theoretical models predicting the behavior of dynamic systems.

In naming this group "logical argumentation," Groat and Wang (2002) were among the first to distinguish its activities as a special research category and to foreground its relevance in architectural research:

> The main characteristic of logical argumentation is that of *system*: its definition, its component parts and how they relate, what delimits the system, and how the system is connected to other systems that, in total, make up the cosmos in a logical manner. . . . Suffice it here to say that, while other research typologies implicitly assume system on their way to demonstrating other things, research in logical argumentation aims to frame the system itself. (2002, 92–3)

This class of strategies deals with a vast range of conjectural structures, such as the creation of virtual realities or ecologies, that are layered, adaptable, and comprehensive in and of themselves. In scientific philosophy, a hypothesis (a positive or negative declaration of expected findings based on accepted theory) is testable on empirical or statistical grounds. In contradistinction to such positive knowability, Karl Popper (1963) used the term *conjecture* to indicate a proposition that (for the purposes of research or practice) is presumed to be real or true, but is actually empirically inconclusive or unknowable. It is precisely the presumption of "reality" that allows for sustained inquiry, articulation, and development of conjectural structures, thus their appeal for designers. In fact, both design and logical systems are partly or wholly dependent on conjecture or proposition.

Although not completely convinced of its descriptive adequacy, for the discipline of landscape architecture we prefer to call this group logical systems (implying axioms, rules, and argumentation). Because systems research is usually governed by a priori theory (based on a theory of organization or function) rather than themes emerging inductively from a collection or sample (like classification), we have placed it in the deductive column of the matrix. Yet because this work is essentially a creative, synthetic, or pragmatic response to such abstractions, we have placed it in the subjectivist row. In this chapter we first explore the structure of logical systems—in particular, the relationships that make them systems. We then examine synthetic logical systems, expanded field analysis, spatial syntax, and indexing languages.

13.2 Logical Relationships

The component parts of a logical system are ideas or things that perform together at a higher level—such as in an organism, architecture, landscape, or language.

> In very general terms, a system is any (circumscribed) object which consists of a number of "parts" or "components" which, in some way or another, work together in order to produce an overall effect or behavior. As immediately can be seen, this concept is so general and all-encompassing, that any attempt to define it in both a complete and logically consistent manner would probably be futile. We can only concede to the obvious: that just about everything in the world would seem to be some sort of "system." (Ritchey 1991, 7)

Indeed, these images are all used at times as metaphors for complex systems (the architecture of the Internet; the landscape of higher education, etc.). And, as in ecology, every system must be understood as the interplay of scales. That is, it is only possible to understand a particular "system" as a whole object or unitary event from a scale order of magnitude higher, whereas "components" or constituent parts can only be understood from a scale order of magnitude lower. The classic short film *Powers of Ten* by Charles and Rae Eames offers a vivid dramatization of this idea. Chaos theory offers a slightly different version of the same idea—that our comprehension of organization or change is always relative to scale, in both time and distance.

Groat and Wang (2002) have proposed a spectrum of logical argumentation that ranges from the most abstract categories to the most situated; from computer programs and mathematical equations on the one hand to treatises and policies on the other. Because landscape architecture is concerned with a somewhat broader range of formal and cultural issues and tends more to the cultural and environmental end, we have modified their "spectrum" to include other categories (fig. 13.1).

Although evaluation research relies on a theory of value embedded within a rubric, the rubric itself is an example of a conjectural structure, developed through and resulting from the strategies of logical argumentation. It may be helpful here to think of the relationship between argumentation and adjudication (practical research methods) and the law or legal code (the structures that are constructed through methodical legal practice). Taking that analogy one step further, it is possible to understand logical systems as both a means and an end for research—a system that generates and articulates rules (best practices), as well as a repository or manifestation of lessons about rules learned from trials using other research strategies. We can see that such logical systems are equivalent to *policy research*—that is, environmental laws, codes, and best practices that exist as conjectural "truths," yet are continually tried, tested, and transformed into empirical knowledge through other means.

Consideration of law and codes highlights the role of decision making and decision trees in shaping a logical system. Like evaluation, decision-making processes take place in every discipline. Professionals, academics, and public administrators use logical systems to assist in guiding decision making and to ensure that decision making is orderly, unbiased, and efficient. Decision models are logical structures or systems developed for the purpose of analyzing and criticizing decisions; essentially they are used to increase efficiency and

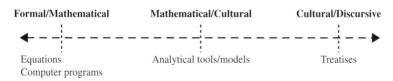

Figure 13.1 Spectrum of logical argumentation

(Adapted from Figure 11.2 in Groat and Wang 2002. Reproduced by permission of John Wiley and Sons.)

output. The purpose of decision models is to suggest the best possible answer to a given set of problems and yield the best set of means to arrive at a desired end.

A decision model is an axiomatic (rules-based) system that contains at least one action axiom (process directive). Decision models often look like a graphic or mathematical model that simulates a real process or system, albeit with simplified and abstracted elements. It often takes the form of a flow diagram, or "tree," with a series of steps or feedback loops that, depending on responses (go/no-go), can direct the decider to either consider the consequences of decisions or alternative actions. Decision trees may offer one or more points of entry, with multiple levels of complexity, depending on the service or level of engagement desired.

Decision models have been commonly developed for business purposes, including the Pure Rationality Model, the Increment Model, and the Bounded Rationality Model. Software engineers and Web designers have also created sophisticated decision model "architecture." Complex decision-making models exist in landscape architecture as well. Figure 13.2 illustrates a decision model developed by Steinitz (1990, 1995) to explain a rational process of site design to beginning students in landscape architecture.

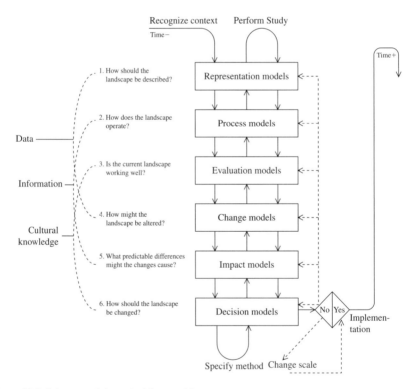

Figure 13.2 A framework for a decision model

(Courtesy of Carl Steinitz. Originally published in *Landscape Journal*, 1995. Reproduced by permission of the University of Wisconsin Press. Copyright 1995 by the Board of Regents of the University of Wisconsin System.)

13.3 Synthetic Logic

In order to address complex problems for which one theory may be inadequate, researchers in landscape architecture often try to reconcile or consolidate features from two or more disparate frameworks, perhaps connecting "unappreciated factors" in new ways. This creates a synthetic logical system. In a framework known as the Ladder of Citizen Participation, Arnstein (1969) classified eight levels of participation, in effect, describing the redistribution of power that enables nonparticipants to become decision makers. Landscape architects, organization researchers, and activists have tried to apply this notion to problems of corporate and community capacity building (Example 13.1). In order to create a hybrid "ladder of community participation" that also addressed certain challenges of community education, Thering and Doble (2000) synthesized Arnstein's "ladder" with Bloom's "taxonomy" on pedagogy (see chapter 8).

Example 13.1:
Theory and Practice in Sustainability
(Thering and Doble 2000)

Arguing that environmental and social sustainability are but two sides of the same coin, investigators sought to develop a new paradigmatic framework that could effectively address both issues and improve public participatory processes.

To gain a better understanding of trends in contemporary political behavior, the authors first explored and considered literature from intellectual history, as well as contemporary community activism and outreach. The challenge/opportunity that emerged from the literature review was to reconcile two potentially comparable or parallel taxonomies—one relevant for evaluating public education (Bloom's taxonomy of cognitive objectives) and the other relevant to evaluating public engagement (Arnstein's ladder of citizen participation).

Both taxonomies were compared and aligned so that their similarities became apparent; Bloom's objectives were proposed as outcomes for a simplified version of Arnstein's "ladder." Finally, the authors expanded and developed new categories (structure, integration, and approach) to describe the relationships between the two. The new approach was then compared or tested by a set of older case studies in community participation and visioning exercises.

For landscape architecture programs in public universities, the study is relevant for several reasons: state-mandated support for public outreach and extension, the prevalence of local community projects for service- and problem-based learning, and the position of landscape architects at the intersection of environmental and social factors for sustainability.

Because of its complexity and range, we included this example within the discussion of logical systems. The investigators have combined research strategies in classification techniques (literature mapping and taxonomy) to develop a new rubric for the evaluation of public engagement and education activities (logical argumentation).

It is interesting to note that although the focus of this study is the problem of evaluation of community-based education, the strategy it engages is synthetic logic—this is evident in the synthetic reconciliation of two taxonometric schemes. Another closely related example by Thering (2009) has been placed in the chapter about evaluation strategies (Example 10.1). That study has a similar motive—to improve schemes for community-based program evaluation—but the rubric, in that case, is grounded in "real-world" applications and feedback from experience. The rubric proposed in this study (Example 13.1) is almost entirely propositional and based on argumentation. Therefore, we have located this example within logical systems because the primary motive of the authors was axiomatic.

13.4 Expanded Field Analysis

Expanded field has been a fruitful analytical structure for mapping and understanding the composition of many fields of inquiry. Adapted from mathematics (Klein Group) as well as structuralism (Piaget), the cultural critic and theorist Rosalind Krauss translated the idea for the art world in the early 1980s. In her landmark essay, "Sculpture in the Expanded Field" (1983), Krauss developed an expanded field diagram explaining the relationship between binary terms of opposition (such as landscape and architecture) and their neutral "mirrors" (not-architecture and not-landscape).

The effect of this conceptual structure (fig. 13.3) on the discourse of landscape architecture was immediate and pronounced. It opened up possibilities for earthworks and other environmental sculpture to be intellectually mediated in the context of other emerging paradigms in the design fields. The terms that Krauss introduced at this time have proven to be highly durable: "marked sites," "site constructions," "sculpture," and "axiomatic structures." Within a few years, a series of new studies had emerged within the discipline of landscape architecture using expanded field diagrams, including those by Jacobs (1991) and Meyer (1997). In reviewing the impact of the concept, Jacobs speculated on its uses for other conceptual problems in landscape architecture.

> What would happen were we to apply the same expanded field analysis to landscape? While I have defined landscape as a concept in which sculpture mediates our idea of nature and of culture. . ., landscape is neither nature not culture, but rather is "suspended" between the two. The quaternary field occupied by culture-not culture and nature-not nature gives rise to a rich periphery of concepts that includes landscape displayed to the north of society, and environment displayed to the west of artifact. (1991, 53–54)

What this diagram suggests, according to Jacobs, is a way to "reintegrate landscape architecture into fields (e.g., environment) from which it has been temporarily excluded," and to rearticulate the values of the field (54). As presented here, the significance of the expanded field is almost purely argumentative or speculative, yet its appeal as an analytic device for a wider range of purposes remains unabated. It is, in itself, a deductive model of possibility.

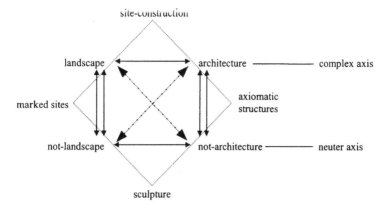

Sculpture in the Expanded Field - Rosalind Krauss

site-construction

landscape — architecture ——— complex axis

axiomatic
structures

marked sites

not-landscape — not-architecture ——— neuter axis

sculpture

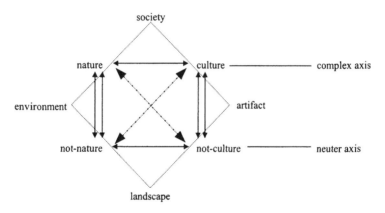

An Expanded Field for Landscape Architecture 1 - Peter Jacobs

society

nature — culture ——— complex axis

environment

artifact

not-nature — not-culture ——— neuter axis

landscape

Figure 13.3 Landscape in an expanded field

13.5 Spatial Syntax as Logical System

Since the 1970s, shape grammar and logic have resided at the abstract intersection of architecture and mathematics, where a wide variety of grammars have been constructed for design and the fine arts. Perhaps because of the tectonic properties of architecture, this set of theories and methods have found particularly fertile ground in architecture. However, the emergence of more sophisticated computational design for landscape architecture suggests that the importance and visibility of research on spatial syntax will only increase.

Knight (2003) writes, "All computational systems display emergence in some sense. Shape grammars (Stiny, 1980) are a computational system in which emergence is a foundational feature" (127). It is this property of emergence—not the emergence of human cognition and capacity, as in engaged action strategies, but the emergence of abstract spatial patterns and relationships that can expand our notions of design—that suggests spatial syntax belongs (with other logical strategies) on the subjectivist row. It is only because of the human ability to question or perceive relevance in abstract patterns that spatial syntax or any other language can develop at all.

The logical bases for this cluster of formal techniques are rooted in spatial and formal topologies. Topological spaces are defined as mathematical structures or geometries "that allow the formal definition of concepts such as convergence, connectedness, and continuity." For this reason they are important in spatial design fields such as architecture, planning, and landscape architecture, as well as in design for communication pathways and social networks. In preparing a site design, for example, landscape architects frequently use topological techniques (e.g., abstract bubble diagrams or flow charts) to analyze the relationships between program elements and circulatory function.

It might also be argued that the syntax of visual and formal elements developed for, say, visual inventory and landscape assessment studies (chapter 10) may comprise a shape grammar specific to landscape conditions. Rather than the abstractions of architectural structure, landscape syntax is rooted in terms of pictorial structure: points/objects (trees, figures, houses), lines (fences, roads, horizons), planes/surfaces (textures, patterns, thickness), and layers (foreground, background, depth, fold). To produce an inventory of these elements belongs to classification; to assess their beauty of coherence belongs to evaluation; to formulate and articulate the visual system is axiomatic—and, therefore, belongs to research in logical systems.

Other systems involving spatial syntax at a site or urban scale include pattern languages and metrology. Metrology may be defined quite simply as the science or system of measurement. In landscape architecture, metrology has been used in archaeological applications as a way of extrapolating or conjecturing site geometries that may have very little material evidence to support them (fig. 13.4). Applied in this way, metrology contributes to a conjectural system that suggests new questions or directions in research.

Two examples below demonstrate how metrology can become hybridized when computational and statistical analyses are combined with spatial analysis. Metrology can be useful in service of landscape ideas that are distinctly formal/geographical and humanistic. Example 13.2 investigates the logic of spatial patterns that appear to govern the location and orientation of ancient temples on Crete (Doxtater 2009).

The metrological study in Example 13.3 offers a conjectural reconstruction of a classical urban building complex in ancient Rome (Gleason 1994). The projection uses perspectival drawing techniques that synthesize evidence from extant city forms, as well as letters, carvings, and known social practices, together with classical urban-design theory and proportional systems. This exemplifies Groat and Wang's original point: that logical systems seek to "interconnect previously unknown or unappreciated factors in relevant ways."

Figure 13.4. Sacred Sites of Crete: Summit of Mount Kofinas (*left*) and Ida Cave (*right*). Figures 3 and 11 in "Rethinking the Sacred Landscape: Minoan Palaces in a Georitual Framework of Natural Features on Crete."

(Photographs courtesy of Dennis Doxtater, 2000. Originally published in *Landscape Journal,* 2009. Reproduced by permission of the University of Wisconsin Press. Copyright 2009 by the Board of Regents of the University of Wisconsin System.)

13.6 Pattern Language

In 1991, Robert Riley, then editor of *Landscape Journal,* challenged readers to identify five books that had most influenced their work in landscape. The resulting editorial, "Most Influential Books," included thirty-seven responses with 228 citations. Only twelve works were cited three or more times; one of them was Christopher Alexander's *A Pattern Language: Towns, Buildings, Construction* (1977). A contributor to Riley's survey, Anne Spirn, remembered Alexander's early work as liberating. "As a visually-oriented person steeped in a highly verbal educational tradition, I found that the diagrams in [an] early version of *Pattern Language* packed a jolt in the way they fused abstract ideas, empirical information, and physical form. A door opened; this was a language more native to me than words" (1991, 185).

Describing the book's contribution to postmodern design thinking, Condon (1988) wrote, "Alexander's (1977) *A Pattern Language* marked the first major comprehensive

Example 13.2:
Rethinking the Sacred Landscape
(Doxtater 2009)

This is an investigation into the deep cultural roots of landscape architecture. The author challenges the long-standing interpretation of the relationship between Greek and Minoan temples and the surrounding landscape put forward by the historian Vincent Scully. Scully argued that the alignment observed between classical temples and adjacent landscape features was the result of the formal *extension* of the sacred architecture outward into the site. The purpose of this research was to test an alternative premise: that Minoan palaces were located primarily in relation to features in the landscape context and connected the landscape to the temple—by *intension,* or drawing in the landscape to the architecture.

Because there are only the merest fragments left of these temple complexes, and no other triangulating evidence, the author must use logical (geometrical) models to argue in favor of this georitual framework. The strategy adopted a metrology—a theory of measurement that uses interpolation to reveal hidden spatial structures and relationships.

First, the author demonstrates that the builders designed and laid out temples based upon good surveys of the landscape. Then he employs a customized spatial-modeling software called Geopatterns to generate all possible mathematical relationships between the temples. Finally, he calculates the statistical probability that the geometries linking landscape to temple sites were random (or, conversely, were intentional).

The first step was to identify and survey the most significant natural features on the island of Crete and to compare the patterns of actual building and orientations with those generated by chance. The author also used plans, photographs, and perspectives of the temples to inform and interpret the results.

Based on metrology, the author concluded that the locations of the major Minoan palaces—Knossos, Mallia, Zakros, Phaistos—appear not to have been randomly oriented, but rather were deliberately and intentionally oriented to natural features. The significance of this finding suggests a need for historians to revise received understanding of Minoan culture and its relationship with nature.

This example is interesting because it shows the way that spatial modeling and logical systems can be used to inform theoretical investigation into wider cultural questions. Although this is not a proof of the proposition, it offers enough evidence of a new "rule" to be plausible and to inform new theoretical models for further development. As a strategy, the research is hybrid as, it includes modeling. The underlying logic is deductive, but the proposition is tested by spatial argumentation, rather than by experimentation.

design theory based on the environmentalist paradigm; the city was viewed. . . as habitat—a complex system of interdependencies that together comprised the 'patterns' of a 'language'" (10). A pattern language may thus be understood as a network of patterns that are linked and interdependent. Used in combination, patterns can create complex forms and typologies. Patterns are analogous to words, relying on syntax (proper grammatical structure and relationships) to create an endless variety of sentences and complex meanings. Individual patterns describe a typical solution to a familiar or perennial problem in any

Example 13.3:
Porticus Pompeiana: A New Perspective
(Gleason 1994)

Most landscape historians are not aware that the origins of the term *porticus,* or colonnade, referred to a type of urban garden in Rome. This study reports on an archaeological site in Rome that once was a luxurious complex of gardens, temples, amphitheaters, political institutions, and markets known as the *opera Pompeiana,* or Pompey's Porticus. Because of the translation of the term porticus (as porch—an architectural feature) and the absence of preserved remnants of the site, it is difficult to understand the character or dimensions and features of the park. However, traces of the contours of the precinct are visible still in the urban form of Rome, and textual and anecdotal evidence is available in historic texts. Also, the marble plan of Rome (210 CE) indicates some of the main features of the space.

The author wonders how such a large structure, expressing the aggressive political ambitions of the owner, could have been designed at this time in Roman history when legal restrictions were placed on structures such as amphitheaters. The study uses metrology, relying on graphic techniques of planimetry and perspectival projection to demonstrate how the space may have been conceived and experienced.

Theoretical constructs for this virtual reconstruction include Vitruvian principles of geometry and proportion that guide the size and arrangement of regulating geometries (circles, grids, rectangles, and axes) inscribed on the probable location of the site. Also, because the probable narrative of the garden was an homage paid to Venus, it suggests the character and the choreography of the spaces.

The significance of this study is to open up new possible interpretations of the urban design of Rome, as well as an alternative understanding of the quality of space and furnishing of Pompey's Porticus and the concept of the public park as a shared democratic space.

This study offers a perfect example of the way that logical argument may be used in landscape architecture to connect disparate ideas and evidence in a new way and to present a coherent conjectural structure.

given context or scale. Patterns are independent of materials, so they can be interpreted freely and adapted as needed for costs or culture.

Combining studies in architecture with transportation theory and computer science at MIT, and cognition and cognitive studies at Harvard, Alexander and his colleagues reasoned that a syntactical architectural system could be formulated to empower anyone to design buildings at any scale. Thus, the work presented a highly theoretical generative grammar that was practical and "user-friendly." Their collaboration anticipated a growing interest in architectural and landscape typologies, influencing not only the design of built spaces but also gardens (Easton 2007), streets, pattern languages in computer science, and the architecture of computer gaming.

The idea of generative grammar that is syntactical and axiomatic is altered, but not unrecognizable in the metaphors of a phenomenological language of landscape, for

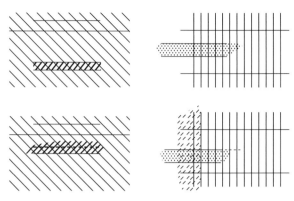

Figure 13.5 Syntactic landscape spatial relations: (*left*) "Throughout an Along an Along—Now/Later"; (*right*) "Between a Far and Near—Today/Tomorrow." Figure 7 in "Land-scopic regimes: Exploring perspectival representation beyond the 'pictorial' project."

(Image courtesy of H. Getch Clarke. Originally published in *Landscape Journal,* 2005. Reproduced by permission of the University of Wisconsin Press. Copyright 2005 by the Board of Regents of the University of Wisconsin System.

instance, in the work of Spirn (1998) and Joan Nassauer (1995). Using the metaphors of patterns and language, Nassauer explains, "[A]pplied landscape ecology is essentially a design problem . . . [that] requires the translation of ecological patterns into cultural language (Eaton 1990 a, b). It requires placing unfamiliar and frequently undesirable forms inside familiar, attractive packages. It requires designing orderly frames for messy ecosystems" (1995, 161).

More recently, there has been continued interest in exploring syntactical spatial relationships in landscape representation. Using the work of Stephen Holl as a point of reference, Getch Clarke (2005) identifies and articulates a landscape system of connections, linkages, adjacencies, and movements (fig. 13.5). In turn, this system supports her rejection of picturesque conventions in landscape architecture in favor of an alternative modality she has termed the *phenomenological picturesque.*

Logical Systems: Summary

Logical systems often provide a neutral, metadisciplinary point of entry for ideas and languages from sister disciplines like painting, sculpture, architecture, music, dance, and other notational arts. They also have strong connections with related "invented" languages or symbolic system-based strategies (e.g., Labanotation, the innovative language for recording natural movements of people used by Anna and Lawrence Halprin). Iconology (chapter 9) may also be understood as a language structure resulting from research in a system of symbols and images.

However, it is important to register different modalities of this type of such broad-reaching research strategy. Recognizing icons and producing iconographic inventories belongs to classification; the application of iconological concepts to draw out complex themes belongs to interpretation, and so on. The research strategy for logical systems lies in recognizing or inventing the language as an emergent phenomenon in itself.

- Logical systems are rules-based strategies; this category of research attempts to make sense of phenomena and ideas and to place them within a coherent system or order.

- As a category for research, logical systems overlap considerably with a variety of other strategies and families.

- Logical systems of spatial syntax and grammars have been adapted for landscape architecture in innovative ways.

The abstraction of axiomatic structures such as language, form, and organization is appealing to many because it offers the possibility for a transcendent, nonspecific meta-discipline that *seems* to be free (for a while) from social, material, and economic constraints. Perhaps, this is why this group of research strategies is among the most complex to explain, and yet it is frequently the most appealing to students of design. However, there is also a significant risk that studies based entirely on logical systems may become overly abstract, seductive but ungrounded in reality, and/or unproductive in terms of landscape utility or performance.

References

Alexander, C. 1977. *A pattern language: Towns, buildings, construction*. New York: Oxford University Press.

Arnstein, S. R. 1969. A ladder of citizen participation. *American Institute of Planners Journal,* 35 (4): 216–24.

Condon, P. 1988. Cubist space, volumetric space, and landscape architecture. *Landscape Journal* 7 (1): 1–14.

Doxtater, D. 2009. Rethinking the sacred landscape: Minoan palaces in a georitual framework of natural features on Crete. *Landscape Journal* 28 (1): 1–20.

Easton, V. 2007. *A pattern garden: The essential elements of garden making.* Portland, OR: Timber Press.

Eaton, M. M. 1990a. *Aesthetics and the good life.* Rutherford, NJ: Farleigh Dickinson University Press.

———. 1990b. Responding to the call for new landscape metaphors. *Landscape Journal* 9 (1): 22–7.

Getch Clarke, H. A. 2005. Land-scopic regimes: Exploring perspectival representation beyond the "pictorial" project. *Landscape Journal* (24) 1: 50–68.

Gleason, K. L. 1994. Porticus Pompeiana: A new perspective on the first public park in Rome. *Journal of Garden History* 14 (1): 13–27.

Groat, L., and D. Wang. 2002. *Architectural Research Methods.* New York: John Wiley and Sons.

Jacobs, P. 1991. De In Re (form)ing landscape. *Landscape Journal* 10 (1): 48–56.

Knight, T. 2003. Computing with emergence. *Environment and Planning B: Planning and Design* 30 (1): 125–55.

Krauss, R. 1983. Sculpture in the expanded field. In *The Anti-Aesthetic,* ed. H. Foster, 31–42. Port Townsend, WA: Bay Press.

Meyer, E. 1997. The expanded field of landscape architecture. In *Ecological design and planning,* ed. G. F. Thompson and F. R. Steiner. New York: John Wiley and Sons.

Nassauer, J. I. 1995. Messy ecosystems, orderly frames. *Landscape Journal* 14 (2): 161–70.

Popper, K. 1963. *Conjecture and refutation: The growth of scientific knowledge.* London: Routledge and Kegan Paul.

Riley, R., and B. Brown, eds. 1991. Most influential books. *Landscape Journal* 10 (2): 173–186.

Ritchey, T. 1991. Analysis and synthesis: On scientific method—based on a study by Bernhard Riemann. *Systems Research* 8 (4): 21–41.

Spirn, A. 1998. *The language of landscape.* New Haven: Yale University Press.

Steinitz, C. 1990. A framework for theory applicable to the education of landscape architects (and other environmental design professionals). *Landscape Journal* 9 (2): 136–43.

———. 1995. Design is a verb; design is a noun. *Landscape Journal* 14 (2): 188–200.

Stiny, G. 1980. Introduction to shape and shape grammars. *Environment and Planning B: Design and Planning* 7 (3): 343–51.

Thering, S., and C. Doble. 2000. Theory and practice in sustainability: Building a ladder of community-focused education and outreach. *Landscape Journal* 19 (1–2): 191–200.

Thering, S. 2009. A methodology for evaluating transdisciplinary collaborations with diversity in mind: An example from the Green Community Development in Indian Country Initiative. *Journal of Extension* 47 (3), online article #3FEA2, www.joe.org.

CHAPTER 14

Research and Practice

14.1 Introduction

The purpose of this book is to empower new researchers and motivate a new generation of scholarly practitioners in landscape architecture and environmental design. Bentz and Shapiro (1998) define a scholarly practitioner as:

> someone who mediates between her professional practice and the universe of scholarly, scientific, and academic knowledge and discourse. She sees her practice as part of a larger enterprise of knowledge generation and critical reflection. . . . The role of the scholarly practitioner involves a two-way relationship. It involves using professional practice and knowledge as a resource for evaluating, testing, applying, extending or modifying knowledge. It involves mastering procedures for generating knowledge, not only to create knowledge but, as important, to become aware of the limits of knowledge. (1998, 66)

Professional practice constitutes a (mostly) untapped research capacity of enormous potential value for the discipline. The numbers are compelling. Practitioners outnumber academics by more than an order of magnitude. In a recent workshop on urban ecology we attended, the majority of participants were practitioners—many of them scholarly in the sense described above. Their interest was in learning and sharing new knowledge about the incorporation of urban ecology concepts into practice. If each participant at that workshop engaged in just one project each year that was structured to formally generate new knowledge—if it incorporated a *research strategy*—our rate of shared new learning and knowledge creation could increase dramatically. One of the main challenges in adjusting to the "new normal" in which new knowledge is a critical feature of successful practice is, therefore, how to more systematically connect the research activity of universities with professional practice, and to better connect scholarly practitioners with a wider research community and enterprise.

It is particularly notable that much of the knowledge transformation in landscape architecture is emerging precisely at the interface of research and practice. Market pressures provide one set of drivers, with design companies competing for brand recognition as innovative problem-solvers. A second set of drivers are related to new models of governance that demand enhanced performance from public policy, investment, and infrastructure. Third, it is important to recognize the impetus from individuals at the interface of practice and the academy—a new and growing generation of practitioner scholars who see themselves as agents of cultural change (Corner 1999). The excitement of innovative design penetrates even the most staid of established research institutions, which are beginning to recognize and value the transformative value of nontraditional research strategies of the sort discussed particularly in chapters 11 to 13.

Transformation of knowledge may occur in several ways and at different levels. Environmental design in general and landscape architecture in particular have been transformed most dramatically through two contrasting yet in some ways complementary traditions—pragmatic innovation and polemic design exploration. Both are responses to changing demands of the context and the times and have led to the discovery and demonstration of emerging theories, principles, and techniques for diagnosing and resolving societal issues and problems.

On the one hand, there is a pragmatic development and testing of knowledge in practice settings—a reciprocal process that links the operational knowledge of the discipline with its systematic knowledge. The movement we consider below is "evidence-based design," a public-policy paradigm that seeks to incrementally enhance the quality of public investment in policy, design, and services. On the other hand, chapter 12 has highlighted the extension and promulgation of conceptual knowledge through polemical scholarship and

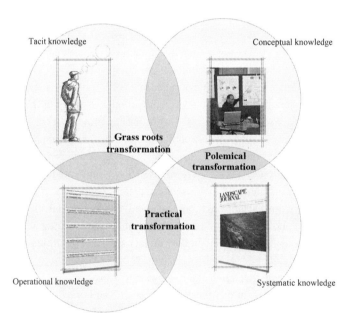

Figure 14.1 Realms of knowledge transformation

its expression in practice innovation, such competitions and exploratory projects. This also informs and transforms the systematic knowledge base of the discipline by challenging conventional categorizations and assumptions.

Between these two processes we also see the work of individuals and networks of scholarly practitioners—observing, reflecting, interpreting, using grounded and community-based techniques such as participatory action research—to build grassroots movements through which knowledge becomes embedded in the context of practice.

In the following sections we examine in turn these three realms of knowledge development—practical transformation through evidence-based design and policy, polemical transformation, and grassroots transformation (fig. 14.1). In all three, there are organizational challenges in connecting research with practice. In the final section of the chapter, we consider organizational issues and opportunities for ways in which research activity of any kind can be integrated into practice.

14.2 Integrating Research Strategies into Practice— Evidence-Based Design

Evidence-based practice is the premise that practice should be based upon systematic knowledge grounded in empirical evidence. It is a concept that has been widely adopted in the health sciences (de Leeuw 2009), and the links between health, well-being, and environment have been critical in extending the paradigm into the design professions (Cooper Marcus and Francis 1998; Harris et al. 2008; Ward Thompson and Travlou 2007). More recently, there have been parallel developments in architecture (Hamilton and Watkins 2009), social science (Young et al. 2002), and public services more generally (Davies et al. 2000).

Evidence-based policy "helps people make well-informed decisions about policies, programs and projects by putting the best available evidence from research at the heart of policy development and implementation" (Davies 1999). The closely related concept of evidence-based design is in a similar way "a process for the conscientious, explicit, and judicious use of current best evidence from research and practice in the making of critical decisions, together with an informed client, about the design of each individual and unique project" (Hamilton and Watkins 2009). Demand for public and private action to be linked to evidence of its efficacy is reinforced by the need to defend and justify expert professional decisions in an increasingly litigious society that opens professional knowledge to the scrutiny of the courts and other quasi-legal processes.

Hamilton and Watkins (2009) review a number of "models" of evidence-based design that also provide insight on the rationale for the emergence of the paradigm. They include project-based research, preparation of broad databases, niche-focused investigations, client-driven research, the use of evidence-based practice as a promotional/ marketing tool, and its role as a new business strategy. They also note a number of levels at which evidence-based design can be undertaken. These range from "pretending" (i.e., using selected research to justify decisions already taken) (Marmot 2004) and following the latest literature, to making more formal commitments to making and testing propositions about practice, sharing the lessons learned, and submitting results for peer-reviewed publication.

There are a number of strategies that can provide the framework for generating knowledge that can claim status as "evidence." In science, the emphasis is upon experimentation, which, as has been noted (chapter 7), can be hard to apply to landscape architectural questions. However, comparative case studies, correlation, alternative futures modeling, classification (particularly typology), and postoccupancy evaluation are all examples of types of strategy described and illustrated in the preceding chapters that are capable of generating knowledge that can withstand scrutiny as evidence in a legal setting or in the public examination of policy or design proposals.

The critical factor in applying any or all of these strategies within practice is the need to formalize the process in a way that meets the quality conventions for that particular strategy (see chapters 4 or 12 for a discussion of quality criteria). So, for example, identification of resilient design configurations for a particular type of situation through a comparison of a series of case studies requires a systematic template for analysis of each case (as illustrated in Francis 2002; see chapter 5 of this book), a framework for comparison of the cases, and a way of recording and reporting the outcomes. These need to be established at the start of the process, not retrospectively.

Similarly, postoccupancy evaluation requires a database of design goals and decisions that must be initiated at the start of the project. Even then, as the example by McWilliam and Brown (2001; see chapter 5 of this book) illustrates, changes in measurement techniques and standards can make longitudinal comparisons difficult. A number of the more "subjectivist" strategies such as action research (chapter 11) offer greater flexibility in adapting to changing research settings and parameters over time, although the selection of a strategy for practice-based research needs to consider the institutional setting (see section 14.5).

14.3 Integrating Research into Practice — Polemical Transformation

Transformative research has been described in radical terms, as "a range of endeavors which promise extraordinary outcomes, such as: revolutionizing entire disciplines; creating entirely new fields; or disrupting accepted theories and perspectives—in other words, those endeavors which have the potential to change the way we address challenges in science, engineering, and innovation" (NSF 2007). The language and the process are very different from the systematic and incremental transformation that results from evidence-based design. In polemical transformation, the style is bold and radical challenge.

Quite beyond critique, polemic means controversy. As such, a polemical practice or text aims to dispute or refute a position or theory (philosophical, sociopolitical, or scientific) that represents generally received opinion. Polemic is intended to provoke significant change. It may be motivated by many things, including a sense of injustice, incorrectness, inadequacy, or unfairness, or a forecast of imminent doom—the sense that "we're headed over the falls and nobody else knows it yet." *Design with Nature* (McHarg 1969), now a classic of the literature of the discipline, was, first and foremost, a polemic that proposed an alternative framework for evaluating land and decision-making processes. Hohmann and Langhorst's "Apocalyptic Manifesto" (2004), cited in Baird and Szczygiel (2008) is another type of polemic, intended principally to challenge and confront what they see as a growing complacency in the profession of landscape architecture.

A large body of work based on polemical design has emerged in the thirty years since Krog lamented the paucity of design innovation in the discipline (1981). In Europe, France and the Netherlands, in particular, have been crucibles of innovation and polemic. Individuals such as Christophe Girot and Georges Descombes, and practices such as West 8 and MVRDV, have projected alternative modes of practice and broad visions of social and urban change through their work and competitions. Similar movements have emerged in North America and around the Pacific (Field Operations, Room 4.1.3, and many others). As reviewed in chapter 12, polemical projects have challenged conventional practice and articulated new possibilities, a process captured best by Corner's formulation of landscape as a "strategic agent of culture" (1999).

The challenge is how to place this work within the discipline's systematic knowledge. At what point does a design proposition embedded in a competition entry, or in the virtual projects so beloved of landscape urbanists, become tested and accepted as part of the wider knowledge base of the discipline? The disciplinary "work in progress" of polemical transformation is the codification of knowledge. If it is created in ways that have credibility with the wider discipline, it will, in due course, inform operational protocols—moving from the design "laboratory" into the design office and the regulatory sphere.

14.4 Integrating Knowledge into Practice—Grassroots Movements

Between these broad movements, driven by public policy imperatives and by leading public scholar-practitioners and their corporate embodiment in large practices, there is the "bottom up" knowledge transformation of the individual scholar-practitioner (Castells 1983). This person is the grassroots of reflection and community engagement, who draws more directly upon Schön's concept of the "reflective practitioner" (1983).

All practitioners engage in such reflection, either willingly or under the duress of crisis, and it is upon this base that the tacit knowledge of the discipline is grounded. However, by its nature, such knowledge is individual, introspective, unformed. It can become integrated into the wider body of knowledge of the discipline in three ways. First, it can be connected through expression in operational knowledge at a grassroots level—through the development of protocols and locally embedded practices that resolve local needs in particular ways. Second, and less frequently, but most important, the knowledge can be codified and publicly expressed in conference presentations, scholarly books, and increasingly, through Internet portals—community Web sites, blogs, and the like. As was noted in chapter 2, much of the discipline's conceptual knowledge has been shaped and communicated in this way, through the books produced over the years based upon an individual's lifetime of experience.

Third, and more challenging, is the need to translate the core knowledge of individual scholar practitioners into the systematic knowledge base of the discipline. This typically depends upon a relationship of some kind between a researcher and one or more practitioners, drawing out characteristic modes of practice, comparing and contrasting, and placing the work into its wider context. This is the work of interpretive research strategies—ethnography, historiography, and biography—that are focused upon our own discipline and its shakers and movers.

14.5 Organizing Practice-Based Research

Historically, there was no distinction between practice and research within the discipline—new knowledge was created by practitioner scholars. It was the creation of specialized university courses and faculty and the emergence of a distinct research culture, guarded by the "gatekeepers" discussed in chapter 1, that has opened a space—and in some places a gulf—between the two. What organizational arrangements can help to reintegrate research culture more fully into practice? In this section, we review a spectrum of relationships that are possible, arguing that the challenge currently faced by the discipline is the need to shift the median of practice-based research activity from passive consumption toward constructive leadership.

The dominant relationship between practice and practitioners and research, as we have outlined it, is that of *passive consumer* (Table 14.1). Most, if not all, practices subscribe to professional magazines—either hard copy or online—and these increasingly include articles that cite research findings. The discussion in *Landscape Architecture* magazine about green roofs, noted in chapter 5, is one example of this process. However, the process here is typically opportunistic—a practitioner may pick up some new knowledge relevant to a project or be inspired to investigate further, but that depends upon the material being featured in an article.

The advent of the Internet has vastly enhanced the potential to be an *active consumer* of research. Search engines such as Google enable practitioners to directly search and, in many cases, access both peer-reviewed research and also the growing volume of grey literature—for example, reports published online by public agencies, nongovernmental organizations, businesses, and practices, as well as by universities and research centers. Some practices and practitioners subscribe directly to research journals. However, the findings of Gobster et al. (2010) on citation indices suggest that the sources most likely to be accessed on research relevant to practice may not be the specialized landscape architecture journals.

Effective search and review also requires an investment of billable time. These types of skills have not been universally mastered in the profession, particularly in practices

Table 14.1 Practice Relationships with Research

Passive consumer	Active consumer	Host	Collaborator	Sponsor	Partner	Leader
Detached			Engaged			Integrated

dominated by staff with undergraduate rather than master's degrees. One real challenge for inexperienced and experienced searchers alike is how to discriminate between credible and less-credible sources and knowledge claims. Therefore, a challenge for the discipline more generally is to achieve greater utility and impact through the specialist journals that publicly represent our "discipline" (Gobster et al. 2010).

Practices that are located in regions with tertiary institutions (universities) that teach landscape architecture are increasingly playing a role as research *hosts*—taking students on placements or scholarships. In a recent initiative in New Zealand, for example, the Tertiary Education Commission funded several hundred summer scholarships for senior undergraduate students on the condition that they involved industry partners. Another type of relationship is a graduate research placement, in which graduates gain credit for completion of a project in association with a practice. We have had productive research relationships with practices following these types of research student-host models (e.g., Ayres et al. 2010), which have scope for much wider application.

Another variation on this type of host relationship involves faculty spending time in practices, undertaking research that is supported in kind by the practice. The type of research undertaken is typically modest in scale and ambition—for example, literature review or post occupancy evaluation. These types of practice-host relationship can then result in coauthored peer-reviewed publications and thereby contribute to the systematic body of knowledge of the discipline. The advantages for the practice include direct engagement with talented and experienced researchers, as well as the build-up of practice-based knowledge on topics relevant to their market plan.

Hosting a researcher can easily translate into research *collaboration.* In many research agencies and schemes, collaboration between a university researcher and an industry organization is a prerequisite for access to public or foundation funding. The collaborator may contribute in kind to the project, by providing facilities or access to sites, but what is typically required by the funding agency is evidence that the findings of the research will contribute to either business success or wider public good and well-being. This requires researchers to have active collaborations with end users of the research— such as practices, industry sectors, and public agencies. Successful research applications almost inevitably now include provisions for knowledge transfer. Correlational research, scenario-based modeling, and alternative-futures research are all examples of research strategies that typically involve collaborations with practitioners in public agencies.

Practice *sponsorship* of academic research expresses another level of commitment. The sponsorship may be modest—perhaps just sufficient to leverage other funding— but the effect can be far-reaching. Many service learning studio projects involve some measure of sponsorship by a community or public agency—which can enable access to other funding sources. The various action research models discussed in chapter 11 offer some models for engagement. Another strategy that can be an effective focus of sponsorship is case-study research, enabling a practice to formalize and share the knowledge embedded in completed projects by following the case-study model exemplified in chapter 5.

Research *partnerships* imply a full involvement by practices and practitioners in the development and implementation of a research project—from initial scoping, through funding applications, implementation, and reporting. A number of practices are recognizing the opportunity to bid for public research projects as an integral part of their business model and actively incorporate funded research projects into their core activities. This may involve a wide range of research strategies—from basic public perception surveys to complex diagnostic investigations. In all cases, the key requirement is that the practice has the appropriate research skills to be a full and equal partner with a research center or university.

The highest level of engagement is for practices to become research *leaders*. This has been increasingly the case in research projects that are focused upon particular regions or locations, or upon policy-related work. An early influential example of research leadership by practitioners was the preparation by Land Use Consultants of the Countryside Character Assessment system (Swanwick and Land Use Consultants 2002). In Europe, large consultancies and consortia of practices are currently undertaking a range of projects related to the implementation of the European Landscape Convention.

Many of these projects are consistent with the paradigm of evidence-based policy and design. Much of the polemical transformation and knowledge creation in the discipline is also undertaken by practices as research leaders. Some style their practices as "research laboratories," and their work as "design experimentation" (Steenbergen 2008). However, in this category of engagement, as in all the less active categories, the critical test remains whether the research outcomes contribute to the systematic knowledge of the discipline. Gaining funding or investing practice time and funds in exploratory studies do not in themselves constitute research. This also requires formal expression as an outcome that meets the quality criteria of research discussed in the first part of this book.

Strengthening the engagement of landscape architectural practice with research and, hence, contributing to the systematic body of knowledge of the discipline faces a number of challenges. These include, first, how to enhance practice-based research skills; second, how to deal with the relationship of intellectual property and published systematic knowledge, when innovation increasingly has a business value; and third, how to more effectively incorporate the "experimental" polemics of the leading practitioner scholars into the systematic body of knowledge of the discipline.

Enhancement of practice-based research skills requires a greater level of attention to the place of research methodology in continuing professional development (CPD) or continuing education (CE) programs. Traditionally, CPD/CE has focused on operational knowledge, with occasional forays into conceptual knowledge through attendance at conferences with inspirational speakers. The critical need for enhancing formal research activity in practices is to build practitioner capacity in research skills. It is our hope that this text will prompt further reflection and development of those potentials.

One fruitful avenue is the development of higher research degrees that can be taken part time, and at a distance, encouraging practitioners to develop research skills and confidence incrementally over a period of two or three years. Another avenue is through the collaborations and hosting arrangements discussed above, in which exposure to experienced researchers helps practitioners develop familiarity with the protocols of disciplined investigation. Development of practice research networks offers a particularly exciting pathway that has been explored with considerable success.

The management of intellectual property issues in research projects is another challenge, but there are precedents in a number of related disciplines, and all universities have protocols and proforma that deal with the outcomes of collaborative research. A common model is to embargo research findings for an initial period—for example, two years—enabling the practice partner to leverage advantage from their collaboration, after which publication in academic journals is allowed. Ultimately, business advantages from innovative practice usually accrue more from broad dissemination of inspirational work than through control of particular patents. However, some certification and benchmarking schemes fall into the category where value can be extracted over a longer period by retaining control of the intellectual property. The relationship between private gain and the public good will become an increasingly important issue as the knowledge base of the discipline deepens.

Translation of the innovation of the leading practitioner scholars from conceptual knowledge into the systematic knowledge base of the discipline offers its own distinct challenges. The individuals and practices that lead innovation through polemical projects have not always made the commitment to report their work in ways that makes it suitable for peer-reviewed publication in journals, although this appears to be changing (e.g., Weller 2008 a, b; Waldheim and Berger 2008). Instead, the role of transformation from conceptual to systematic knowledge falls to those theorists and others who undertake critical reviews of the work.

The research strategies used for this transformation typically fall within the middle-lower part of the classification matrix. In particular, the development of logical systems, typologies, and historical and theoretical interpretations help to situate polemical projects in their wider disciplinary and social context. The commentators and critics involved in this mediation include a growing number of knowledge brokers. Some translate the work of polemic and innovative practitioners into more formal systems of knowledge, while others translate the systematic knowledge of the discipline into more accessible forms of operational and conceptual knowledge.

The caricature of this role is the "media don"—the academic who popularizes science or scholarship and becomes a commentator in the popular media. There is growing recognition of the need to encourage and support the role of faculty who undertake this "outreach" role —acknowledging the scholarship required (Milburn et al. 2003)—but there are few institutional arrangements that provide the practical support required for effective extension into the design professions, when compared with the programs that service agriculture, for example. Nonetheless, research agents and knowledge brokers will be a critical part of the discipline over the coming decades.

14.6 Reprise

In assembling this text, we set out to offer researchers in landscape architecture a place to begin shaping their research program. We started by asking what research strategies are appropriate and effective for the discipline, and by what criteria should new knowledge be evaluated. Our investigation has been structured by a focus upon strategy rather than method, and we have adopted a process of survey, classification, and commentary upon recently published research within English-speaking parts of the discipline. It is, thus, only a partial survey, but the global extent is wide, drawing examples from Australia and New Zealand, North America, and across Europe.

The opening chapters reviewed the nature of knowledge "gatekeeping" within the discipline and the debates that have revolved around the definition of theory and research in landscape architecture. We have adopted a broad and inclusive, rather than a narrow, approach to these questions of definition. We have nonetheless grounded our approach to research quality in established institutions—drawing examples from peer-reviewed journals and research quality criteria and thesis requirements from established protocols within our respective universities.

The core of the book—the nine chapters that lay out a series of research strategies, with each explained and illustrated by examples—has revealed a rich and varied terrain of research activity in landscape architecture. One of the main conclusions we draw from this review, which is relevant to the debate about the definitions and limits of research and for new researchers shaping a research strategy, is that no strategy will satisfy all possible criteria of research quality. This is well known by experienced researchers. Research design is, above all else, a work of trade-offs and compromise, balancing the desirable with the possible and the useful.

Our approach to the vexed question of whether design can be research draws upon this contextual understanding. Rather than excluding design research on the basis that it cannot (or perhaps more accurately has not yet) met *all* conventional research quality criteria in all respects (Milburn et al. 2003), we have taken the view that all research strategies are a process of balancing different needs and demands. Design as research provides a different profile of quality measures than conventional strategies—but this generates other advantages, as we explain in chapter 12. Indeed, design research, when crafted and practiced appropriately, is no further from mainstream science than are other emergent research strategies—a number of which are included elsewhere in our classification matrix. The key is to ensure that the balancing of aims and criteria is undertaken deliberately, carefully, and contextually, in order to maximize the overall value and effectiveness of the research enterprise.

In this final chapter we have reviewed the ways in which research and practice interrelate, and suggested how they might cooperate better in the future. In particular, we have explored three realms across which knowledge is transformed by and through its relationships with practice and have identified challenges and opportunities in each. Our concluding hope is that this overall process of survey, review, and commentary upon research strategies and their practice context will empower all researchers in the discipline. We have specifically targeted the next generation of researchers—graduates in landscape architecture programs—but we also hope that the map we have created and the commentaries we offer will encourage and empower the many scholarly practitioners who can contribute to enhancing the knowledge of the discipline. If we have managed to inspire new researchers—young or old—we will have succeeded in our goal. If we have stimulated experienced researchers to reflect further upon their practice, that is an added bonus.

References

Ayres, II., P. Burns, T. Church, S. Davis, and S. Swaffield. 2010. Research and development of a conceptual framework for sustainability indicators used in structure planning. *LEap Report* no. 13. Christchurch, New Zealand: Lincoln University.

Baird, C. T., and B. Szczygiel. 2008. Sociology of the professions: The evolution of landscape architecture in the United States. *Landscape Review* 12 (1): 3–25.

Bentz, V. M., and J. J. Shapiro. 1998. *Mindful inquiry in social research.* Thousand Oaks, CA: Sage.

Castells, M. 1983. *The city and the grassroots.* Berkeley: University of California press.

Cooper Marcus, C., and C. Francis, eds. 1998. *People places: Design guidelines for urban open space.* 2nd ed. New York: John Wiley and Sons.

Corner, J. 1999. *Recovering landscape.* Princeton, NJ: Princeton University Press.

Davies, H. T. O., S. M. Nutley, and P. C. Smith. 2000. *What works? Evidence-based policy and practice in public services.* Bristol, U.K.: Policy Press, Bristol University.

Davies, P. T. 1999. What is evidence-based education? *British Journal of Educational Studies* 47 (2): 108–21.

Francis, M. 2002. Village Homes: A case study in Community design. *Landscape Journal* 21 (1): 23–41.

Gobster, P. H., J. I. Nassauer, and D. J. Nadenicek. 2010. *Landscape Journal* and scholarship in landscape architecture: The next 25 years. *Landscape Journal* 29 (1): 52–70.

Hamilton, D. K., and D. H. Watkins. 2009. *Evidence-based design for multiple building types.* Hoboken, NJ: John Wiley and Sons.

Harris, D., A. Joseph, F. Becker, K. Hamilton, M. Shepley, and C. Zimring. 2008. *A practitioner's guide to evidence-based design.* Concord, CA: Center for Health Design.

Hohmann, H., and J. Langhast. 2004. An apocalyptic manifesto. Unpublished discussion paper. Department of landscape Architecture, Iowa state University. www.iastate.edu/nisi/dead.

Krog, S. 1981. Is it art? *Landscape Architecture Magazine,* May, 373–76.

de Leeuw, E. 2009. Evidence for healthy cities: Reflections on practice, method and theory. *Health Promotion International* 24:19–36.

Marmot, M. G. 2004. Evidence-based policy or policy-based evidence? Editorial. *British Medical Journal* 328:906–7.

McHarg, I. 1969. *Design with nature*. New York: Doubleday.

McWilliam, W. J., and R. D. Brown. 2001. Effects of housing development on bird species diversity in a forest fragment in Ontario Canada. *Landscape Research* 26 (4): 407–19.

Milburn, L-A., R. D. Brown, S. J. Mulley, and S. G. Hilts. 2003. Assessing academic contributions in landscape architecture. *Landscape and Urban Planning* 64:119–29.

National Science Foundation. 2007. *Important notice no. 130: Transformative research.* http://www.nsf.gov/pubs/2007/in130/in130.jsp.

Schön, D. 1983. *The reflective practitioner: How professionals think in practice*. New York: Basic Books.

Steenbergen, C. 2008. *Composing landscapes: Analysis, typology, and experiments for design.* Basel: Birkhauser Verlag.

Swanwick, C., and Land Use Consultants. 2002. *Landscape character assessment: Guidance for England and Scotland*. CAX 84. Cheltenham, U.K. and Edinburgh, Scotland: Countryside Agency and Scottish Natural Heritage.

Waldheim, C., and A. Berger. 2008. Logistics landscape. *Landscape Journal* 27 (2): 219–46.

Ward Thompson, C., and P. Travlou. 2007. *Open space people space*. Abingdon, U.K.: Taylor and Francis.

Weller, R. 2008a. Landscape (sub)urbanism in theory and practice. *Landscape Journal* 27 (2): 247–67.

———. 2008b. Planning by design: Landscape architectural scenarios for a rapidly growing city. *Journal of Landscape Architecture* (Autumn):18–29.

Young, K., D. Ashby, A. Boaz, and L. Grayson. 2002. Social science and the evidence-based policy movement. *Social Policy and Society* 1 (3): 215–24.

Index

Note: Italicized page numbers indicate figures, examples, notes on method, boxes, and tables.

integration of projective design with, 221
interpretive, 217
of landscape perception and preference, 118
large-scale scenario-based, 124
quasi-experimental, 122, *123*
theoretical, *233*

Journal of Architectural Education (JAE), 38
Journal of Landscape Architecture (JOLA), 34, 84
Journeys through landscapes, as observational
    strategy, 68

Key informant interviews, 154–55, *156*
Knowledge:
    in autonomous disciplines, 18
    baseline of available, 146
    conceptual, 19, 24
    constructed, discourse analysis and, 161
    generation of, 6–8, 13–15, 239–40
    integration into practice, 24, 241–42
    in landscape architecture, 1–2, 4, 33–34, 237–39
    situated, *171*
    systematic, 35–37
    theoretical, 33–34
    theorizing through design exploration and
        testing, 38
    transformation from conceptual to systematic,
        237–38, *238,* 245
    types of, *19,* 19–21
Knowledge domains, 19, 21–26, *25*

LABOK (Landscape Architecture Body of Knowledge)
    project, 21–26, *25*
Ladder of citizen participation, 137, 227, *227*
LAF (Landscape Architecture Foundation), 26, *84,* 86
    Land and Community Design Case Studies Series
        (LAF), 26
Landing, in design process, 216
Landscape architecture:
    compound themes, 142
    core competencies, 22
    critique styles, 42–43
    debates over theoretical base, 30
    discourse analysis, *162*
    experimentation in, 117
    "experiment-like" research, 119–22
    graphic representation in, 164
    research productivity by faculty, *91*
    as scholarly discipline, 13–14
    theory in, *31*
    values in practice of, *164*
Landscape Architecture Magazine, 84, 242
Landscape assessment, 184–87
Landscape-based historical narrative, 165
Landscape biography, *169–71*
Landscape change, *76, 160–61*
Landscape Character Assessment approach, *75*
Landscape coherence, *99*
Landscape design theory, 32

Landscape development, local, *121*
Landscape Futures Initiative, 26
Landscape Journal, 13, 22–26, *25,* 83, *132*
Landscape patterns, *72–73*
Landscape planning research, 124, *184*
Landscape preference and place attachment, *97*
Landscape quality, *73–74*
Landscape Review, 41
Landscape sensitive planning: a benefit/cost
    assessment, *184*
Landscape syntax, 230
Landscape theory, representations of, *34*
Landscape transformations, potency of, 210–12
Landscape urbanism, projective design and, 212–13
Landscape visual analysis, *147*
Landscape visualization for predictive modeling, *103*
Land Use Consultants, 244
L diagram, *168*
Learner-centered education model, 194
Learning assessment guidelines in general
    education, *177*
Learning by teaching, *196*
Learning outcomes assessment rubric, 176–78, *177*
Le Notre project, 21–22, *22,* 24–26, *25,* 28, 85
Life-cycle costs and benefits theories, 183
Life-history research, 158, *160–61*
Likert scale, *77, 118*
Linnaean classification, 137
Literature reviews, 144–46
Logical argumentation, 224, *225*
Logical frameworks, 51, 227–29, *229*
Logical systems research, 51, 223–24, *233,* 235

Mapping, *71,* 71, 213–15
Matrix of research strategies, 9
McHarg, Ian, 67, *212–13,* 240–41
Mean (average), *93*
Measurement, *92, 123,* 126, *178–79*
Median, defined, *92*
Meta-analysis, 147–49
Methodological variety, 13
Methods, in hierarchy of terms, 3
METLAND, *184*
Metrology, 230, *232–33*
Migration, *159*
MLA (master of landscape architecture) degree, 53–55
Modal category, *92*
Mode, defined, *92*
Models and modeling:
    overview, 50
    of action research, 192
    analytical, *91,* 92–94
    in benefit/cost assessments, *186*
    computer, *187*
    correlation, in quasi-experimental strategy, *123*
    descriptive, *89,* 89–90
    hypothetico-deductive, of science theory, 32–33
    inductive and interpretive, of social sciences and
        humanities theory, 44

Suitability analyses, 181, 183
Surveys:
    field, *72–73*
    intercept, *81*
    postoccupancy, *72–73*
    predevelopment, in areal studies, 71
    in preference studies, *95*
    social, 65, 72–77, *76, 78, 81*
Sustainability, 183, *227*
Synthesis, 148, 210
Synthetic logic, 227–28
Synthetic models, 89–90, *90*
Systematic knowledge, in applied research, 19–20
Systems, 225

Tacit knowledge, in applied research, 19
Target populations, *130,* 146
Taxonomies, 136–40, 145
    Biological taxonomy, 137
    Taxonomic classification of Siberian tigers and
        Romaine lettuce, *140*
TDAR (transdisciplinary action research), 202
Teacher-centered education model, 194
Teaching, in categories of scholarship, 39
Tenure, research productivity and, *96*
Tertiary Education Commission, New Zealand, 243
Theoretical assumptions embedded in standards,
    codes, rubrics, and ranks, 176
Theoretical basis for landscape biography,
    170–71
Theoretical investigation, *233*
Theoretical taxonomies, 137
Theories of life-cycle costs and benefits, 183
Theory:
    and critique, 42–43
    debates over nature and content of, 31–32
    defined by Silverman, 37
    in design disciplines, 35
    evaluation research in relation to, 174
    frameworks *vs.,* 32–33
    interpretive approach to, 33
    in landscape architecture, *31*
    roles of, 30
Theses and thesis proposals, 54–57, 60–61, *61–63*
"Thinking Eye" (JOLA), 34
Topological spaces, defined, 230
Transects, 67–68, *68*
Transdisciplinary, as term, 202
Transdisciplinary collaborations, *178–79*
Transformative research, 240–241

Transparency in design research, 56, 207
Transportation research literature citation
    analysis, *144*
Triangulation, 79, *80*
Truth value, 56, 206
Tuning, use of term, 22
Typology, 133–36, *138–39*

"Under the Sky" (JOLA), 84
United Nations Rio Summit, 202
United States Department of Health, Education, and
    Welfare (USDHEW), 193–94
United States Environmental Protection Agency
    (USEPA), 148
University systems, and research performance, 39
Urban design and planning, nonlinear systems
    thinking in, *210–11*
Urban greenway trails preference study, *118*
Urbanization effects on woodlands, *75*
Urban resilience principles, 210–12
Urban spaces, design and use of, *67*
U.S. Forest Service, 116, 187

Valid, as term, 56
Valley sections, 67–68, *171*
Values in evaluation, 174
Village Homes, Davis, California, *82–83,* 181, *182*
Virtual landscape tour, 117–19
Virtual reality laboratory, *118*
Visitor Itinerary Planning and Perception Survey
    (VIPPS), *76*
Visual studies and assessments:
    computer-generated, for rehabilitation projects, *95*
    critical, 217, *218*
    in ecosystem management, *104–5*
    evaluative research in, 186–87
    for predictive modeling, *102*
    public involvement in, *188–89*
    resource management, *147*
    simulations in correlational research, *96*

Water-conservation policies, unintended
    environmental consequences of, *185*
Web of Science, 142
Women in landscape architecture, *170*
Woodland changes and landscape structure, *75*
Wungong Urban Water (WUW) Landscape Structure
    Plan, *212–13*

Xeriscape, *185*